BORDER OF WATER AND ICE

A volume in the series

The Environments of East Asia

Edited by Ann Sherif and Albert L. Park
Editorial Board: Anna L. Ahlers, David Fedman, Eleana J. Kim, and Micah Muscolino

This timely series brings an interdisciplinary lens to the study of the environments of East Asia, approaching questions of human-environment relations by bringing together scholars from social science, humanities, and STEM fields to challenge entrenched paradigms about East Asian societies' relationship with the environment. The series interrogates past and present societies, cultures, and environments with the aim of imagining and forging ways to a more sustainable and equitable future. Books in the series are freely available in open access through the generous support of the Henry Luce Foundation.

A list of titles in this series is available at cornellpress.cornell.edu.

BORDER OF WATER AND ICE

The Yalu River and Japan's Empire in Korea and Manchuria

Joseph A. Seeley
Foreword by Albert L. Park

CORNELL UNIVERSITY PRESS   ITHACA AND LONDON

Thanks to generous funding from the Luce Foundation, the ebook editions of this book are available as open access volumes through the Cornell Open initiative.

Copyright © 2024 by Joseph A. Seeley

The text of this book is licensed under a Creative Commons Attribution-NonCommercial-NoDerivatives 4.0 International License: https://creativecommons.org/licenses/by-nc-nd/4.0/. To use this book, or parts of this book, in any way not covered by the license, please contact Cornell University Press, Sage House, 512 East State Street, Ithaca, New York 14850. Visit our website at cornellpress.cornell.edu.

First published 2024 by Cornell University Press

Library of Congress Cataloging-in-Publication Data

Names: Seeley, Joseph A., 1989– author. | Park, Albert L., writer of foreword.
Title: Border of water and ice : the Yalu River and Japan's empire in Korea and Manchuria / Joseph A. Seeley.
Description: Ithaca, NY : Cornell University Press, 2024. | Series: The environments of East Asia | Includes bibliographical references and index.
Identifiers: LCCN 2024011461 (print) | LCCN 2024011462 (ebook) | ISBN 9781501777370 (hardcover) | ISBN 9781501777387 (paperback) | ISBN 9781501777400 (epub) | ISBN 9781501777394 (pdf)
Subjects: LCSH: Water boundaries—East Asia—History—20th century. | Yalu River Region (China and Korea)—Environmental conditions—Political aspects. | Korea—Boundaries—China—Manchuria. | Manchuria (China)—Boundaries—Korea. | Korea—History—Japanese occupation, 1910–1945.
Classification: LCC DS518 .S386 2024 (print) | LCC DS518 (ebook) | DDC 951/.8805—dc23/eng/20240403
LC record available at https://lccn.loc.gov/2024011461
LC ebook record available at https://lccn.loc.gov/2024011462

To Margaret
Thanks for putting up with me

Contents

Foreword by Albert L. Park	ix
Acknowledgments	xi
Note on Transliteration	xv
Introduction	1
1. Reeds, Fish, Timber, and Defining the Yalu Border	17
2. Bridging the Yalu	41
3. Seasons of Yalu River Border Policing	65
4. Environments of Yalu River Smuggling	91
5. Dam Construction and "Manchurian-Korean Unity"	115
Conclusion	140
Abbreviations Used in the Notes	149
Notes	149
Bibliography	181
Index	195

Foreword

The defining marker of border construction in the twenty-first century has been the "reinforcement and fortification of borders" through the construction of walls, barriers, and fences.[1] Buttressing borders through massive physical materials has been part of the long history of the modern era in hardening boundaries to build and enforce territorial sovereignty for states and maintain their control of flows and movements. Border construction has been a complex geographical process for the order and reordering of natural bodies through the detailed mapping of bodies of land and water and the human-led placement and stabilization of material barriers. Yet, disruptions and cracks have always appeared within any fortification, regardless of its scale or degree, and these developments have unsettled border landscapes to produce different forms of openings for the movement of goods, ideas, human bodies, and nonhuman life.

These simultaneous ebbs and flows of movement have become even more visible through the happenings along the Yalu River between North Korea and China. Since the start of the COVID-19 pandemic in 2020, there were reports of the North Korean government building "hundreds of kilometers of new or upgraded border fences, walls and guard posts," with the intention of "tighten[ing] the flow of information and goods into the country, keep foreign elements out and its people in."[2] At the same time these reports were published, news agencies also provided accounts of a rise in smuggling operations along the Yalu. A built environment of lax security has allowed for a smuggling trade market of minerals—such as coal, aluminum, and copper—medicinal herbs, and livestock between China and North Korea.[3] In the midst of this vibrant exchange of goods, different plants have grown wildly and animal species have continued to move back and forth along the border, including the wild fauna of the region such as deer, foxes, birds, wolves, and fish. The human and nonhuman movements across the river have attested to the emergence of unplanned happenings and worlds at the fortified border.

As Joseph Seeley's *Border of Water and Ice* masterfully shows, unplanned happenings and worlds along the Yalu River have been seen, experienced, and encountered from the premodern to the modern period despite several state efforts to harden borders. The book specifically investigates these unplanned happenings and worlds and their relationship to state drives to control and reinforce borders through a study of Japanese imperialism along the Yalu River from the late nineteenth century into the twentieth century. *Border of Water and Ice* is a layered story of the turmoil and challenges of building a stable political order and secure border along the Yalu River in the face of "the fluid motion of peoples, goods, water, ice, sediment, and other human and nonhuman elements." At the center of the story, *Border of Water and Ice* employs the concept of "liquid geographies" to make visible and sense of the tension, conflict, violence, and contradictions that emerge between Chinese political forces; Japanese authorities in Korea, Manchuria, and Japan; and the flora and fauna in the Yalu region. It introduces a transnational, multispecies framework for tracing and interpreting the formation and dynamics of borderlands and the agents behind them. In line of recent works in the fields of science and technology studies (STS) and New Materialism, *Border of Water and Ice* is a platform to rethink and expand the concept of agency because it shows how different agents—human and nonhuman bodies and nonhuman matter—overlapped and interacted to create the material conditions of the Yalu area. These different agents formed and became forces of change through their webs of interactions and interconnections and not before; the arrangement of a specific context determined the production, nature, scale, and degree of agency. Hence, Seeley's detailed study demonstrates that agency does not just belong to and reside in humans but is a process of change that involves nonhumans through entanglements with human bodies and forces.

In covering agency in border-making, *Border of Water and Ice* persuasively reminds readers about the vital necessity to connect the environment and the overall nonhuman world to the study of the construction of an imperium and political order and boundaries. Regardless of the amount of force used by Japanese imperial forces in Korea and Manchuria to dominate and control the Yalu region for the empire, nonhuman elements, including different aspects of seasonal weather, continuously disrupted carefully calculated plans and unsettled their execution in the material world. The contingency of the nonhuman world produced unexpected outcomes and forced Japanese authorities into uneasy situations that derailed their carefully made plans. Japanese authorities held immense resources and exercised extensive powers, but the water and ice of the Yalu River showed the limits of those powers. *Border of Water and Ice* leaves readers with effective tools and platforms to unravel the complexities of making and sustaining borders and the limits and difficulties of planning, creating, and sustaining empires.

—Albert L. Park

Acknowledgments

It's been a decade-long journey for this book from initial idea to completion, and I am indebted to the many individuals who helped me out along the way.

This work had its beginnings at Stanford University, where I was lucky enough to write about the icy Yalu River while benefiting from mild California winters and wonderful mentors. Jun Uchida always encouraged me to "let the sources guide," and my writing and scholarship are all the better for her sharp, critical eye. Yumi Moon was an indefatigable leader of Korean studies at Stanford while pushing me to think critically about my own contribution to it. Kären Wigen was incredibly generous with her time and energy, as she not only carefully pointed out many quirks in my writing but also mentored me about life and academia from her office and over dinners at her home. Thomas Mullaney supported my forays into modern Chinese history while pushing me toward greater conceptual ambition. At the same time Mikael Wolfe helped me get my bearings in the immense literature on environmental history. I also benefited immensely from courses and conversations with other Stanford faculty including Dafna Zur, Matthew Sommer (special thanks to Matt and Ih-hae Chang for their dinner parties!), Zephyr Frank, Keith Baker, Martin Lewis, Steven Carter, Momoyo Lowdermilk, and Laura Stokes.

Life at Stanford was also made possible by many long hours of laughter, conversation, and commiseration with the many people I met there, including graduate students, postdoctoral scholars, and visiting researchers. I am grateful to David Fedman for first suggesting that I research the colonial Yalu, and for blazing a path forward for me as my *sŏnbae* in Korean and imperial Japanese environmental history. Koji Hirata probably spent way too much time chatting with me after lunches and over Facebook than he should have (which is my fault), but for a *kōhai* trying to navigate scholarship and a crazy job market, the support was essential. Other scholars of East Asia I befriended at Stanford also provided incalculable scholarly and personal support, including Jon Felt, Yvon Wang, Philip Thai, George Qiao, Gina Tam, Andrew Elmore, Hajin Jun, Russell Burge, Riley Brett-Roche, Michelle Chang, Peter Hick, Yunxin Li, Claudius Kim, Tristan Brown, Sixiang Wang, Cyrus Chen, Seiji Shirane, Mei Li Inouye, David Hazard, Jacob Reidhead, Eun Seo Jo, Andrew Nelson, Preetam Prakash, and Luther Cenci. Finally, I would be amiss to neglect the tremendous help of Art

Palmon and the other History Department staff for making the administrative aspects of scholarly life at Stanford as smooth as possible.

In 2019, I had the incredibly good fortune to move from one US coast to another to immediately begin working at the beautiful University of Virginia. UVA's Corcoran Department of History has been a warm and welcoming home for this transplant from the Western United States. I am also grateful to UVA's East Asia Center and area studies colleagues in the Department of East Asian Languages, Literatures, and Cultures for their support. All of my colleagues at UVA have enriched my life and scholarship in various ways, but I want to give special thanks to those who read and provided me feedback on portions of the manuscript, including Lean Sweeney, Chad Diehl, David Singerman, Fahad Bishara, Neeti Nair, Ellen Cong Zhang, Xiaoyuan Liu, Brad Reed, and S. Deborah Kang. Special thanks go to the PhD students who read the manuscript or worked patiently alongside me as I fumbled my way through courses as a newly minted professor, including Mina Lee, Wu Qu, Hao Chen, and Yuchen Zhao. The staff of the Corcoran Department of History also deserve many thanks for their administrative help.

Any historian knows that our scholarship is only as good as the sources that are made available to us. From the time I began the research that would become this book (in 2014), I found myself reliant on the good graces and generous support of archivists, librarians, and scholarly mentors at institutions throughout the United States and Asia. Regan Murphy Kao, Kyungmi Chun, and Zhaohui Xue at Stanford's East Asia Library were always willing to go the distance to track down obscure sources for me and point me to other useful materials. Elsewhere I was helped at critical junctures by archivists at the Hoover Institution, Sonoma State University Special Collections, and the Presbyterian Historical Society, and since coming to UVA I have been indebted to East Asian Studies librarian Wei Wang. Across the Pacific in Japan, Asano Toyomi graciously hosted me at Waseda University while I benefited from the patient help of librarians and archivists at the National Diet Library, National Archives of Japan, Kanagawa Prefectural Archives, Imperial Household Agency archives, Waseda University Library, University of Tokyo Libraries, Takushoku University Library, Yūhō Bunko of Gakushūin University, Shiga University Library, Kyoto University Library, Osaka City University Library, and Fukui Prefectural Library. Conversations with Kimura Kenji, Yuting Dong, and the late Aaron Stephen Moore were also critical in shaping my archival explorations in Japan. In South Korea I was helped by staff at the National Archives of Korea, National Library of Korea, National Assembly Library, the Busan Metropolitan Simin Municipal Library, and the Seoul, Yonsei, and Korea University libraries. Meanwhile, successful research trips in China would have been impossible without the support of Li Jiao at

Tsinghua University, her students in modern Chinese history at the School of Marxism, and archivists and librarians at the Liaoning Provincial Archives, National Library of China, and the Liaoning and Jilin Provincial libraries.

Over the years I have been given many opportunities to present the findings of my research and solicit feedback for improvement. Special thanks go to brilliant scholars and colleagues who attended talks at the Asia and the Anthropocene Workshop, D. Kim Foundation for the History of Science and Technology in East Asia Workshop, Korea at Nature's Edge workshop, various conferences sponsored by the Association for Asian Studies, and presentations at Waseda University, Georgetown University, UVA, the Northeast Asian History Foundation, and the Institute for Far Eastern Studies at Kyungnam University.

I must also thank the amazing editorial team at Cornell University Press. Emily Andrew responded to my initial query to CUP with enthusiasm, while Alexis Siemon capably guided the manuscript through the entire review and publication process. The editors of the Environments of East Asia book series, Albert L. Park and Ann Sherif, were champions of the book from its earliest stages and helped me incorporate the instructive feedback I received from anonymous peer reviewers and those scholars who participated in a series-supported book manuscript workshop at Claremont McKenna College, including Eleana Kim, David Fedman, and Char Miller. I am also grateful to India Miraglia, Susan Specter, Kristen Bettcher, and Michelle Asakawa for further editorial help and Mike Bechthold for the book's maps, and to Springer Nature for allowing me to reprint parts of my article "Reeds, River Islands, and Inter-imperial Conflict on the Early Twentieth-century Sino-Korean Border," *Water History* 12 (2020): 373–384, in chapter 1 of this book.

This book, and my career as an academic in general, also owes a significant debt to additional experiences and mentors. My time at Brigham Young University was punctuated by a two-year mission for the Church of Jesus Christ of Latter-Day Saints in South Korea. Whether my assignment was the result of God's will or bureaucratic chance, I ended up abandoning my early plans to study medieval European history and became an eager student of East Asia. Upon my return to BYU, Kirk Larsen and Aaron Skabelund were exceptional mentors who not only taught me about East Asian history and historiography in the classroom but also thought it worth their time and energy to collaborate with me on coauthored journal articles. As a first-generation college student, I could not have achieved my dream of becoming a history professor without their early help and those of other BYU mentors, including Mark Peterson and Shawn Miller.

Finally, I want to share my deepest gratitude to my family members. Siblings and parents in Idaho and Utah provided immeasurable support for my seemingly esoteric academic pursuits. In completing this book, I am especially reminded of the love of learning instilled in me by my late mother, who adored reading and literacy but always worried I would be corrupted (as I perhaps have been) by secular academia. Margaret Mengxi Seeley read every word of this book before anyone else did and was both my sharpest critic and warmest ally. I dedicate the book to her—she certainly deserves as much. Our daughters Xile and Xiai were welcome distractions from writing and are a reminder that some things matter much more than scholarship. And while their older brother Shutian could only be with us for the briefest of moments, his presence will forever be felt in our lives.

Note on Transliteration

Japanese-language words have been transliterated according to the modified Hepburn system, Korean-language words according to the McCune-Reischauer system, and *pinyin* for Chinese. Exceptions are made for well-known toponyms such as Tokyo or Seoul or historical figures with well-established English forms of their names that follow different conventions, such as Kim Il-sung. East Asian names are listed with surname first, according to East Asian custom, except in cases where individuals choose to reverse that order. Place names on maps and in the text generally follow historical convention, including Andong for the name of the major Sino-Korean border city renamed Dandong in 1965. There are just a few exceptions to this, such as occasionally using Seoul to describe the Korean capital rather than Keijō/Kyŏngsŏng, the city's official name under Japanese rule. All translations from the Japanese, Korean, and Chinese, unless otherwise noted, are my own.

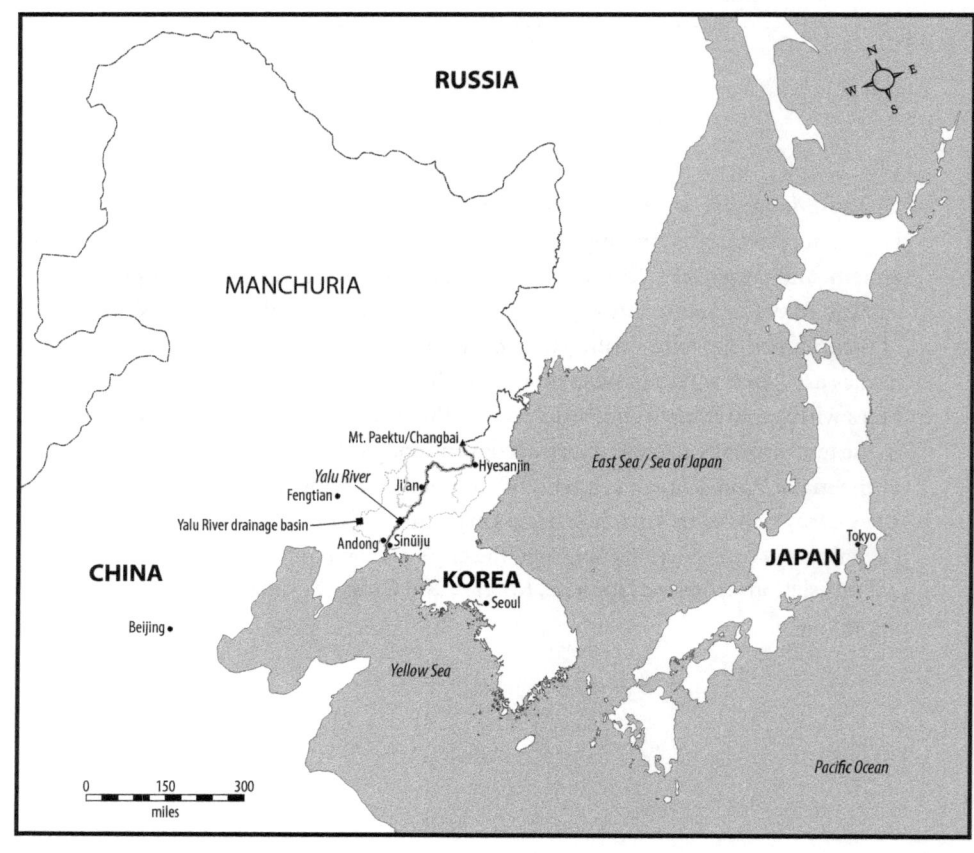

FIGURE 0.1. The Yalu River in early twentieth-century Northeast Asia.

INTRODUCTION

Navigating the Yalu River on a raft of timber and twine was not for the faint of heart. Throughout the early twentieth century, rafters piloted logs cut from upstream forests to processing plants downstream. Cutting rapids with churning plumes of whitewater threatened to impale them on sharp rocks. With skill and a well-timed prayer to the "water gods," most hoped to make it past the rapids and onto more placid parts of the river's course.[1]

In addition to natural obstacles, timber rafters had to be wary of the river's human dangers. Today the Yalu River forms part of the border between the Democratic People's Republic of Korea (North Korea) and People's Republic of China. During the early twentieth century, the Yalu was a border between colonial Korea, annexed by the Japanese Empire in 1910, and the northeastern region of China historically known as Manchuria—also a target of Japanese expansionism.

On May 29, 1935, a Korean timber raftsman was piloting his craft near the town of Yongyŏn. Having passed the Yalu's upstream rapids, the raftsman likely anticipated a restful end to his weary journey. But his voyage was suddenly interrupted when an anti-Japanese militia based in Manchuria stormed the riverbank and began exchanging shots with colonial Korean border police on the opposite side. For fifty minutes bullets flew between imperial Japanese agents and their opponents, transforming the Yalu's surface into a maelstrom of blood and water. As reported in a Korean newspaper, the timber rafter was heavily injured in the ensuing melee.[2]

The Yalu River's dangers were hardly limited to the warmer months when timber rafts plied its surface. Colonial police portrayed the frozen wintertime Yalu River border as a pathway freely traversed by smugglers and anti-Japanese rebels. But those who did cross the Yalu in winter spoke of a landscape far more treacherous than convenient. In 1933, Yi Ok-hyun (Yi Okhyŏn) traveled north across the Yalu border so that her husband, a Korean independence activist blacklisted by Japanese authorities, could find work in Manchuria. After an initial attempt to cross the border by rail was hindered by Japanese border police, Yi decided instead to traverse the frozen Yalu on foot. Years later Yi recalled the following:

> A passerby took us to a spot along the riverbank where people got to Manchuria by walking across the frozen Yalu River. A path stretched ahead of us, beaten down through the snow, exposing the slippery, treacherous ice. Lights blinking on the far shore guided us. I had on cotton socks, my feet were bitter cold, but somehow they did not freeze. I was terrified that the ice would crack beneath us.[3]

Yi lived through this ordeal, but the trauma of this icy crossing would survive for many decades to come.

The following account places these life-and-death experiences with water, ice, and violence along the Yalu River border in a larger historical frame. With the Japanese annexation of Korea, the Yalu River became part of the longest formal, non-maritime border of the Japanese Empire. The Yalu border was a pivotal site for shoring imperial control over Japanese-occupied Korea and for projecting imperial power further into Manchuria.

Drawing on primary sources in Japanese, Korean, Chinese, and English, this book analyzes how Japanese border agents attempted to harness the fluid movements of bodies, goods, water, and ice across the Yalu River border. These seasonally contingent human and nonhuman mobilities, which I call the Yalu's *liquid geographies*, defined the limits of Japanese imperial expansion in Northeast Asia. Colonial police and customs officials tried to make this strategic river border, with its seasonal patterns of receding, flooding, freezing, and thawing, into a selectively permeable membrane that would allow certain goods and people to pass while blocking others. Japanese engineers also tried to channel flows of water and ice to productive ends by building infrastructure such as bridges, embankments, and dams. These various forms of Yalu border-making succeeded in promoting Japan's wider political and economic power in the Sino-Korean borderland and beyond. But the unpredictable movements of summertime floods, wintertime ice, timber cutters, anti-Japanese guerrillas, smugglers, and other human and nonhuman borderland actors also repeatedly spilled outside the bounds set by Japanese colonial regimes until the ultimate collapse of the Japanese Empire in 1945.

By emphasizing the tenuous, environmentally contingent nature of imperial border governance, this story bears critical lessons not only for East Asian history but also for how we understand border-making processes globally. This book argues that nonhuman environments play an active role in border creation and maintenance. Environments are more than static backdrops to interhuman dramas. A more-than-human history of the colonial Yalu River border also demonstrates the importance of considering how border-making and frontier state formation unfold across different seasons, as well as years, decades, and centuries. In the case of the Yalu River, a distinct seasonal cycle of water and ice shaped the actions of both border crossers and the state agents who endeavored to police their mobility, with violent consequences for all involved.

The Yalu as River, as Border

The Yalu River (Chinese: Yalu Jiang; Korean: Amnokkang; Japanese: Ōryokkō) begins as a trickling stream and ends as one of Northeast Asia's major waterways. The longest river on the Korean Peninsula, the Yalu has multiple major tributaries and is almost twice as long as its longest counterpart in Japan, Shinano-gawa. On a map it is easy enough to trace the river's serpentine course from its headwaters on the slopes of Mt. Paektu/Changbai (2,500 meters above sea level) to its wide, gaping mouth at the Yellow Sea some 803 kilometers to the west.

Of course, the river is far more than a cartographic abstraction. Throughout the Yalu's history, most locals knew the river through their livelihoods and labor.[4] The experience of the Yalu River for a fisherman on its wide, sandy delta was quite different from the hunter or timber cutter who crossed a much narrower river that carved deep mountain canyons further upstream. Others, like the aforementioned timber rafters, directly witnessed the Yalu's transformation from narrow and swift upstream rivulet to wide downstream river. Because of the river's relatively shallow depths and steep gradient from its mountain headwaters to oceanic mouth, in its middle and upper spans the Yalu is impassable to larger boats outside of shallow-bottomed craft like timber rafts. The region around the Yalu River is also characterized by a continental climate with extreme seasonal variations in temperature and precipitation. Frigid temperatures cause much of the river to freeze in the winter, while summers are marked by intense heat as well as seasonal floods caused by monsoonal climate patterns.[5] Throughout the Yalu's history, human life and politics have had to adjust to these seasonal variations.

For centuries, the Yalu held symbolic significance for state-builders in what is now China and Korea. The river flowed centrally through early Northeast Asian polities such as Koguryŏ (first-century BCE–668 CE), a proto-Korean state that controlled parts of what is now northern Korea as well as northeast China. Koguryŏ erected several major monuments along the Yalu's banks, including several royal tombs as well as the King Kwanggaet'o Stele, a stone monolith that detailed the accomplishments and conquests of the Koguryŏ king Kwanggaet'o (whose name literally means "Expanding the Domain"; r. 391–413).[6] The Yalu also flowed through the center of the Koguryŏ successor state Parhae (698–926). The earliest textual references to the name Yalu/Amnok stem from around this period, using Chinese characters meaning "duck-green." The exact etymological origins of the name are debated, including whether it was an allusion to the color of the river's water, derives from a Jurchen/Manchu language term for boundary, or is a transliteration of an even older term of unknown meaning.[7]

By the tenth century the Yalu came to assume the border status that it would hold for centuries following. In 936 CE the Korean Peninsula came under the unified rule of the Koryŏ dynasty (918–1392). The southern part of the Yalu River served as a boundary between Koryŏ and various political entities in Manchuria, including the Khitan Liao dynasty and Jurchen Jin dynasty. The Khitans and Jurchens would periodically cross the river to raid Koryŏ, thus also marking the beginning of the river's status in Korean history as a site of existential anxiety about unwanted border crossers. But Koryŏ soldiers also fought back against the northern invaders, and by the fourteenth century successive conquests and military campaigns brought most of the river's southern bank under Koryŏ control.[8]

The significance of the Yalu border to premodern Korean history is further cemented by its role in the origins of Korea's last royal dynasty. The Chosŏn dynasty (1392–1910) began with an act of mutiny on the Yalu's banks. In 1388 the Koryŏ king dispatched military leader Yi Sŏnggye to take part in a punitive mission against the recently founded Ming dynasty in China. But after traveling north from the Koryŏ capital of Kaesŏng and reaching Wihwa Island in the middle of the Yalu, Yi abandoned his original mission and instead returned to Kaesŏng, where, with the help of powerful allies among the Koryŏ bureaucracy, he overthrew the ruling monarch and began the process of creating a new kingdom. By the late 1400s Yi's successors would complete the conquest of the Yalu's southern banks as well as those of the neighboring Tumen River, giving Korea the approximate northern boundaries that would define it until the present.[9]

During the Chosŏn dynasty the Yalu was known as a rugged frontier periphery home to bandits, ginseng poachers, timber cutters, and wild animals. This frontier status was not a simple consequence of the region's mountainous topography or geographic distance from the Chosŏn capital of Hansŏng (modern-day

Seoul). Rather, it was the deliberate result of borderland policies enacted by rulers in Chosŏn Korea and premodern China. In 1459 the Chosŏn court closed the upper Yalu to settlement. This region became known as the "four closed counties"—a buffer zone between Chosŏn and the Jurchen "barbarians" to the north.[10] Settlement on the Chosŏn bank of the Yalu was restricted to the river's lower reaches, where the walled city of Ŭiju remained a critical border entrepot throughout the dynasty's history.

Similar policies meant to dissuade people from settling along the Yalu's banks were also enacted by the Qing (1644–1912), China's last imperial dynasty. The Qing dynasty was the creation of the Manchu people, successors of the Jurchen tribal confederation that previously ruled north of the Yalu. Following the Manchu conquest of the Ming dynasty, Qing leaders gained control of China proper, but they never forgot their Manchurian origins. Geomantic discourses promulgated by the Qing court highlighted the centrality of Mt. Paektu/Changbai, the location of the Yalu's headwaters, in the dynasty's imperial landscape.[11]

The upper Yalu River basin was also a key source of wild ginseng, a valuable medicinal herb whose trade helped fuel the dynasty's rise. Thus, in an effort to preserve their sacred ancestral homeland from the polluting influence of Han Chinese and Korean settlement, as well as to protect the lucrative ginseng monopoly from outside poachers, Qing rulers "sealed off" (*fengjin*) a circumscribed portion of territory abutting the Yalu River. Qing and Chosŏn officials on either side of the border enacted various strict punishments, including death, for illegal border crossings. But as scholars of Qing-era frontier policies have shown, *fengjin* was more aspiration than achievement.[12] Indeed, the threat of punishment failed to dissuade waves of Korean and Chinese migrants lured by the region's rich natural resources—especially ginseng, furs, and timber.[13]

Illicit border crossers encountered a dynamic landscape that shifted with the seasons. With the passing of the year, ginseng grew and ripened, while the Yalu border also froze over and thawed, receded and flooded. As a result, a distinctive seasonal cycle governed the actions of both furtive border crossers and those defending against them. In Kanggye, a key area of ginseng production, Chosŏn guard posts were most heavily staffed against Manchurian ginseng poachers during the summer ginseng-harvesting season, while Korean ginseng poachers also traveled north across the Yalu to harvest wild ginseng that grew on the slopes of Mt. Paektu/Changbai.[14] During these same summer months monsoonal rains would engorge the river's banks, resulting in frequent flooding.[15]

Flooding and ginseng poachers together proved a constant administrative headache along the summertime border, but officials were also concerned about the winter, when hunters crossed the frozen Yalu River to pursue their quarry. Not only did hunters ignore border regulations, but much like ginseng poachers during the summer, they also created semi-permanent camps in further violation of frontier prohibitions and despite Chosŏn complaints to the Qing court.[16] Prohibitions against long-term settlement and illegal border crossings clearly did not work, no matter what the season.

The already limited ability of Chosŏn and Qing officials to police the Yalu border collapsed even further in the nineteenth century. Centuries of overharvesting made wild ginseng and fur-bearing animals increasingly rare by this period. But the Yalu region was still rich in timber, a sylvan effect of enforced isolation eagerly exploited by timber cutters. It also abounded in another increasingly precious resource—land. Population pressures in both Qing China and Chosŏn Korea caused more and more people to move to the border region and establish permanent agricultural communities. Despite continued prohibitions, settlement still occurred—often with the full knowledge of local officials. When Chosŏn officials traveled to the Yalu border on an official expedition in 1872, they found Korean migrant communities eking out a hardscrabble existence from the land while defending themselves from corrupt military officials as well as bandits.[17]

Bandits were a perennially troublesome feature of the nineteenth-century Yalu border for migrants and state officials alike. Popularly known as "mounted bandits" (Chinese: *mazei*; Korean: *majŏk*, though the actual use of horses was not universal among these groups), these brigands took advantage of the rugged terrain and absence of strong local authority to prey on frontier communities. At the same time, they occasionally formed client-patron relationships with local landowners, and the Qing state was not above occasionally drawing officials from the bandit ranks.[18]

With nineteenth-century changes to the Yalu frontier's socioeconomic composition also came a shift in the seasonal cycles of unsanctioned border crossings. Early modern officials were well aware that the river was easier to cross in winter. In the winter of 1636, Qing invaders crossed the frozen Yalu River border to launch a successful invasion of the Chosŏn state. Traditionally, however, concerns about summertime ginseng poachers weighed heavier than worries about rarer wintertime invasions. This changed in the nineteenth century. As agricultural settlers and bandits took the place of ginseng poachers, these new groups were all too eager to take advantage of the frozen river border's accessibility.

Writing in 1860, one Chosŏn border official explained that "winter defense (*tongbang*) had now become more anxious than summer defense," and recommended that the number of sentries guarding the border during the winter be increased.[19] Authorities north of the Yalu also worried that newly arrived Korean migrants would use the frozen river for subversive purposes. As one Chosŏn official wrote in an 1872 report, Korean migrants in one community had their guns taken away from them at the beginning of winter, only to be returned at the very end of winter as the river unfroze.[20] These concerns about how the seasonally changing river environment affected border security would continue well into the modern period.

As illegal migration grew, nineteenth-century Qing and Chosŏn authorities reconsidered their former prohibitions. With state ginseng monopolies no longer as lucrative as they once were, increased settlement along with timber harvesting could mean greater tax revenue for cash-strapped dynasties in Korea and China. The cultivation of lands along the border also provided relief to populations affected by various natural and human disasters, including famine in Chosŏn Korea or the disastrous Taiping Rebellion (1850–1864) in Qing China. Chosŏn officials began officially opening up the "Four Closed Counties," and by the 1870s Qing authorities created counties (*xian*) in Andong and Tonghua on the northern bank of the Yalu.[21] Cross-border trade expanded accordingly, with the Qing and Chosŏn courts concluding a new trade agreement in 1883 that authorized the creation of border customs stations to monitor this trade and crack down on smuggling (which had long flourished in the region).[22]

Foreign imperialism was also a decisive factor that drove Qing and Chosŏn officials to encourage settlement of the Yalu River basin. Preoccupied with the violence of the Taiping Rebellion and other internal uprisings, the Qing state was unable to stem increasing Russian encroachment into Manchuria, which grew more robust by the mid-late nineteenth century. The 1858 Treaty of Aigun saw the Qing cede large swaths of its imperial territory to the Russian Empire, and by the 1890s the Russian Empire also used strong-arm tactics to force the Qing court to cede major Manchurian railway concessions.[23]

The late nineteenth century also saw the entrance of a disruptive new element into the politics of the region: imperial Japan. After Japanese leaders embarked on ambitious modernizing programs at home following the 1868 Meiji Restoration, the Yalu River basin emerged as an important frontier of the country's imperial expansion into Korea and Manchuria. Following decisive victories against the Qing during the Sino-Japanese War (1894–1895) and imperial Russia in the Russo-Japanese War (1904–1905), Japan not only gained railway concessions in southern Manchuria but also cemented control in Korea. In 1905 the Yalu River and neighboring Tumen River became the northern boundary of the newly formed Japanese protectorate of Korea. With the official Japanese annexation of Korea in 1910 there was no longer any doubt as to Japan's political stake in the region. Not only was Korea Japan's largest formal colony, but its northern border was also a key gateway for projecting power into Manchuria.

With imperial Japan's victories against the Qing and Russia, the Sino-Korean border at the Yalu and neighboring Tumen River became part of the Japanese Empire's longest, as well as economically and militarily most significant, terrestrial border. In the eyes of Japanese observers, colonization of the Yalu River basin transformed the country's geopolitical imagination. Writing in 1941, one Japanese geographer argued that prior to the late nineteenth century ordinary Japanese had "strikingly no conception of borders"—a virtue of the Japanese archipelago's separation from surrounding countries by miles of ocean.[24] The appearance of the new imperial border with China thus marked a milestone in the country's transformation from an isolated "island nation" to a global power able to project its influence far outside the archipelago. This statement ignored, of course, a more complex premodern history of Japanese frontier expansion to and fluid territorial boundaries along spaces such as Ezochi (later Hokkaido) and Ryukyu (Okinawa).[25] But the imperial conceit of the "island nation" becoming a continental power was alluring, explaining how the Yalu became a symbolically as well as strategically significant periphery for Japanese imperialists.

The seasonal dangers of this fractious riparian borderland would not disappear under Japanese rule. Indeed, throughout this new imperial era the Yalu would remain a dynamic landscape marked by distinct seasonal cycles. It would also take on new meanings as a site of both heady imperial ambition and profound imperial anxiety. Rather than sealing off the Yalu boundary, as the early modern Chosŏn and Qing had tried to do, the Japanese government completed the first permanent railroad bridge across the Yalu in 1911. This bridge linked Japanese-built railways in northern Korea and Manchuria and the frontier boomtowns of Andong (modern-day Dandong) and Sinŭiju, which became the most important cities along the border.

As part of a broader campaign to strengthen control over Korea and extend influence into southern Manchuria, the Government-General of Korea encouraged trade as well as the migration of Koreans across the river border. By the mid-1930s, millions of yen worth of goods traveled across the border annually, while the number of people who made daily journeys across the railroad bridge exceeded ten thousand.[26] But despite the best efforts of imperial Japanese customs and police officials to limit exactly who and what could cross this border of water and ice, the heavily militarized border with China was a space where smugglers, bandits, and anti-colonial rebels openly and violently clashed with Japanese authority. Local Korean and Chinese farmers and itinerate woodcutters protested over issues like limits on access to forests or the trafficking of homegrown opium, while at the same time ice, shifting riverbeds, and other features of the Yalu River's ecology continued to defy efforts to control the region.

Even after Japan occupied Manchuria and created the puppet state of Manchukuo in 1932, the process of assimilating and controlling the Yalu border would remain fraught up to the Japanese Empire's collapse in 1945. Before the Japanese takeover of Manchuria in 1931, state authority along the Yalu was fractured between the colonial government in Korea, Japanese railway concessions in Manchuria, and various Chinese regimes including the Qing and later Zhang Zuolin's Fengtian Clique. Following the Japanese invasion of Manchuria in 1931 and the creation of the puppet state of Manchukuo, the Yalu River was putatively transformed from an international border into an intraimperial boundary. Yet despite the official rhetoric of "Korean-Manchurian unity," Japanese imperialists' insistence on Manchukuo's "sovereign" status provided ample fodder for bureaucratic infighting and cross-border tensions. Even as the overall goals of the Japanese Empire demanded the economic and political integration of Manchukuo and colonial Korea, disputes over smuggling regulation, fishing rights, and other issues underscored the persistence of border conflicts that originally predated 1931. Such tensions were only exacerbated by the difficulty of dividing the Yalu border's fluid and seasonally contingent topography into discrete Korean and Manchurian zones.

Liquid Geographies

This book proposes the concept of *liquid geographies* to narrate how the fluid motion of peoples, goods, water, ice, sediment, and other human and nonhuman elements of the Yalu borderland together shaped the politics of the colonial Sino-Korean border. The use of "liquid" evokes not only the physical properties of the Yalu's riparian environment but also the fluid mobility of the different groups of people that variously upheld or challenged the political boundary haphazardly imposed on the Yalu's surface. The plural term "geographies" emphasizes the multiple ways the river border was constituted and experienced across different sites and temporal frames. The physical topography of the river varied dramatically depending on location upstream or downstream. It also changed according to the season, with the springtime "thawing season," summertime monsoonal flooding, and wintertime "icebound season" being particularly salient moments of riverine transformation.

Liquid geographies describe not only the fundamental characteristics of the Yalu environment but also the process and ambitions of imperial border-making. Imperial Japanese border police, military, and customs officials encouraged liquid cross-border flows of people and goods as a means of extending the reach of imperial authority beyond this boundary. Officials' projection of power along and beyond the Yalu hinged on their own ability to move fluidly across this space. At the same time, they attempted, through surveillance and violence, to constrain the liquid movements of other border crossers within officially proscribed channels. This included keeping out so-called rebellious Koreans or other people and illicit goods that threatened imperial control. Border river infrastructure such as bridges, embankments, and dams were also key in trying to channel and contain flows of people, goods, water, and ice in ways that serviced the goals of imperial expansion.

Building on recent environmental humanities scholarship, this book draws attention to the ways human societies and politics are created by the dynamic interactions between human actors and nonhuman entities. In narrating "more-than-human" histories predicated on "relational views of the world," scholars have shown that the older Man vs. Nature binary of Enlightenment-era thought is insufficient for understanding the world around us.[27] Rivers have proven to be particularly salient sites for breaking down these barriers, as shown by scholarship such as Richard White's study of the Columbia River as an "organic machine" and Sarah Pritchard's work on the "envirotech" nexus between ecological and technological systems on the Rhone River.[28] Dilip da Cunha's study of the Ganges also reminds us that the idea of the "river" itself is a human construction rooted in the artificiality of a clear line between water and land.[29] I am engaged in a similar project of narrating a "more-than-human" history of the Yalu River, but with a specific emphasis on how interactions between people, water, and land shaped the river's politics as border. Rather than treating the Yalu River border as a creation of individual historical actors (human or nonhuman), the concept of liquid geographies foregrounds their complex and dense interrelationships. Through their interlacing movements, multiethnic human actors such as colonial police, smugglers, anti-Japanese guerrillas, opium growers, fishermen, timber cutters, and nonhuman "actors" (a term reflecting their dynamic role in shaping human action)[30] such as animals, plants, mountains, sediment, water, and ice together constituted the animating force of the border.

Previous border studies have largely highlighted human actors' mobility as the primary mechanism for defining state boundaries. Scholars have shown how political borders are not straightforward lines on a map but multi-sited, "complex social institutions" articulated through interpersonal encounters between mobile border crossers and state agents.[31] These encounters between mobile human agents are as important to border construction and maintenance as physical infrastructure like walls, gates, or boundary markers. Border studies scholarship also emphasizes, much as this book does, how borders serve as tools of inclusion as well as exclusion that promote the circulation of goods and peoples as much as they serve as barriers for entry.[32]

These studies provide a valuable theoretical and empirical basis for any scholarly treatment of borders, yet the following narrative joins other recent works of environmental border history in pushing border studies scholarship toward a greater embrace of nonhuman stories and mobilities.[33] As Xavier Oliveras-Gonzalez notes in a recent study of the Rio Grande border between the United States and Mexico, a persistent "anthropocentrism" pervades border studies, treating physical landscapes as mere backdrops rather than dynamic central actors in border histories.[34] In terms of how border regimes are constructed and physically experienced, a state border is more than the sum of its human parts. Rivers, forests, mountains, deserts, and other environments act in concert with human actors as challenges to the rationalizing impulses of state control while adhering to their own seasonal rhythms. This is as much true for the Yalu River, with its seasonal patterns of water and ice, as it is for other arcifinious frontiers such as the US-Mexico border, where migrants and wall-builders alike confront a bewildering array of desert, mountain, and riparian landscapes that can suddenly flood during the rainy season, or the Mekong River bordering multiple Southeast Asian states, with its extreme seasonal variations of monsoon rain and drought.[35]

Understanding imperial Japanese efforts to channel the liquid geographies of the Yalu border for their benefit demands special attention to the role of seasonal change in shaping imperial border creation and maintenance, a process I call *seasonal border-making*. The logic and rhythms of borderland life and state surveillance along the Yalu were compelled to adapt to the river's seasonal cycles of springtime thawing, summertime monsoonal flooding, and wintertime freezing. Smugglers, timber cutters, fishermen, anti-Japanese guerrillas, and other border crossers encountered the Yalu border not only as checkpoints and watch towers but also as a landscape that literally shifted underfoot with changes in the weather and the freezing and unfreezing of the river. Seasonal changes in the river affected the permeability of the border to river crossers, such as during the wintertime "icebound season" when the frozen river was easier to cross and Japanese police and customs officials accordingly posted more border agents along the river's frozen reaches. Yet accumulative human activities also had the power to transform the riverine environment over time and shape these seasonal rhythms. For example, the felling of timber upstream could, and did, exacerbate flooding downstream, while the Japanese-led construction of the massive Sup'ung Dam (1937–1944) altered water temperatures in ways that prevented parts of the river from freezing over in the winter.

This focus on the seasonality of the Yalu's liquid geographies and border-making joins other environmental histories in highlighting weather and climate as important drivers of historical change. Most works of the growing subfield of climate history take a *longue durée* view of climate's effects, examining how long-term variations in average temperatures shaped human societies and civilizations over time.³⁶ But just as important to historical actors as these macroclimatic changes were the micro-effects of seasonal weather patterns. Seasonal change was an essential aspect of historical lived experience, and yet conventional historical narratives often resemble the climate-controlled spaces where many modern historians write their works. As one scholar writes in a recent history of winter in colonial New England, there is a pressing need to address historians' "uneven attention to all twelve months of the year."³⁷ Sensitivity to seasonality illuminates the visceral experiences of historical daily life and ebbs and flows of state power in regions like the Yalu. Recapturing this seasonal contingency has become all the more important as anthropogenic climate change prompts contemporary concerns about water, ice, and shifting weather patterns worldwide.

Transnational Histories of East Asia

Much like a river gathering water and sediment from multiple sources along its long course, this book gathers inspiration from multiple scholarly literatures, including transnational histories of Manchuria, Korea, and the Japanese Empire. It joins other recent scholarship in narrating a multilingual, multinational story of Northeast Asia's past that resists the traditional tripartite division between "Chinese," "Japanese," and "Korean" national histories. In the case of Manchuria, scholars are increasingly drawing on multilingual archives to show how this multiethnic frontier and "cradle of conflict," situated at the seeming periphery of competing Chinese, Russian, Japanese, and Korean states, was very much central to the modern development of all these competing polities.³⁸ Environmental approaches have also been prominent in recent studies of the region's history, showing that Manchuria's politics cannot be separated from its mountains, forests, plains, and rivers.³⁹

This book extends such ecological sensitivity to an analysis of the modern Sino-Korean border, with attendant ramifications for how we understand the exercise of state power in colonial Korea. Scholars of the Korean past have looked with increased interest toward the twentieth-century history of the peninsula's northern borderland. Groundbreaking multilingual studies have contributed important perspectives about the role of border-crossing human actors, including Japanese police, Chinese "mounted bandits," and Korean migrants, in articulating conceptions of sovereignty and territoriality along the Tumen River border in particular.⁴⁰ This book builds on these insights while also foregrounding the nonhuman forces of Sino-Korean border-making through a focus on the Yalu, the largest of the two Sino-Korean border rivers. In doing so, it shows that states' articulations of sovereignty and territoriality and the visceral, everyday experiences of border crossers were intertwined with the Yalu's geophysical environment. A focus on the Yalu borderland also invites scholars of colonial Korean history more broadly to glean insights that are only possible when moving beyond a previous "urban bias" toward spaces like Keijō/Seoul.⁴¹ When considering colonial state-society relationships from the peninsula's northern periphery, for example, the ideological hegemony and moral suasion central to the influential "colonial modernity" framework seem far less salient.⁴² What becomes quickly evident instead is the everyday violence behind imperial efforts to coerce the Yalu's human and nonhuman flows into sanctioned channels.

This book also joins newly emerging studies of frontiers, borders, and border-making in the Japanese Empire in shedding light on the profound intraimperial tensions engendered at empires' edges. Whether examining marine borderlands like those between Taiwan, Okinawa, and the South Chinese littoral, or terrestrial frontiers in places like Manchukuo and Inner Mongolia, new scholarship on Japan's colonial empire has increasingly foregrounded its "frayed edges and fluid interstices" as critical sites for articulating imperial power.⁴³ Much as this book does in its examination of the Yalu River boundary, these scholars have shown how imperial borders acted as "gateways" for Japanese expansion that facilitated the movements of certain individual people and goods while simultaneously constraining the movements of others.⁴⁴ This scholarship has also shown how borders were sites of competition not just between imperial Japan and neighboring countries, but also between different Japanese colonial regimes and agencies.

In a similar vein, this book reveals profound intraimperial discord between Japanese-controlled regimes in Korea and Manchuria that belied the official rhetoric of "Manchurian-Korean unity" that predominated after the Japanese takeover of Manchuria in 1931. Prior studies have noted overlaps between Japanese imperial projects in Korea and Manchuria, but few have focused on Manchurian-Korean border environments as sites for both sustaining these projects and exposing their internal contradictions.⁴⁵ The seasonally inflected patterns of Yalu border violence and surveillance that existed prior to Japanese occupation of Manchuria persisted for years afterward, as local residents and colonial regimes in Korea and Manchuria alike mobilized the intraimperial border of water and ice to zealously guard their own conflicting interests.

Sources and Chapter Outline

Over the past several decades, flows of migration, colonization, decolonization, war, and bureaucratic procedure have deposited Yalu-related materials into libraries and archives throughout East Asia and across the Pacific. The story told here is drawn from documents in four languages (Japanese, Korean, Chinese, and English) housed in archives and libraries throughout Japan, South Korea, mainland China, Taiwan, and the United States. These sources include official documents produced by the Government-General of Korea and Chinese regimes in control of the northern bank of the river until 1931, as well as the records of the Manchukuo puppet-state created afterward. I also draw on accounts of border raids, smuggling, and other aspects of Yalu politics that featured prominently in Korean, Chinese, and Japanese newspapers, magazines, and fiction published throughout this period. Finally, I use surviving private diaries of border officials as well as published oral histories for documenting the more elusive seasonal patterns of local life and the impacts of border engineering and surveillance. Such records, especially those of former Korean and Chinese residents of the Yalu River basin, provide an important counterpoint to the self-aggrandizing archive of officials who tried to erase local voices and violently impose their own sense of order on a recalcitrant landscape.

The book's narrative chronologically traces the evolving interaction between Japanese colonial expansion and the Yalu's liquid geographies. Decades of Japanese imperial border-making along the Yalu resulted in an increasingly far-reaching surveillance apparatus and profound transformations in the river border's social and natural ecosystems, but it also invoked fierce resistance from local populations and a continually challenging river environment until the empire's collapse in 1945.

The first two chapters analyze the origins of imperial Japanese efforts to channel the Yalu's liquid geographies, especially during the period of the Japanese protectorate of Korea (1905–1910), and the seasonality of these same campaigns. While the Korean Empire retained its nominal independence during this period, control of its foreign affairs (and increasingly its internal governance as well) was ceded to imperial Japan, which meant that Korea's northern border with Qing-dynasty China was now a matter of Japanese statecraft and interest. Chapter 1 shows how the wintertime harvesting of reeds on newly formed river islands, the springtime movements of fish populations, and scattering of fallen logs by summertime floods posed both opportunity and obstacle to Japan's border-making efforts during the protectorate era. By analyzing disputes over these different river resources, the chapter shows how a variety of local human and nonhuman actors reacted to Japan's attempts to push the outer limits of its emergent empire in ways that defined imperial power in the border region for years afterward.

Chapter 2 examines a key infrastructural aspect of early imperial efforts to channel the liquid movements of peoples and goods across the Yalu River: bridge construction. Japanese military engineers battled the Yalu's seasonally variable lows and highs and wintertime ice to erect temporary bridges across the river to transport troops and supplies during the Sino-Japanese War and Russo-Japanese War. These bridge construction efforts culminated in the completion of an iron bridge linking colonial rail lines in Korea and Manchuria. Begun during the protectorate period in 1909 and finished in 1911, one year after the official Japanese annexation of Korea, this railway bridge had to overcome significant challenges from human and nonhuman borderland actors to become a keystone of imperial border-making for decades afterward.

Chapters 3 and 4 examine the work of colonial border police and customs agents to control flows of peoples and goods across the Yalu during the 1910s–1930s. As these chapters show, the post-annexation Yalu River border was defined by seasonally inflected patterns of violence and surveillance that persisted even after Japanese forces occupied Manchuria in 1931. Chapter 3 focuses on the seasonality of border policing against so-called bandits (Japanese: *hizoku*), a broad term that included traditional brigand groups as well as anti-Japanese guerrillas. From the 1910s until the 1931 Manchurian Incident, anti-Japanese dissidents made thousands of raids across the Yalu during the late spring and summer, periods known locally as the "thawing season" and "flourishing season." Japanese officials' aggressive policing of rebels during this same period, which included frequent trespassing into Chinese territory, incited the alarm of Chinese officials on the opposite side of the border. Following the creation of Manchukuo, the wintertime "icebound season" emerged as the greatest threat to Yalu border security in the eyes of Japanese officials trying to control the frozen river crossings of a reinvigorated anti-Japanese guerrilla movement.

Chapter 4 engages with another critical type of mobility that helped define the Yalu's liquid geographies—the movement of illicit goods and money. Smugglers used boats during the spring through fall or crossed the river on sledges or on foot during the winter, a time of particular flourishing for the contraband trade. Repeated pleas by Chinese officials on the northern bank of the Yalu prior to 1931 for Japanese help cracking down on bootleggers fell on the deaf ears of Japanese authorities, who exploited the border's liquidity to weaken Chinese sovereignty while enriching the Japanese merchants who profited from smuggling. But after Japanese-controlled Manchukuo officials seized the Yalu customs in

1932, tensions erupted between Manchukuo authorities and Japanese authorities in Korea reluctant to prosecute illegal cross-border exchange as seasonal patterns of border smuggling continued.

The fifth and last chapter focus on construction of the Sup'ung Dam, second largest in the world at the time of its completion, as a culminating effort to make the river border's liquid geographies work for, and not against, imperial expansion. Harnessing the Yalu River's energy and motion to power Japanese-built factories and industrial sites throughout Korea and northeast Asia, the dam was part of a broader attempt to reshape the Yalu into a politically stable industrial corridor at the height of World War II in Asia (1937–1945). In contrast to the early years of the Japanese occupation of Manchuria that saw persistent border conflict, the outbreak of full-scale war with China in 1937 led to increased cooperation between authorities in Manchukuo and colonial Korea on a number of fronts, including smuggling enforcement, "bandit" suppression, and construction of the dam. Yet despite the rhetoric of "Manchurian-Korean unity," border tensions never truly disappeared, as continued regional rivalries and Japan's own insistence on maintaining some semblance of Manchukuo sovereignty undermined cross-border cooperation. Meanwhile, the mercurial nature of the Yalu and its peoples continued to subvert Japan's imperial aims as smuggling increased in intensity and floods and ice challenged hydroelectric projects even as dam construction forever altered the river's seasonal cycles.

The final chapter is followed by a brief reflection on the legacies of the colonial Yalu River in the post-1945 period and the contest for regional supremacy between American and Chinese forces during the "longest winter" of the Korean War. For both Japanese imperialists and their American successors, the possibilities and perils of empire-building were glaringly exposed at the Yalu River border.

1

REEDS, FISH, TIMBER, AND DEFINING THE YALU BORDER

In a 1908 preface to his book *Yalu River: The Manchurian-Korean Border Situation* (*Ōryokkō: Man-Kan kokkyō jijō*), Japanese Army major Ōsaki Mineto proclaimed that the "waters of the Yalu" were "intimately connected" to the growth of Japanese national power. Mineto's book sought to address lingering "insufficient knowledge" about the Yalu River border between Qing-dynasty Manchuria and Korea, which had become a protectorate of the Japanese Empire in 1905. Japanese troops had just waged two bloody wars, the Sino-Japanese War (1894–1895) and Russo-Japanese War (1904–1905), to establish Japan's presence in a border region Mineto described as the "inner sanctum" of Korea and strategic "gateway" to the rest of the Asian continent. Black-and-white photographs accompanying Mineto's account showed the border towns of Andong and Sinŭiju, products of wartime railway construction, swelling with newly arrived Japanese settlers and Korean and Chinese migrants. Mineto's account also featured two images of the Yalu River that intersected these borderland boomtowns. The first was of the frozen river during the wintertime "icebound season," complete with sledges plying its frozen surface. The second was of ice breaking along the Yalu during the "thawing season" (see figure 1.1). As these images of the seasonally changing river attested, the "waters of the Yalu" were far more than just a static, unchanging line dividing the territorial maps of Manchuria and Korea.[1]

Japanese efforts during the Korean protectorate era (1905–1910) to channel the human and nonhuman mobilities of the Yalu River border—what I call the Yalu's liquid geographies—defined imperial power in the region for years afterward. While Japanese intervention in Sino-Korean border politics was ostensibly

FIGURE 1.1. "Scene of the Ice Thawing on the Yalu River."
Source: Ōsaki Mineto, Ōryokkō: Man-Kan kokkyō jijō *(Tokyo: Maruzen, 1910).*

on behalf of the nominally independent Korean Empire (*Taehan cheguk*), in practice these efforts were crucial to demarcating a new imperial Japanese border, one later formalized by the annexation of Korea in 1910. This chapter's three case studies show how Japanese officials tried to delineate the Yalu border in such a way that harnessed river-borne flows of nonhuman and human actors for the benefit of imperial expansion. First, Japanese authorities intervened in ongoing Sino-Korean sovereignty disputes over Yalu River islands—islands that had emerged only decades earlier due to river flooding and sedimentation—by trying to control the harvest of reeds on the islands of Hwangch'op'yŏng. Second, Japanese imperialists sought to drive Chinese fishermen from the river and monopolize access to the lower Yalu's fisheries. Third and finally, Japanese tried to strengthen their emerging monopoly over the borderland timber industry by creating new rules for the dredging of timber scattered by Yalu floods. These episodes of imperial border-making followed the seasonal cycles of the river, from the wintertime harvesting of reeds on river islands during the "icebound period," to the springtime harvesting of Yalu icefish, to the summertime floods that regularly disrupted the Yalu timber industry.

The unruly dynamism of the Yalu's liquid geographies gave space for Japanese to insert themselves into the region, yet it also invited resistance from those who contested these new attempts at imperial boundary-drawing. Korean and Chinese reed harvesters, timbermen, fishermen, and other members of local frontier society were mobilized to shore up Japan's political and economic control over Korea and project it further into Manchuria. But these same mobile crossborder actors also could, and did, resist Japanese attempts to control their livelihoods. An additional complicating factor for border diplomacy was the vigilante activity of Japanese "continental adventurers" (*tairiku rōnin*), who pushed protectorate officials toward greater intervention by forming alliances with local collaborators along the border but also carried their own competing agendas. Also involved in these border encounters were the riparian dynamics of the Yalu itself, which set the stage for moments of violent confrontation and helped define their outcomes.

Sediment, Reeds, and the Origins of a Territorial Dispute

From 1906 to 1908 two small reed-covered islands in the Yalu River delta, collectively named Hwangch'op'yŏng (Chinese: Huangcaoping, literally "field of yellow grass"), became the site of a violent territorial dispute between the Qing and Japanese empires. Studies of Sino-Korean border politics in the protectorate era typically focus on the Tumen River border and the "Kando question," drawing attention to the 1909 agreement that saw Japanese officials forfeiting Korean claims to the lands north of the Tumen (Kando) in exchange for railroad concessions linking Korea to Manchuria.[2] Irridentist Korean nationalists still bemoan the Korean loss of territorial claims to Kando as part of a larger loss of sovereignty under Japanese rule.[3] But as the following case of Hwangch'op'yŏng suggests, protectorate officials' strategic calculus meant pressing some territorial claims along the Sino-Korean border just as they were forfeiting others. Hwangch'op'yŏng, now known as Hwanggumpyong and firmly under the sovereignty of the Democratic People's Republic of Korea (North Korea), would possibly be Chinese territory today had it not been for the actions of Japanese imperial agents during the protectorate period. Japan's imperial intervention, part of a larger campaign to control the Yalu's liquid geographies, would transform marshy Hwangch'op'yŏng from an area of previously disputed Sino-Korean sovereignty (see figure 1.2) into one controlled by the Japanese colonial regime in Korea.

Explanation for how these reed-covered islands came to be a Sino-Japanese battleground must first be sought in the seasonally shifting, sedimentary landscape of the Yalu River. Like all rivers, the Yalu collects and carries eroded sediment from its upper reaches and deposits it further downstream. Much of this sediment ends up in the river's lower delta, where it forms numerous sandbars and river islands. Sedimentation occurs year-round, though the amount of

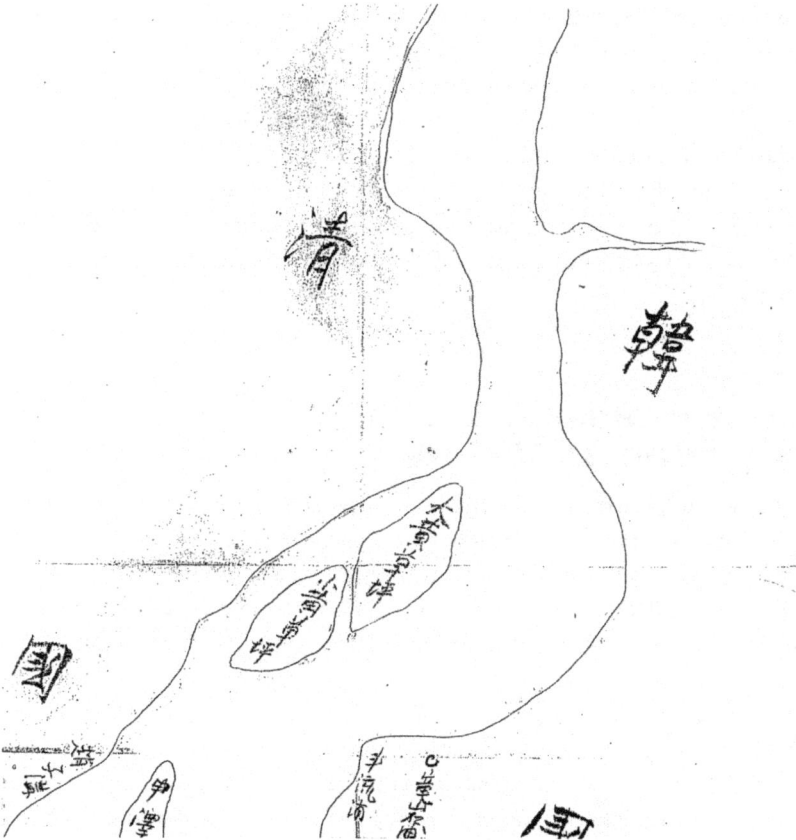

FIGURE 1.2. Japanese sketch of lower Yalu River delta showing islands marked as "Greater Hwangch'op'yŏng" and "Lesser Hwangch'op'yŏng" in center, 1907. Larger characters on left of map read "Qing" while those on right read "Korea."

Source: Japan Center for Asian Historical Records (Holding Institution: Diplomatic Archives of the Ministry of Foreign Affairs of Japan), Ref. B03041223900.

sediment in the river can also be affected by seasonal variations in climate and precipitation. The greatest amount of sedimentation along the Yalu occurs in the summertime months and coincides with monsoonal rains and flooding that erode the river's banks at greater rates.[4] Sedimentation in the river can also be affected by human activities. By the late nineteenth to early twentieth centuries, the harvesting of the upper Yalu River basin's rich timber stands by newly arrived migrants was exacerbating erosion and sending an ever-increasing amount of silt and sediment into the river and further downstream.[5]

Small river islets and submerged sandbars in the Yalu delta where this sediment accumulated grew in size over time and became more prominent river islands. The largest, and most contested, of the river islands to emerge in the Yalu delta was Hwangch'op'yŏng. Hwangch'op'yŏng was technically composed of two closely adjoining islands known as So-Hwangch'op'yŏng (Lesser Hwangch'op'yŏng) and Tae-Hwangch'op'yŏng (Greater Hwangch'op'yŏng), though official discourse typically grouped the two together under one term.[6] Testimony from local Korean and Chinese residents stated that the islands first began featuring more prominently above the river's surface around the 1860s–1870s.[7] Even then Greater Hwangch'op'yŏng would continue to disappear at high tide. It was only after significant flooding in 1888 that it became a fixed feature of the Yalu's above-water landscape.[8]

Hwangch'op'yŏng's emergence coincided with local Korean and Chinese officials' evolving attitudes toward river island sovereignty. Prior to the late nineteenth century, when the Qing dynasty proscribed settlement along the northern bank of the Yalu River, river islands were more troublesome as potential hideouts for illicit border-crossers than as sites of contested sovereignty.[9] The island of Sindo at the Yalu's mouth, for example, was from an early point inhabited by Koreans and traditionally considered within Korean jurisdiction.[10] At repeated points throughout the Chosŏn dynasty, Chinese migrants traveled to the island to engage in fishing or to harvest timber from prohibited regions elsewhere along the border.[11] In response to repeated Korean entreaties, in 1803 the Qing emperor Jiaqing issued an official proclamation banning Chinese travel to the island. The Qing ruler also promised to punish officials who negligently permitted border crossings to happen.[12] Korean officials would cite this edict in later negotiations over Hwangch'op'yŏng as evidence of the Qing court recognizing their control over the river and its islands. The original circumstances behind the proclamation, however, demonstrated that the Qing authorities were more interested in preserving peace between the two countries than asserting sovereignty claims to spaces within the Yalu River.

Attitudes toward the Yalu River islands changed in the wake of nineteenth-century foreign invasions and mass migration to the region. On the Chinese side of the river, the threat of Russian and Japanese invasion caused Qing authorities to reverse their former isolationist policies and actively encourage Han Chinese colonization of the region.[13] As Han settlers from the Shandong Peninsula and other parts of northern China poured into the Manchurian frontier, the Qing government officially incorporated the areas north of the Yalu into counties beginning in the 1870s. Meanwhile, imperialist threats from the West and Japan encouraged the ruling Taewŏn'gun in Korea to station additional troops on Sindo in 1868 as part of a larger bid to improve Chosŏn's coastal and border defenses. In order to fund the increased military presence along the lower Yalu, Chosŏn officials declared the river islands surrounding Sindo to be "public lands" and the property of the Chosŏn government, with taxes and tenant revenue from these islands helping to sustain Chosŏn border defense.[14]

Hwangch'op'yŏng's emergence just as the Qing and Chosŏn governments revised their frontier policies led to clashes over the islands' sovereignty. Especially at stake in this debate was the question of who would be allowed to control the reeds that grew in abundance on the islands' marshy surface. These reeds, which grew throughout the Yalu estuary, were grouped by contemporaries into two varieties: *tianshuiru* (freshwater reed) and *yanshuiru* (saltwater reed). Their durable bark was valued for use in a number of products—including baskets, shoes, roofing material, fuel, and material for straw mats.[15]

Like other aspects of the Yalu border environment, reeds had their own seasonal cycle. Reeds flourished in the salty and marshy wetlands of the Yalu delta during the hot summer months, growing several meters tall by the time they reached maturity in autumn. By October the tall reed stalks started to dry and become ready for cutting and use, but most harvesting actually occurred in the winter during the "icebound period." Given the typically marshy and muddy conditions of the Yalu wetlands, it was far easier for reed cutters to move around and work when the ground was covered in ice and snow.[16]

In 1872 Chosŏn officials declared Hwangch'op'yŏng's reeds to be state property, charging license fees to Korean harvesters to fund new military installations on Sindo. But in 1883 Qing officials protested, claiming that Koreans were illegally crossing the border by harvesting reeds on the islands.[17] In 1896 the Chinese governor of Dongbiandao ("Eastern Circuit"—a political unit encompassing the region along the northern bank of the Yalu) authorized a group of businessmen led by local Chinese resident Wang Choushan to plant and harvest reeds on Hwangch'op'yŏng. In exchange, Wang was to pay an annual tax of 1,200 *diao* on his island holdings.[18] Chinese reed cultivators working on the islands encountered the fierce opposition of local Koreans, however, and the former sandbar once again became the subject of diplomatic debate. In negotiations with the Qing, Korean officials claimed that the islands fell under the jurisdiction of Sindo, pointing to the 1803 imperial proclamation preventing illicit border crossings on Sindo as evidence of Korea's long-standing control over Hwangch'op'yŏng and other islands in the Yalu delta. Qing diplomats countered these claims by arguing that Wang had been granted legal authorization to collect the islands' reeds. Qing officials also cited a 1779 Qing gazetteer, the *Shengjing tongzhi*, which stated that Korea's territory began to the south and east of the Yalu, suggesting that the river itself, including its islands, fell completely under Chinese jurisdiction.[19]

Attempts to conclusively resolve the Hwangch'op'yŏng issue were postponed by the outbreak of the Russo-Japanese War. In November 1904, only months after this imperial contest between Russia and Japan brought bloodshed directly to the Yalu's banks and other parts of Korea and Manchuria, the Japanese ambassador to the Qing court urged the Qing and Chosŏn governments to delay discussion of ongoing territorial issues until after the war's end.[20] Korean officials forged ahead with their attempts to resolve the issue, even going as far as to send an unsuccessful diplomatic mission to the lower Yalu in May 1905. But the sovereignty question remained unresolved until after the war's end, when Japanese officials decided to intervene in the long-standing dispute for the benefit of their own expanding empire.[21]

The actions of Korean collaborators provided a convenient pretext for Japan's initial involvement in the Hwangch'op'yŏng conflict. Whereas many in Korea saw the signing of the December 1905 Japan-Korea Protectorate Treaty as a damning loss of national sovereignty, others, especially along Korea's northern border region, saw a chance to enlist Japanese military power for their own profit.[22] In May 1906, An Kyŏngha, a Korean resident of the border town of Yongamp'o, received permission to harvest reeds on Hwangch'op'yŏng from the Korean Nongsanggongbu (Ministry of Agriculture, Commerce, and Industry). Collaborating with An were two Japanese settlers, Mine Hachirō and Kitamura Keisuke, who together organized the Ch'ŏksik Hyŏphui (Colonization Association).[23] By November 10 the Ch'ŏksik Hyŏphui contracted with a local Japanese businessman, Kondō Seikei, to lead a group of Korean laborers to Hwangch'op'yŏng to harvest reeds growing on the islands. This action fueled protests from Qing authorities, who claimed that Kondō had forcibly stolen the reeds from their original Chinese cultivators. The initial response by Japanese authorities was to mitigate potential conflict by suppressing the Ch'ŏksik Hyŏphui's claims and putting an end to Kondō's unilateral reed harvest.[24] But the attitudes of Japanese authorities soon shifted as they saw a chance to intercede to Japan's benefit in this long-simmering border dispute.

A few days later, on November 15, Kwŏn Chunghyŏn, the pro-Japanese head of the Ministry of Agriculture, Commerce, and Industry that originally authorized the Ch'ŏksik Hyŏphui's claims, raised the issue of Hwangch'op'yŏng in a high-level meeting between Korean cabinet ministers and the Japanese resident-general, Itō Hirobumi. Kwŏn explained that these "small islands in the middle of the Yalu River" were originally Korean territory, but due to Korea's "weakness" the islands had been occupied by the Qing. Kwŏn then asked for Itō's help intervening in the dispute. Itō responded affirmatively by requesting that Kwŏn send him materials buttressing Korea's claim to the islands. He also promised to have the Japanese consul in Andong, Okabe Saburō, appointed to an additional position as resident of the Korean border city of Sinŭiju, which would allow him to negotiate on Korea's behalf in the dispute.[25]

Itō's decision to authorize Japanese intervention in the Hwangch'op'yŏng dispute reflected a growing consensus among Japanese authorities that these small, marshy islands held the key to controlling flows of river traffic, and thereby, the Yalu River border. Between May and August 1906, Narita Sei, a Japanese military officer stationed in Andong, conducted a thorough survey of the lower Yalu delta that was later sent to Tsuruhara Sadakichi, general affairs secretary of the residency general in Seoul.[26] Included in Narita's report was a history of the Hwangch'op'yŏng territorial dispute.[27] In an addendum to his report, Narita elucidated the difficulties facing attempts to resolve the border island issue while simultaneously offering a new interpretation of Hwangch'op'yŏng's significance beyond just reeds. Narita noted that Hwangch'op'yŏng's close proximity to the Chinese bank split the river in such a way that all river traffic was compelled to travel on the east side of the islands. If the islands could successfully be brought under Korean control, then a significant portion of the lower Yalu River shipping route would also fall within the control of Korea, and by extension, officials in the Japanese protectorate government. "The issue of Hwangch'op'yŏng sovereignty may seem unimportant," Narita explained, "but as it is connected to the question of Korea's potential possession of the lower Yalu river route, I believe that it must be quickly resolved."[28]

Just a month later, Narita's conclusions were echoed in a telegraph from Andong consul Okabe to Japanese foreign minister Hayashi Tadasu that was also sent to Resident-General Itō. Although Hwangch'op'yŏng seemed to be "little more than an uninhabited, reed-covered sandbank," Okabe similarly argued it held the key to controlling the lower Yalu River route. With an eye toward future trade opportunities and the extension of Japanese imperial hegemony along the river, Okabe stated: "I believe these small islands bear immense value to our empire."[29]

With the upper echelons of the protectorate government united behind the need to intervene in the Hwangch'op'yŏng dispute, the question now became one of appropriate tactics. The bulk of this decision-making fell to Andong consul Okabe, the person initially suggested by Itō as a suitable intermediary in the dispute.[30] In a November 16, 1906, telegraph to General Affairs secretary Tsuruhara, Okabe offered his assessment of the Hwangch'op'yŏng situation and the most appropriate means for Japanese authorities to respond. According to Okabe, Chinese "precedent" to ownership of the islands' reeds, though "regrettable," had to be recognized as stronger than preexisting Korean claims to the islands. Okabe thus suggested that the sovereignty issue be momentarily set aside while he tried to purchase the rights to the islands' reeds from Chinese interest-holders. If local Chinese could first be convinced to relinquish their claim to the islands' reeds, Okabe reasoned, then the bargaining position of Korea (and by extension Japan) in future sovereignty disputes would be considerably strengthened.[31]

Okabe's initial attempts to convince Chinese stakeholders to sell their claims to Hwangch'op'yŏng's reeds met with little success.[32] By December, Okabe identified a joint-stock company with thirty-four local stockholders as main claimants to the islands' reeds. Realizing that it would be difficult to convince each of the stockholders to sell their shares on an individual basis, Okabe focused his efforts on persuading the company's general manager, Sun Jingtang. Sun, a local landowner who had already invested thousands of yen into the islands' reeds, rebuffed Okabe's offer, declaring that not only was Hwangch'op'yŏng Chinese territory, but Koreans and Japanese had no business interfering in the islands' management.[33] In Okabe's eyes, Sun's obstinance was not just an act of individual resistance but a direct response to pressure from the Qing state. In later correspondence with Tsuruhara, Okabe blamed the unwillingness of Sun and other stockholders to sell their claim to the islands' reeds on Chinese authorities' determination to prevail in the ongoing sovereignty dispute.[34]

Wintertime Violence and the Dispute's Resolution

Unable to achieve his desired resolution of the Hwangch'op'yŏng issue through more peaceful means, Okabe turned instead to violence. The timing of this decision coincided with the arrival of winter, the prime harvesting season for reeds and a time when the normally uninhabited islands would be traversed by hundreds of reed gatherers. The coming of winter also meant Hwangch'op'yŏng's increased accessibility to the Korean and Chinese sides of the now-frozen Yalu River, as well as a ready supply of local labor during what was otherwise an agricultural slack-season. With conditions ripe for confrontation, Okabe recruited the help of local Japanese to forcibly drive Chinese reed harvesters from the islands. When these Japanese arrived at Hwangch'op'yŏng at the head of a group of nearly a hundred Korean laborers, however, they were soon repelled by a determined force of approximately three hundred scythe-wielding Chinese reed harvesters.[35]

Rebuffed in his initial attempt to forcibly settle the Hwangch'op'yŏng question, Okabe tried to once again drive out Chinese reed harvesters by recruiting the help of local Japanese settlers Nonaka Yūichi and Shibata Rinjirō. Nonaka and Shibata had previous experience organizing armed bandits to fight against

Russian forces during the Russo-Japanese War.³⁶ Shibata's additional membership in the Genyōsha league of violent ultranationalists marked them both as "continental adventurers" (*tairiku rōnin*), a term applied to a loosely associated group of Japanese Pan-Asianists, entrepreneurs, spies, and agent provocateurs who variously supported both revolutionary movements in Asia and the advance of Japanese colonialism on the continent. Eiko Siniawer groups such adventurers among the "violence specialists" who she argues formed a "deeply rooted element of modern Japanese political life," especially during the Meiji period as the use of formal and informal violence went hand in hand with Japan's imperial expansion in Korea and Manchuria.³⁷ As Okabe's recruitment of Shibata and Nonaka shows, such "violence specialists" were also a volatile component of Sino-Japanese competition over the Yalu River basin. Invading Hwangch'op'yŏng with a combined force of approximately one hundred Korean laborers at their command, Shibata and Nonaka tried to forcibly turn the tide of the ongoing dispute. Chinese reed harvesters proved once again successful at repelling such advances, however. The Japanese-Korean force met the fierce resistance of Chinese reed harvesters, who had armed themselves this time with firearms as well as scythes.³⁸

The successful Chinese repulsion of two waves of militia violence led Okabe to make a final appeal to the Japanese military. On surreptitious orders from Okabe, troops stationed in the Japanese concession in Andong, ceded to Japanese forces after their victory in the Russo-Japanese War, decided to engage in outdoor "field exercises" on Hwangch'op'yŏng. In reality, the "field exercises" were little more than an excuse to occupy the islands by force. With two autocannons in tow, the garrison destroyed eighteen Chinese reed harvesters' huts, allowing Korean harvesters to follow and access the islands' reeds in their wake. When part of this garrison traveled from the islands to the home of Sun Jintang, however, he calmly rebuffed the force of Japanese threat. According to a later report by Okabe, Sun asked the assembled troops why they had come, and that "if they had come for the islands, I am already an old man of sixty. . . . Even if I die, I will not let the islands fall into the hands of another."³⁹

When successive violent raids failed to convince Sun and other stakeholders to relinquish their claims to the islands, Okabe at last resorted to imprisoning Sun and meeting with the other reed cultivators on a one-by-one basis. After a violent argument erupted between Sun and local Japanese and Koreans claiming access to the islands' reeds, Okabe used this as a pretense to pressure local Chinese officials to imprison Sun. With Sun behind bars, Okabe unsuccessfully tried to convince the other stake-holders to sell their claims to the islands' reeds.⁴⁰ In the meantime, Nonaka and Shibata purchased thirty junks, which they used to collect reeds gathered by the Chinese laborers and move them to the Korean side of the river.⁴¹

The forceful actions of Okabe and his Korean and Japanese collaborators caused understandable alarm for Chinese authorities and diplomats. Telegrams from officials in Manchuria to the Qing Foreign Ministry identified the ill-defined Sino-Korean border in particular as the source of the repeated violence. In a July 12, 1907, telegram, Andong officials argued that the threat of violence would be unending until the island sovereignty question was settled and the Yalu border definitively defined.[42] Yet Japanese authorities were reluctant to agree to Qing demands to clearly define the border until they could shore up their own claims to Hwangch'op'yŏng. In a June 1907 telegram to Seoul, Japanese ambassador to the Qing court Abe Moritarō suggested delaying negotiations until after local Japanese authorities settled greater numbers of Koreans on the islands or undertook other means to strengthen their bargaining position.[43]

As the thorny question of border demarcation remained unresolved, local Qing officials began to press for more immediate, practical compromises on the issue of Hwangch'op'yŏng's lucrative reed harvest. On April 23, 1907, representatives from the Andong governor and Japanese consul in Andong met on Hwangch'op'yŏng and agreed to split the remaining proceeds from the reed harvest. The Andong governor also raised the possibility of continued joint administration of the islands in another meeting with Japanese officials nearly six months later.[44]

In his detailed Japanese-language study of the Hwangch'op'yŏng dispute, Yi Chusŏn points to such compromises to express doubt as to whether Qing authorities regarded the question of Hwangch'op'yŏng sovereignty as ultimately important to their strategic interests.[45] Analysis of Qing correspondence, however, suggests that the proposal for joint administration was born more out of pragmatic calculation than indifference. In their own correspondence local officials recognized that the island dispute was a "major international issue" (*wei guoji yi da wenti*).[46] But at the same time, Qing administrators expressed greater concern over protecting the livelihood of local reed harvesters threatened by Japanese and Korean violence than enforcing Chinese territorial claims.[47] The Qing state, which would collapse only a few years later and give way to the short-lived Republic of China, was also beset with a number of external and internal crises that necessitated uncomfortable compromises with Japanese power. Rather than reading the Qing approach to Hwangch'op'yŏng as evidence of disengagement, it might be more accurate to describe it as a calculated concession in the face of a powerful rival.

While the Andong governor called for joint administration of Hwangch'op'yŏng, Japanese consul Okabe continued to plot means by which the (ostensibly) Korean claim to Hwangch'op'yŏng could be strengthened. One step was to find new local collaborators. An Kyŏngha's Chŏksik Hyŏphui helped initiate Japanese intervention in the island dispute, but they were deemed less than reliable after they expressed a willingness to negotiate with Chinese stakeholders.⁴⁸ Okabe instead turned to representatives from the Ilchinhoe, a pro-Japanese Korean reformist organization with strong ties to the Sino-Korean border region. Although traditional assessments of the Ilchinhoe stress its collusion with Japanese power and active support for colonization, recent revisionist scholarship by Yumi Moon also highlights the organization's populist agenda, which included campaigns to resist taxation and organize new tenant relationships on "public lands."⁴⁹ Hwangch'op'yŏng's status as public land formerly claimed by the Korean royal family helped attract the Ilchinhoe's interest in this dispute. In addition, Yi Chusŏn speculates that the appointment of Ilchinhoe head Song Pyŏngjun as minister of agriculture, commerce, and industry influenced the choice of Ilchinhoe as Okabe's local collaborators.⁵⁰

In July 1907 an agreement on Hwangch'op'yŏng reed harvesting was drafted between Ilchinhoe representative Kim Chintae and Japanese continental adventurer Shibata Rinjirō.⁵¹ This contract called for the joint investment of 12,000 yen into the settlement of Hwangch'op'yŏng by Koreans who would engage in rice agriculture, fishing, and the collection of stray floating timber from logging sites upstream. This plan outlined not only the Korean colonization of the islands to help settle the long-standing sovereignty question but also the ecological transformation of Hwangch'op'yŏng through the construction of irrigation ditches, levees, and other infrastructure necessary to accommodate rice cultivation.⁵² Ilchinhoe resentment at the unequal terms of the agreement, however, which specified that 8,000 of the 12,000 yen in starting capital would be provided by Ilchinhoe members while designating Shibata the primary contract-holder, led its signers to later renegotiate the terms.⁵³ In a November 12 Seoul-based conference between Okabe, Shibata, Ilchinhoe chief Yi Yonggu, and Ilchinhoe advisor Uchida Ryōhei, a more equal contract was agreed upon by the two sides, though the absence of any Chinese negotiators from the bargaining table remained salient.⁵⁴

The fate of Hwangch'op'yŏng colonization would be settled in an unexpected way, however, by a diplomatic about-face that followed Okabe's temporary departure from his post as Andong consul. Soon after his meeting with the Ilchinhoe in Seoul, Okabe left Korea to briefly return to Japan. Further planning for Hwangch'op'yŏng fell in the interim to the Andong vice-consul and other Japanese officials in Andong and Sinŭiju, who together attempted a new breakthrough in negotiations for the islands' control.⁵⁵ Their plan, ultimately endorsed by Okabe as well, called for neither the involvement of the Ilchinhoe nor the violent occupation of the islands. It also did not involve the joint administration suggested by the Qing, as the Japanese goal of achieving hegemony over the Yalu River route remained constant. Instead, these officials sought to recognize the

Qing desire for access to the islands' valuable reeds while extracting an implicit recognition of Korean sovereignty by having the primary Chinese stakeholders pay an annual tax to local Korean authorities.[56] At a February 1908 meeting between Chinese claimants and Japanese officials, an agreement was reached to have Chinese stakeholders pay the Korean protectorate government an annual sum of 2,000 yen in exchange for ten years of uninhibited access to the islands' reeds.[57] This decision was further reaffirmed in a July meeting with the governor of Andong, who agreed that joint administration of the islands was no longer necessary under the terms of this new agreement.[58]

In exchange for temporarily forfeiting Korean claims to the islands' reeds, Japanese authorities secured implicit Qing recognition of the Korean claim to sovereignty over Hwangch'op'yŏng. Thus ended several decades of tense and violent disputes over the pair of river islands since their first appearance in the sandy Yalu delta—at least for a moment. Following the formal Japanese colonization of Korea in 1910 and the fall of the Qing dynasty in 1912, the issue of Hwangch'op'yŏng sovereignty would periodically resurface as a point of tension in Sino-Japanese relations. Heightening these tensions was the steady narrowing of the river channel separating the islands from the Chinese bank through increased sedimentation. In 1926 Japanese officials in the region even reported an alleged "scheme" by local Chinese to artificially fill in the remaining gap with stones, thus conjoining the islands to the Chinese side of the river and negating Japanese claims to the territory.[59] In response to these and other concerns, colonial officials in Korea began exercising more direct control over the harvesting of the island's reeds in 1928. The Hwangch'op'yŏng question would remain in flux until 1962, when any and all doubts about sovereignty were officially resolved by a treaty between the Democratic People's Republic of Korea (North Korea) and the People's Republic of China that officially recognized Korean control of the islands—a diplomatic victory for local Korean interests that must be seen at least partially as a legacy of Japan's imperial intervention.[60]

Even though Japanese officials were unable to monopolize access to the island's reeds, the brandishing of violence during the winter of 1906–1907, when reeds dried out for harvesting and the frozen river bridged the gap between the island and riverbank communities, helped secure implicit recognition of their larger sovereignty claims. Intervention in the Hwangch'op'yŏng dispute, ostensibly done in the name of the Korean government, was a key aspect of the protectorate government's efforts to control the Yalu River trade route and channel the border's liquid geographies. But as the following sections show, controlling the border during this period involved more than just river islands or reed harvesters.

Disputes over Yalu Fishing Rights and Springtime Harvests

Humans were not the only organisms whose seasonally contingent cross-border mobilities mattered to Qing-Japanese imperial competition along the Yalu River. For millennia the river has been home to dozens of fish species. The first comprehensive fish survey of the Yalu River, conducted by Japanese colonial officials in 1938, documented some seventy-four species total whose scaly bodies inhabited the different lengths of the river.[61] After the creation of a Japanese protectorate over Korea in 1905, the aggressive policing of Japanese and Korean fishing rights in the Yalu became an important means for Japan to challenge China's sovereignty along the Sino-Korean border. While imperial Japan's pursuit of marine fisheries has received greater scholarly attention, the case of the Yalu shows that Japan's piscatorial colonialism also extended into the riparian arteries of its growing continental empire.[62]

Compared to river island disputes that reached their violent apex in winter, fishery disputes were primarily a springtime phenomenon. The fish populations of greatest commercial significance had long been two species that thrived in the saline waters of the lower Yalu estuary, shrimp and icefish (*Salangidae*). Icefish, a thin, translucent fish native to freshwater environments throughout East and Southeast Asia, were considered a particularly notable "specialty product" of the river. Yalu icefish were valued for their size, which was larger than in many other parts of Northeast Asia. They were also harvested in greatest numbers during the early spring, when they would travel upstream to spawn, which lent them the moniker "cherry blossom icefish."[63] During this time fishermen from all over Korea's northwestern provinces would congregate on an eight li (roughly thirty kilometer) stretch of the Yalu near the river's mouth at the Yellow Sea. Period accounts reported, with perhaps only slight exaggeration, that the fishing boats during this few weeks period were "as thick as a forest."[64]

In 1908 Japanese protectorate officials pressed the Korean government to accept their proposal for a new "Korea Fisheries Law" that would go into effect on April 1, 1909. One of the primary provisions of the new law was an extensive licensing system that would prevent unauthorized fishing within Korean territorial waters. Done in the name of "protecting" Korean fishery resources, the new law in practice accelerated exploitation of Korean fisheries by making it easier for ambitious Japanese entrepreneurs to gain licensed access to Korean fisheries. The provisions against unlicensed fishing also empowered Japanese colonial officials to more aggressively guard against "poaching" by third-party entities, which in the Yalu border region meant Chinese fishermen in particular.[65]

Competing Chinese and Japanese claims to jurisdiction over the Yalu icefish harvest led to increased diplomatic tensions soon after the proclamation of the new fisheries law in spring 1909. In May 1909 Japanese officials in Andong and Sinŭiju pursued the case of six Korean fishermen whom they claimed had been "illegally" extorted by Chinese fisheries officials.[66] According to police interviews, the six fishermen were harvesting icefish from the lower Yalu when they were approached by three Chinese, one in uniform and two in ordinary dress, identifying themselves as representatives of the Andong branch of the Fengtian Fisheries Bureau. The Chinese officials then asked the fishermen to pay taxes for their right to fish in the river. While some of the fishermen agreed to pay taxes on the spot, others refused. Those who refused were then taken to the Andong Fisheries Bureau branch and compelled to pay the tax by force.

To the Japanese colonial officials monitoring this case, the actions of the Chinese officials were an egregious offense against Korean fishermen operating in Korean territorial waters. To the Qing, however, the tax collection was an acceptable administrative step in a border zone where the location of the international boundary line was itself fluid and ambiguous. When interrogated by Japanese police about the rationale behind his actions, the accused Chinese fisheries official replied that he had simply been told to collect taxes on "all Korean fishermen" operating along the Yalu, admitting that there was no clear precedent for defined Chinese or Korean fishing districts within the river.[67]

The differing responses to this issue revealed a fundamental conflict in Qing and Japanese sovereignty claims over the Yalu estuary, with both sides wanting to control access to the river's fisheries. The advantage in this dispute ultimately belonged to the Japanese, who, as was the case with river islands, proved willing to back up their claims with greater force. As part of a larger push to enforce the 1908 Korean Fisheries Law, the Japanese government deployed naval torpedo ships to Korean coastal waters to intimidate Chinese fishermen.[68] It also conducted extensive surveys into Chinese "poaching" in the lower Yalu and nearby coastal islands.[69]

Chinese observers, including Qing officials, responded to these new developments with alarm. Newspapers and magazines as far away as Shanghai began publishing articles in spring 1909 highlighting the Japanese seizure of the Yalu fisheries and the corresponding loss of Chinese "sovereignty" (*zhuquan*).[70] Chinese officials in Manchuria launched an investigation into the matter after one such article in the *Beijing ribao* (Beijing daily) claimed that Korean and Japanese fishermen on the Yalu now outnumbered their Chinese counterparts seven to three. In a telegraph to the Qing Foreign Ministry, members of the survey team described how it was simply impossible for Chinese fishermen working along the border to avoid straying into Korean waters (which were nebulously defined to begin with) and being harassed by Japanese colonial officials. Furthermore, protectorate officials' vigilance in limiting access to parts of the river near the Korean bank meant that even Chinese fishermen who had previously operated with the full consent of Korean officials were now cut off from prior sources of income. These included one Mr. Zhao, a Chinese shrimp harvester who operated in Korean coastal waters near the Yalu and had long paid rents on his boats. Japanese warships were also traveling to the region and disturbing Chinese fishermen, all of which led the author of the telegraph to express dissatisfaction at the "extremely unfair" (*shu bu ping*) nature of border relations.[71]

The fluid cross-border movements of fish and fishermen alike provided an avenue for enterprising officials in the protectorate to bolster their sovereignty over the Yalu River border. Yet just as fish beneath the river's surface moved irrespective of national boundaries, fishermen would also exploit gaps in colonial border governance to show that the dual-edged nature of "poaching" as an issue that could harm as well as help imperial interests. Even after the official Japanese annexation of Korea in 1910, the issue of poaching in the Yalu fisheries remained a difficult one for regimes on both sides of the river. A May 7, 1916, article in the *Maeil sinbo*, a Korean-language mouthpiece of the colonial government, related how the Sinŭiju police station was intensifying its efforts to crack down on rising numbers of "poachers" during the springtime icefish harvest.[72] Meanwhile, Chinese government reports continued to complain about Japanese and Korean violation of Chinese sovereignty in the Yalu estuary.[73] The patrolling of the porous border proved a continued challenge for regional authorities, with springtime fishing just one battlefront in this larger border conflict.

Liquid Geographies of the Yalu Timber Industry

Within a few months of protectorate authorities enforcing new anti-poaching laws in the Yalu River delta, other border conflicts were erupting along the Yalu's upper reaches. This time, however, the items of competition were not springtime fisheries or reeds harvested in the icy cold Yalu winter but fallen logs thrown into disarray by late spring and summertime Yalu flooding.

The extensive forests of the upper Yalu River basin comprised a rich and hotly contested prize in the imperialist politics of early twentieth-century Northeast Asia. The expansive stands of pine, fir, and other trees that awed travelers to the region were a direct legacy of centuries of Qing isolationist policy that sought to restrict migration to the region.[74] But while early modern empire-building had encouraged the forests' growth, modern imperial regimes' insatiable appetite for natural resources led to their rapid exploitation.

A conflict over Yalu timber known as the "Yalu River Crisis" was one of the original *casus belli* of the Russo-Japanese War leading to the creation of the Korean protectorate. In 1896 the Qing empire, recently defeated by Japan in the Sino-Japanese War, sought to check Japanese expansion in northeast China by allowing Russia to build an extension of the Trans-Siberian Railroad across Manchuria.[75] That same year, the Korean monarch Kojong fled to the Russian embassy in Seoul following the Japanese assassination of his wife Queen Min. Grateful for Russian protection but also compelled to heed his protectors' demands, Kojong began granting a number of key economic concessions to Russian politicians and businessmen. Among the concessions Kojong granted was the rights to rich stands of virginal timber along the upper reaches of the Yalu and Tumen River basins to Russian businessman Y. I. Briner.[76] The Russian government quickly purchased this concession from Briner, seeing the region both as a source of valuable timber for railway construction and a foothold for securing Russian power in Korea.[77] This purchase attracted immediate attention from Japanese leaders, who not only feared this threat to Japan's position in Korea but were also beginning to express similar interest in the Yalu's sylvan bounty.[78] No sooner had Japanese forces driven Russian troops from the region during the Russo-Japanese War than they began asserting their own monopoly over local timber-felling.[79]

After the end of the Russo-Japanese War, Japanese leadership moved quickly to solidify control over the Yalu's forests. In 1908 an unequal Sino-Japanese treaty created the quasi-governmental Yalu River Timber Company (C: Yalu jiang caimu gongsi; J: Ōryokkō Saiboku Kōshi). Five percent of the company's profits would be paid as a direct royalty to the Qing government, while the company's leadership would ostensibly be in the hands of the local Qing governor and two directors, one Japanese and the other Chinese.[80] On paper, such provisions allowed for equal Sino-Japanese control of the company's management. In reality, however, the Yalu River Timber Company remained a largely Japanese-managed operation run by government-selected directors under the oversight of the Japanese consul in Andong.[81] Similar unequal arrangements were made to control forests on the Korean side of the Yalu. In 1907 the protectorate government created the Forest Management Bureau (J: Eirinshō; K: Yŏnglimch'ang). This constituted a network of field offices and processing stations created to oversee the direct management of national forestlands (*kokuyūrin*).[82] As was the case with the Yalu River Timber Company, the Forest Management Bureau was presented as a collaborative transnational operation: in this case between the Japanese protectorate leadership and the Korean government, which retained nominal control over domestic affairs. In reality, both the Forest Management Bureau and the Yalu River Timber Company were a means of strengthening Japan's timber hegemony over the Sino-Korean borderland.

The daily lived experience and actual success of the Yalu timber industry were tied to the river's annual seasonal cycle. Running like a pulsing artery through the sylvan heart of the Sino-Korean borderland, the Yalu River fulfilled a critical role in the local timber industry as a means of transport. During peak timber-harvesting season in the winter, timber cutters would transport fallen logs by sledge over the frozen earth and stockpile them near the banks of the Yalu and its various tributaries. With the thawing of the river in the spring, these logs would then be tied up into large rafts and floated downstream to the major trading ports of Andong and Sinŭiju at the mouth of the river (see figure 1.3). The springtime melting of ice along the early twentieth-century Yalu River border brought not only the icefish harvests discussed earlier but also the beginning of this near-constant flow of timber rafts from the logging regions of the upper Yalu River.

The Yalu River's role in the local timber industry was indispensable, but the river's friendliness to this commerce was also susceptible to sudden variations in the region's seasonal climate. If the ice on the river melted too early, or if too little rain fell during the spring, water levels would be too low to allow the

FIGURE 1.3. Timber rafters pilot their craft down the Yalu River.

Source: Hantō no suiryoku (Keijō [Seoul]: Chōsen Sanrinkai, 1926). Image courtesy of the Seoul Museum of History.

floating of log rafts, thus crippling the timber trade for that year. Conversely, an overabundance of rain, which was common during the summer due to monsoonal rain patterns, had the threatening potential of breaking apart and scattering already assembled timber rafts and log stockpiles.[83] The seasonal precarity of the Yalu's lumber economy is captured in the words of a contemporary British trade report: "An unlooked-for thaw in the early spring, a dry, early summer, with a consequent insufficient supply of water in the upper reaches to float the rafts down, and floods in July or August are all varying unknown quantities with which to be reckoned in any lumber district; but the Yalu seems particularly well endowed in this respect."[84] There was also the problem of treacherous rapids. Despite Japanese attempts to remove boulders, build levees, and otherwise improve the river course, timber rafters still appealed to the "water gods" for help traversing the river's turbulent waters.[85]

Just as the Yalu River's flow was necessary to the timber industry but also subject to precarious and unpredictable shifts over time, local Chinese timber cutters were necessary parts of Japan's cross-border timber monopoly, but their mobile actions could also cut against timber imperialism. Since the late nineteenth century, migrant seasonal laborers from the Shandong Peninsula, most of them single men, provided the back-breaking labor necessary to harvest the upper Yalu's rich timber reserves. This work was typically done by crews of five to eight contract timbermen, known locally as *muba*, working under the direction of a foreman (*batou*).[86] The border-crossing proclivities of *muba* and their hard-edged resistance to outside control led to recurrent confrontations between timbermen and border officials. During the late nineteenth century, Chinese lumberers frequently crossed over the Yalu border to collect timber scattered by floods or even harvest trees from Korean forest stands. This incited the anger of Korean officials, who labeled the offenders *mokpi* or "timber bandits."[87] Japanese officials also adopted the term "timber bandit" to castigate Chinese woodcutters for their hard-edged resistance to the Japanese monopoly over the Yalu timber industry.[88]

As reliant as Japanese agents were on migrant woodcutters for providing much of the labor to exploit the upper Yalu's forests, these same laborers were not always eager to play by the rules imperial authorities set. Starting in 1906, when the logging monopoly was still under the control of a "military-use timber garrison" first created by Japanese military officials during the Russo-Japanese War, a coalition of Chinese timber cutters began launching armed attacks against Japanese timber raftsmen. After one high-profile attack in spring 1906, when a group of *muba* allegedly fired upon a Japanese raftsman and seized his raft, Japanese military officials responded by demanding a hefty reparation of 25,000 yen from Qing administrators and assurances that logging operations would be protected from future attack. After repeated negotiations, Qing officials reluctantly supplied the sum demanded.[89] This incident would hardly be the last case of *muba* violence, however, against Japanese timber raftsmen.

1909 Yalu Flooding and Muba Resistance

In 1909 the determined resistance of Chinese timber fellers, the disruptive hydrology of the Yalu River, and the sylvan ambitions of imperial Japan collided with particularly explosive consequences around the issue of dredging scattered timber. In April 1909 the newly created Yalu River Timber Company inked an agreement with the Korean protectorate's Forest Management Bureau regarding the disposal of fallen logs that were scattered by the river's frequent late spring and summer floods. The new agreement sought to strengthen Japanese control over the regional logging industry by dictating that all scattered timber that floated over to the Korean side of the river should be collected by the Forest Management Bureau, while scattered wood on the Chinese side of the river belonged to the Yalu River Timber Company.[90] While the new regulations ostensibly allowed for independent timbermen to reclaim fallen logs that had brands or other clear marks of ownership once they had been gathered, the process was more bureaucratic than the previously laissez-faire system of fallen log reclamation. In addition, the routine levying of fees for the cost of organizing these logs and transporting them to designated holding sites before they could be reclaimed further engendered timber cutters' resentment.[91] As a result, the question of collecting logs scattered by floods became a touchstone for mounting *muba* resistance to the Japanese lumber monopoly.

Flooding in late May 1909 provided the final catalyst for this latent rage to detonate. On May 31, 1909, two Chinese timbermen crossed the upper Yalu River near Chunggangjin to collect timber that had been scattered by heavy rains only a few days earlier.[92] They were promptly met by Japanese military police—a prominent fixture of the border region since the Japanese dissolution of the Korean Army two years earlier. Reports differ on the events that followed. Japanese military police officials claimed that one of the two timber cutters was arrested but escaped soon after, while Chinese officials claimed that the arrested lumberer, Wang Bingtai, was tortured and held indefinitely by Japanese authorities.[93]

On June 10, nearly two weeks after Wang's arrest, a group of Chinese timber cutters attacked and kidnapped six Japanese rafters employed by the Forest Management Bureau. These rafters were contract employees from traditional Japanese logging regions like Kiso and Yoshino, recruited for their expertise in Japanese-style rafting techniques by foresters who deemed Chinese timber rafts too cumbersome and slow.⁹⁴ The Japanese timber rafters were traveling downstream on rafts made from scattered logs that had floated over to the Korean side of the river when they were attacked by Chinese timbermen armed with guns and polearms.⁹⁵ A few days later, Chinese timber cutters also destroyed a branch office of the Yalu River Timber Company at Mao'ershan and kidnapped six more timber rafters. After tense exchanges between Japanese and Chinese authorities, the governor of the Chinese border county of Linjiang helped negotiate the release of the Japanese timbermen.⁹⁶ By targeting both the Japanese timbermen employed by the Forest Management Bureau and the Yalu River Timber Company, Chinese timbermen demonstrated their resentment at these twin entities of Japanese lumber hegemony along the Yalu.

The outbreak of violence along the upper Yalu provoked accusatory exchanges between Chinese and Japanese officials as well as finger-pointing within the Japanese protectorate bureaucracy. Chinese officials identified the violence as a predictable consequence of long-standing *muba* animosity toward Japanese timber imperialism. A July 5 telegram from the viceroy of the Three Eastern Provinces (the late Qing administrative name for Manchuria) to the Qing foreign ministry explained that the capture of Japanese timbermen was "all due" to the Forest Management Bureau's charging of fees to dredge and collect Chinese-felled timber as well as their arrest of Wang.⁹⁷ Such violence was not entirely unanticipated. As early as January 1909, an American diplomat in Andong quoted a Chinese Yalu River Timber Company official who predicted "serious disturbances" and "armed resistance" from Chinese timbermen with the arrival of the rafting season.⁹⁸ This idea of official foreknowledge became a sticking point for Japanese officials, some of whom claimed that local Qing police and county officials were encouraging, if not directly instigating, the *muba* violence for their own benefit.⁹⁹

Among Japanese officials in Korea, internal reports chided the Forest Management Bureau and Yalu River Timber Company for their overly aggressive pursuit of scattered timber. A June 14, 1909, report by one Japanese police official further identified the Forest Management Bureau's practice of drilling holes in scattered logs as another source of *muba* resentment, a criticism also raised by Chinese authorities. Japanese raftsmen drilled these holes in order to tie logs together and float them downstream to designated collection sites. But in the eyes of Chinese *muba*, the allegedly careless drilling of these holes irrevocably destroyed the resale value of this timber.¹⁰⁰ A July 7 Japanese military police report called for a return to "previous custom" that would allow for the unregulated collection of scattered timber as a means of quelling *muba* violence, a step that if followed would have threatened forestry officials' Yalu timber monopoly.¹⁰¹ In the meantime, large numbers of Japanese military police and troops were deployed to the upper Yalu in the name of protecting Japanese interests—a move that amplified preexisting tensions along the border.[102]

Japanese forestry officials themselves vehemently denied their own culpability in the outbreak of violence. A June 26 telegram from Forest Management Bureau chief Tokio Zenzaburō to Japanese Resident General Sone Arasuke defended the actions of his subordinates by explaining that modifications to scattered logs were necessary in order to float them downstream during the warmer months of the year, and that Chinese timbermen for their part had stolen over 15,000 *shaku* (roughly equivalent to 450,000 feet) of scattered timber from the Forest Management Bureau over the course of the previous year. Furthermore, Tokio argued that there was "no specific evidence" to support the Chinese account linking Wang's detention by Japanese authorities to the outbreak of violence, claiming that this was merely a "pretense" invented by Chinese officials to conceal their own negligence.[103]

Further large-scale flooding and Chinese timber cutters' lingering dissatisfaction ignited another wave of violence along the Yalu later that summer. On July 31, 1909, the Seoul-based *Hwangsŏng sinmun* (Capital Gazette) reported successive days of heavy rain along the Sino-Korean border region, which was a common enough occurrence that time of the year along the Yalu.[104] Around two weeks later, on August 15, a small group of Chinese lumberers fired upon Korean timbermen near Cho'san County and stole their rafts. Two days afterward, Chinese lumberers on a raft bearing the insignia of the Mushang gonsuo, a *muba* trade guild, captured a raft and tools belonging to a Japanese Forest Management Bureau technician and a fellow Korean employee. Confrontation between the parties resulted in heavy injuries, with the Forest Management Bureau claiming that both men had been cruelly bound and beaten after they tried to reclaim the raft.[105]

As repeated confrontations occurred between timbermen along the Yalu River border, sensationalized reporting on the ongoing violence appeared in media outlets throughout China, Japan, and Korea. Such coverage reflected the ethnic biases of these media organs, with the Chinese press offering a more sympathetic portrayal of the Chinese timbermen's plight while Japanese media and censored Korean newspapers stressed their uncontrolled violence. A June 20, 1909, article in the Shanghai-based *Shen bao*, for example, reported the hardships and poverty that *muba* were enduring under the Yalu River Timber Company monopoly as reasons for their protest.[106] In contrast, an August 22 article in the *Japan Times* noted that Chinese timbermen were "acting in an outrageous manner," while a report published two days earlier in the *Hwangsŏng sinmun* described how the "extreme violence" of timbermen was "causing widespread fear" among the local population.[107] Reports of "riots" along the Yalu River even reached the pages of the London-based *Times*, demonstrating the extent to which Yalu timber politics reverberated on a larger stage.[108]

The divergent attitudes displayed in these media reports closely mirrored those held by Japanese and Chinese officials in negotiations over scattered logs. A July 14, 1909, telegram from Manchurian Viceroy Xiliang to the Qing foreign ministry emphasized the need to protect the livelihoods of Chinese timbermen while resisting the "bullying" of the Forest Management Bureau.[109] Meanwhile, in an August 25 piece of correspondence with the resident general, Andong consul Okabe stated disparagingly that the *muba* were little more than "timber bandits" threatening the peace and stability of the border region.[110]

Noticeably absent from high-level discussions and media reports were the voices of Chinese timbermen themselves. When *muba* were discussed, it was often in collective terms that emphasized their large numbers (nearly 20,000 according to more sensationalized reports) and volatility rather than their individual role in the complex social ecology of the Yalu River border.[111] Illiterate and impoverished, these timber fellers used collective violence and protest as one of the limited range of "weapons of the weak" available to them in the face of Japanese timber imperialism.[112]

The obstinate resistance of Chinese timbermen eventually compelled Japanese officials to renegotiate the timber raft issue. The first set of negotiations took place after the earliest wave of June attacks. A July 6 agreement between the Japanese consul at Andong, the governor of Dongbiandao, and the Yalu River Timber Company put a one-year moratorium on the latter's monopoly over lumber sales on the Chinese side of the river. While this addressed ongoing resentment over the Yalu River Timber Company's actions, noticeably absent from this agreement was any discussion of the flooded timber question, which had wider, cross-border dimensions.[113] In the wake of additional outbreaks of violence in August 1909, the same group of officials and representatives from the Yalu River Timber Company concluded an additional agreement with the Forest Management Bureau on the collection of scattered logs on August 29, 1909. This agreement clarified the procedures by which individual Chinese timbermen could reclaim logs dredged by the Yalu River Timber Company or Forest Management Bureau. Japanese officials also agreed to hire more Chinese timbermen to float timber rafts down the river.[114]

While new negotiations over flooded timber did not ultimately unseat Japanese control over the Yalu timber industry, they demonstrated that the defining of new borders of Japanese power in the Sino-Korean borderland would not go unchallenged. Just as had been the case with Hwangch'op'yŏng negotiations, Japanese imperial officials modified their initial ambitions in the face of fierce local resistance. The question of scattered timber would remain a source of cross-border tension in subsequent years, as seasonal flooding and the resistance of Chinese timbermen continued to move the liquid geographies of the Yalu River to the forefront of Sino-Japanese diplomacy.

With the conclusion of the Japan-Korea Annexation Treaty on August 22, 1910, the Yalu and neighboring Tumen River became a formal border of the Japanese Empire. In terms of border administration, however, the treaty did little more than formalize a colonial boundary that had been constructed over the preceding Korean protectorate period (1905–1910). As this chapter has shown, protectorate officials intervened at multiple occasions in disputes over access to the natural resources of the Yalu borderland. While ostensibly done on behalf of the nominally independent Korean government, the real intention was to shore up Japanese control over the Korean Peninsula and use the Yalu River border as a stage for increasing Japanese economic and political power into Manchuria. This attempt to mobilize the liquid geographies of the Yalu border had clear limits. Japanese officials encountered serious challenges from local populations, officials on the Chinese side of the border, internal disagreements, and the Yalu River itself, which posed obstacles as well as opportunities to imperial border-making by flooding, depositing sediment, and providing a home to boundary-crossing fish populations. The result was a series of violent confrontations and compromises that showed the unstable nature of Japanese governance along this imperial frontier.

The construction of the Yalu River Railway Bridge from 1909 to 1911, covered in the following chapter, further illustrates how Japanese officials tried to make the Sino-Korean border a gateway for the flows of people and goods reinforcing Japanese imperial expansion in Korea and Manchuria. But these infrastructural aspirations would first have to face the seasonally protean Yalu River.

2
BRIDGING THE YALU

Fin di siècle Japanese imperialists attempting to bridge the Yalu River came face-to-face on multiple occasions with the river's capricious nature. Japanese troops first crossed the river using temporary pontoon bridges during the Sino-Japanese War. Ten years later, Japanese military engineers were tasked with bridging the Yalu once again during the Russo-Japanese War. The river they encountered in spring 1904, however, was very different from that in autumn 1894. As one Japanese official related to a foreign military observer:

> "We thought at first the reconnaissance would have been easy, as we crossed the river at the same place in 1894, but the changes had been too great. Our carefully prepared map was useless, as channels had changed; spots where fords had existed required bridging, and points out of range of the right bank were now within range of it, so our labour and money had been wasted."[1]

Seven years later, Japanese engineers completed a permanent steel bridge across the Yalu River, linking imperial railways in northern Korea and southern Manchuria. Here too engineers faced challenges from the seasonally changing river. An account of the bridge's construction related how engineers had faced "great depth, strong tidal flows, terrible floods, and ice—a truly uncommon conjunction of difficulties."[2]

This chapter analyzes bridge construction as a key aspect of imperial border creation and early managing of the Yalu River's human and nonhuman mobilities, or liquid geographies. The chapter begins by examining earlier military river crossings and temporary bridges built during the Sino- and Russo-Japanese Wars. The remainder of the narrative then focuses on construction of the Yalu River Railway Bridge, which officially commenced in 1909, while Korea was still a Japanese protectorate. The bridge's completion came in 1911, one year after the official Japanese annexation of Korea. It was one of the most important pieces of infrastructure along the Yalu border and, along with the protectorate-era imperial interventions detailed in the previous chapter, defined imperial power in the region for years afterward.

For Japanese colonizers seeking to not only cement control over Korea but also project power into Manchuria, bridge construction was an essential means of moving troops and supplies—the building blocks of empire—across the natural obstacle of the river. By providing a regulated, spatially fixed means of passage and transport over an otherwise dynamic and seasonally changing landscape, imperial boosters even claimed that the 1911 railway bridge "obliterated" the border itself.[3] Bridge construction transformed the borderland by fostering the creation of new settlements along the river, spurring further cross-border trade (not all of it licit), and giving military planners a strategic, if costly, pathway for the empire's "northern advance."

Of course, as the stories that opened this chapter highlight, bridging the Yalu River was never a straightforward proposition. Colonial bridge construction followed in the bloody wake of successive military campaigns, diplomatic confrontations, and the large-scale mobilization of manpower in the form of Japanese soldiers as well as Japanese, Chinese, and Korean laborers. Additionally, the Yalu River itself challenged Japanese efforts by seasonally flooding, freezing over, unfreezing, and shifting its course. In this way, bridge construction was characteristic of imperial Japan's larger imbrication in the Yalu River border's liquid geographies. When properly channeled, the mobile cross-border flow of people and goods ensured that the Sino-Korean political boundary was no practical boundary to Japanese military and economic ambitions. Nonetheless, the mobilities of borderland human and nonhuman actors and their seasonal cycles did not always behave in ways that suited the colonialist agenda.

Autumn 1894 and the Japanese Military Bridging of the Yalu

Japanese attempts to bridge the Yalu River began with temporary military bridges constructed during the Sino-Japanese War (1894–1895). As part of their bloody campaign against Qing China for regional supremacy, Japanese bridge builders mobilized physical and human resources in a battle with the river and Qing soldiers. Bridges allowed Japanese to transport troops and supplies across the Yalu in a more spatially fixed and reliable way than other methods of crossing, including the use of ferry boats. But the makeshift nature of these military bridges also rendered them susceptible to seasonal transformations in the river's surface. The physical presence of these bridges would ultimately be fleeting. Yet they provided knowledge about and experience with the Yalu River environment that Japanese military engineers would try (unsuccessfully) to mobilize in later military campaigns.

Growing tensions between the Japanese Meiji state and the Qing court over a number of issues, including competition for hegemony in Korea, culminated in the outbreak of the Sino-Japanese War in July 1894. Only months after Chinese media had proclaimed the need to punish Japanese "arrogance" in Korea, Qing leaders found themselves pushed from Korea to the Sino-Korean border after a series of military defeats.[4] Following the fall of the Qing garrison at the strategic northern city of Pyŏngyang in mid-September, Qing soldiers withdrew to the Yalu's northern bank, where troops under the command of Qing general Song Qing quickly began constructing earthen walls and other fortifications against the expected Japanese advance.[5] In anticipation of a potential Japanese attempt to cross the river, Qing generals also ordered the removal of boats that could be used to ferry troops.[6]

The Qing retreat to the Yalu came during a time of autumnal transition, when the hot, humid days of summer were replaced with rapidly dropping temperatures and water levels in the river were also retreating from their summertime highs. By November, the river would begin freezing over, a process that typically started at the river's narrowest, uppermost reaches and gradually moved downstream. All of these environmental factors weighed on Qing strategists, who worried that the Yalu was not a reliable barrier against Japanese invasion.[7] Should the river freeze over, the icy Yalu could provide Japanese forces a ready footpath to Qing fortifications. The length of the river also made it difficult to defend. While certain parts of the Yalu were deep, its neighboring tributary the Ai River was shallow and easily forded.[8] Qing military commander Song Qing ultimately headquartered the bulk of the Qing forces in Jiuliancheng, a lower Yalu fortress town across from the Korean walled city of Ŭiju. In anticipation of a Japanese river crossing, a further contingent of Qing troops was stationed near Sugujin, fifteen kilometers upstream. An advanced guard was also dispatched to Hushan, a Chinese mountain fortress directly across the easily fordable Ai River.[9]

The Yalu River near Ŭiju posed its own unique set of topographical considerations to advancing Japanese soldiers. As the river neared its mouth at the Yellow Sea just thirty miles downstream, it split into multiple channels intersected by numerous small river islands. It was at this point that the Ai River also joined the Yalu's course. The transport of Japanese troops and supplies across the shifting banks of the delta required the construction of multiple bridges as well as the fording of smaller rivulets. On the morning of October 24, an advance force of Japanese troops secretly crossed the river near Sugujin and ambushed Chinese troops.[10] With Qing forces distracted by this attack, construction of pontoon bridges to bring the bulk of Japanese troops across the river began that same day.

As described in the report of military engineer Yabuki Shūichi, building pontoon bridges across the Yalu River required military engineers to partially submerge themselves in the Yalu's frigid autumnal waters.[11] The stockpiling of materials to construct the bridges began under the cover of darkness on the evening of October 23. By the next morning, Yabuki received orders to build two separate bridges. The first spanned a short, twenty-meter-wide arm of the river and was completed in only an hour.[12] Construction of the second began at 8:00 p.m., as the Japanese sought to make darkness their ally against Qing detection. Japanese soldiers encountered a serious obstacle when the iron boats they had brought to use as supports for their pontoon bridge were discovered to have warped over weeks of transport across the Korean interior. The added difficulty of lashing these warped boats together delayed the completion of the bridge until 6:00 a.m., two hours after the deadline originally set by Japanese military commanders.[13] Yet even with the delay and cold, Japanese soldiers completed the bridge and overwhelmed the Qing force at Hushan. When they arrived at the walled city of Jiuliancheng, they found that it had already been abandoned by Qing forces, who had fled further northward.[14]

While official reports like those penned by Yabuki stressed the ability of soldiers to overcome environmental challenges in orderly (if slightly delayed) fashion, later Japanese-language accounts highlighted the dangers and volatility of the Yalu River crossing. One story of the Yalu crossing reprinted in numerous unofficial war histories and newspapers as far afield as Aspen, Colorado, was the drowning of Private Mihara Kunitarō.[15] As the story went, Mihara was a young soldier and "commoner" (*heimin*) from rural Tokushima prefecture. As military engineers prepared to bridge the Yalu, there was a call for soldiers to help measure the width of the river channel by swimming across the frigid water and laying a rope on the other bank. Courageously volunteering to complete the task, Mihara began the arduous swim across the river, all while trying to avoid the watchful eyes and ears of nearby Qing guards. By the time he reached roughly half the distance of the river channel, however, the frigidness of the water and the unexpectedly strong pull of the current sapped his strength. Unwilling to call for help lest his cries betray the position of his comrades, Mihara was quietly subsumed by the river's flowing current.[16] Inspired by Mihara's devotion, an onlooking sergeant, Miyake Heikichi, volunteered to complete the task and successfully swam across the river, allowing Japanese military forces to complete the pontoon bridge and lead their forces to victory in what became known as the Battle of Jiuliancheng. Woodblock prints from the period depict the stoic Miyake tying a rope to his chest and braving the river's frigid water out of patriotic duty and in memory of his fallen comrade (see figure 2.1).

Narratives of Private Mihara's tragic death stand in stark contrast with tamer official accounts of the Yalu crossing. Yabuki's report does not mention either Mihara or Miyake by name, while a contemporaneous account by a fellow Japanese officer lists zero deaths and only one injury incurred during bridge construction.[17] Whether Mihara's story was an embellishment of actual events or official accounts felt compelled to downplay unnecessary loss of life is uncertain. This story highlights, however, many of the obstacles facing military engineers in their attempt to construct pontoon bridges across the Yalu, including the frigid temperatures of the late autumn river.

Once completed, pontoon bridges across the Yalu provided a valuable military transport route for Japanese forces penetrating further into the Manchurian interior. Over the course of the war, approximately 154,000 Japanese and numerous Korean and Chinese laborers were mobilized to transport food, clothing, armaments, and other supplies from bases in Japan and Korea to the

FIGURE 2.1. Woodblock print depicting Sergeant Miyake Heikichi's crossing of the Yalu River.

Source: Migita Toshihide, Ōryokkō ni Miyake gunsō no gōtan *(Sergeant Miyake's Courage at the Yalu River)*, 1895, Princeton University Art Museum Collection. Image courtesy of Princeton University Art Museum.

battlefront.[18] Goods moving from occupied positions in Korea to battlefields in Manchuria inevitably flowed across the Yalu River, where bridges hastily built in the heat of battle were modified, supplemented, and otherwise refurbished to serve as conduits for military supplies.[19] Yet the makeshift nature of these military bridges posed other logistical challenges to the maintenance of Japanese supply lines across the Yalu's seasonally changing landscape.

Unlike the permanent metal structures that transported later travelers across the river, pontoon bridges floated precariously at the waterline. Thus, when winter carved the Yalu's surface into a craggy landscape of floating ice, it would take additional effort to ensure that the bridges were not destroyed. A series of articles published in the *Asahi shinbun*, a major Japanese newspaper, relayed to metropolitan readers the struggles of soldiers to clear ice from the Yalu bridges.[20] Based on the report of Sixth Army Division military engineer Imasawa Yoshio, one article described how ice began appearing on the Yalu in late November, putting pressure on the pontoons and causing some of them to break and float away. Soldiers were stationed all across the bridges, making repairs and breaking up the large blocks of ice. Iron anchors and chains were used to strengthen the structure of these bridges. To install these anchors and perform other necessary repairs, soldiers entered the frozen river, which, the newspaper recorded, caused them to lose sensation in their limbs. As one article stated, the Yalu was but one of the many continental rivers Japanese soldiers had forded over the course of the conflict, and other rivers brought additional geographic challenges.[21] But the uniqueness of the Yalu lay in its role as the boundary between two strategic zones of new-found Japanese imperial interest, Korea and Manchuria. Japanese Army planners were intent on using bridges to ensure that this political boundary would not be a practical boundary to their own military ambition. Military bridges gave Japanese authorities a reliable method of transporting military supplies across the border, making them necessary to maintain even at the cost of great human effort.

Spring 1904, Useless Maps, and a Second Military Crossing

The bridging of the Yalu River during the Sino-Japanese War had effects that outlasted war's end and the removal of these temporary bridges. As Korea became firmly enmeshed in Japan's growing sphere of informal empire, the Yalu assumed further strategic importance. Nevertheless, the weakening of Qing power did invite a new imperial contender into the region—imperial Russia. Japanese leaders were alarmed by Russia's rapid expansion into Manchuria and northern Korea. This included the opening of a Russian timber concession along the Yalu River, which sparked the so-called Yalu River Crisis that saw the two empires move closer to open conflict. On February 8, 1904, three hours before Japan's official declaration of war was received by the Russian government, Japanese naval forces launched a surprise attack on Port Arthur, a strategic and heavily fortified Russian port on the Liaodong Peninsula in southern Manchuria. In the immediate weeks following the declaration of war, Japanese military leaders feared a Russian occupation of northern Korea.[22] Russian leaders decided instead, however, to concentrate their troops, much as Qing military forces had done a decade earlier, along the northern bank of the Yalu.

Ten years later, Japanese soldiers returned to the banks of the Yalu River in a pitched battle against imperial Russia. Russian troops under the command of General Mikhail Zasulich quickly abandoned a lumber camp on the Korean side of the lower Yalu and split into two contingents: one stationed at Andong, where Zasulich expected Japanese forces to make the river crossing, and another at Jiuliancheng, the same walled fortress where Song Qing's army had defended against a Japanese advance ten years earlier. Zasulich's orders from chief Russian military commander Aleksey Kuropatkin were to avoid making a decisive military stand at the Yalu, holding the Russian position only as long as it took to assess the size of the Japanese advance and inflict significant losses.[23]

Japanese strategy during the first months of the war mirrored that of the earlier Sino-Japanese War. Not content to simply solidify Japan's position on the Korean Peninsula, Japanese military leaders also sought to secure a foothold in southern Manchuria, particularly the Liaodong Peninsula, which had been occupied by Japanese during the Sino-Japanese War but later abandoned after a "Triple Intervention" of diplomatic pressure from Russia, France, and Germany. To accomplish this, Japanese leaders decided that the First Army would cross the Yalu from Korea to engage with Zasulich's troops, while the Second Army would land at the Liaodong Peninsula to begin a siege of the Russian stronghold at Port Arthur, a two-prong strategy also used during the Sino-Japanese War. Echoes of the earlier conflict were also seen in the decision to cross the Yalu not at Andong, where Russian forces were expecting a crossing to occur, but in the supposedly familiar riparian landscape near Jiuliancheng.[24]

Japanese military engineers soon realized, however, that the Yalu River they confronted in April 1904 had little in common with the river bridged by Japanese forces in late October only a decade earlier. As contemporary reports noted, springtime runoff from melting ice upstream raised water levels higher than those encountered a decade earlier in late autumn. Natural shifts in the river channel over the years as well as seasonal fluctuations frustrated engineers' attempts to capitalize on previously acquired experiences.[25] Such frustrations were encapsulated in the remarks to foreign military observers shared in the introduction to this chapter, where one Japanese military officer noted that a map prepared on carefully gathered intelligence from ten years earlier was now "useless."[26] As a result of unforeseen changes in the river's topography, military engineers found they had insufficient supplies to build the necessary bridges. In this respect, however, they received unwitting help from their enemies. In the lumber camp abandoned earlier by retreating Russian forces, Japanese soldiers found anvils and forges, which helped make up for their material deficiencies.[27]

In the space of just ten years the riparian topography of the Yalu River had changed dramatically, necessitating an entirely different approach to bridging the river than before. After gathering critical information about Russian defenses from repeated scouting missions, Japanese troops quickly occupied two river islands between the Korean and Chinese banks of the Yalu.[28] Once these two islands were in Japanese possession, military engineers began surveying the channels between the islands and the main banks for bridge construction. The construction of a first bridge spanning the gap between the island of Kŏmjŏngdo and the Korean bank of the Yalu began on April 26.[29] The bridge soon came under heavy artillery fire from Russian forces, who relentlessly pounded at the engineers who worked on the bridge over the next few days. As a result of this barrage, the 258-yard-long trestle bridge took some forty-five hours to complete, and three Japanese military engineers died in the process. Once finished, however, the bridge was never actually used to transport troops across the river. The whole process was a strategic diversion—while Russians expended their ammunition on this dummy bridge and gave away the position of their guns, other Japanese military engineers stockpiled materials for the bridges that would actually be used by the First Army to cross the Yalu.[30]

Between April 27 and April 30, a total of nine additional bridges were built across the various channels of the Yalu and neighboring Ai River (figure 2.2).[31] The majority of these were trestle bridges composed of fir trunks bound together with straw rope and bolted together with iron nails and supported by wooden trestles that were sunk into the river bottom. The largest of the nine bridges, which spanned the main Yalu channel at 380 yards long, utilized fifty-foot-long pontoon boats that were transported by ship to northern Korea as well as thirty-foot-long boats procured locally.[32] During the bridging process, a small flotilla of Japanese naval gunboats traveled up the river from its mouth at the Yellow Sea to provide support for the First Army advance by bombing Russian positions downstream.[33]

Once constructed, these bridges seemingly promised a stable path across the river. Yet while nails, planks, and boats had reduced the volatility of the river's flowing surface, the life-death contingency of crossing a river in the heat of battle

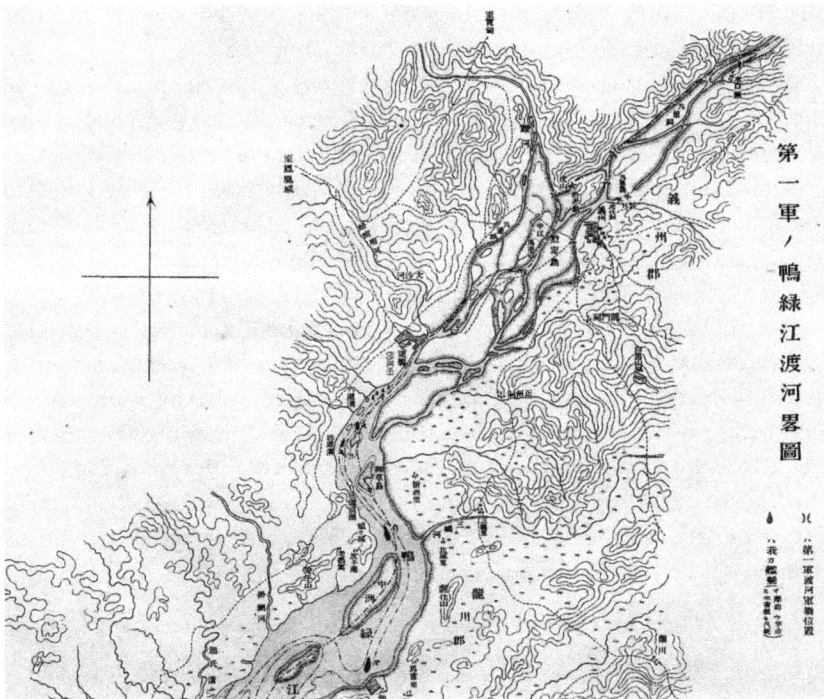

FIGURE 2.2. Detail from Japanese map showing the sites (marked by x-like lines) where the First Army crossed the Yalu River.

Source: https://commons.wikimedia.org/wiki/File:Map_of_the_Battle_of_Yalu_River.jpg.

remained. For Japanese soldiers preparing to cross over these newly constructed bridges, the Yalu River was an unavoidable reminder of the foreignness and danger of the wartime landscape they encountered. "I was taken aback by how large the Yalu River truly was," recorded officer Jimon Tarō in his journal. "At the same time, I was frightened by the thought of how we were supposed to cross that large river right in front of the enemy."[34] The immensity of the landscape and the scale of the conflict was also expressed in the diaries of military doctor Mizokami Sadao: "The landscape was so continental. It was the first time I truly realized that we Japanese were simply frogs in a well."[35]

Although the Yalu's unpredictability presented a significant environmental barrier to advancing Japanese troops, in other respects they enjoyed tangible advantages over defending Russian forces. The Japanese troops led by First Army commander Kuroki Tamemoto easily outnumbered the Russian troops under Zasulich's command, which were spread all over the Yalu's Chinese bank.[36] On

April 30 the First Army officially crossed the Yalu River, quickly overwhelming the outnumbered and outgunned Russian defending forces.

Five thousand Russian soldiers and two thousand Japanese soldiers were killed or injured during the Battle of the Yalu River.[37] Civilian populations along the river were also hard-hit by the violent repercussions of this battle. While Chinese and Korean governments had both officially declared their neutrality in the conflict, they were powerless to shield their subjects from the fallout of imperialist war waged on their soil. The Russian military exercised effective control over northeast China since first stationing troops there in 1901 to protect Russian rail lines and had begun moving into northern Korea by 1903. Only days after the declaration of war, Japanese forces swiftly moved to invade and occupy Korea. As one Seoul-based Korean newspaper related, Russian troops torched Korean farmers' homes and stole livestock, clothes, and other goods in their retreat across the Yalu from the Japanese.[38] Similar brutalities were also perpetrated by Japanese soldiers. Traveling through the war-ravaged landscape of northern Korea and the Yalu River delta, famous American author and Russo-Japanese war correspondent Jack London wrote:

> Northern Korea was a desolate land when the Japanese passed through. Villages and towns were deserted. The fields lay untouched. There was no ploughing nor sowing, no green things growing. . . . I rode down upon the sandy islands of the Yalu. For weeks these islands had been the dread between-the-lines of two fighting armies. The air above had been rent by screaming projectiles. The echoes of the final battle had scarcely died away. The trains of Japanese wounded and Japanese dead were trailing by.[39]

The spring 1904 military crossing of the Yalu was part of a longer, violent process of Japanese imperial expansion in Korea and Manchuria in which this seasonally protean boundary played a key part. In the wake of the Russo-Japanese Battle of the Yalu River (Ōryokkō kaisen) Japanese colonial engineers would set aside pontoon bridges and "useless maps" and begin plans for a more permanent, all-weather bridge to facilitate Japan's increased colonial presence in Northeast Asia.

Planning a Railway Bridge and the River Border Environment

For military planners seeking a quick, efficient, and all-weather military supply route into the Manchurian interior, the hastily built trestle and pontoon bridges of a former period failed to provide a sufficiently stable channel of transport across the seasonally variable Yalu River. Just months after the battle's end, the Japanese military began drawing plans for an iron railroad bridge across the river border. This bridge would link newly built Japanese railroad routes in southern Manchuria and Korea, weaving these regions further into the fabric of overseas empire.[40]

The push for a more permanent and predictable means of passage across the river accelerated after Japan coerced the Korean court into signing the Japan-Korea Protectorate Treaty in December 1905. With the conclusion of this treaty, the ruling Korean Empire nominally maintained its sovereignty, but in practice all decisions regarding foreign affairs, and eventually all domestic administrative and military decisions, were made by the Japanese.[41] The creation of the Korean protectorate made the Yalu into a literal edge of empire, and as the expansionist logic of empire dictated, solidifying the imperial border meant being able to efficiently and quickly transport goods and people across it. Such a strategic calculus had little tolerance for the uncertainties of wind, currents, shifting riverbanks, and seasonal flows of water and ice.

Construction of the Yalu River Railway Bridge, completed in 1911, signaled Japanese imperialists' even more protracted commitment to surmounting the Yalu's natural barriers than the military bridges that preceded it. Challenges encountered by bridge builders included diplomatic protests from Western powers, ice, floods, the task of mobilizing massive amounts of international labor and expertise, and the deployment of new pneumatic caisson technologies to transport workers below the river's surface. Once completed, the bridge was hailed by Japanese commentators as a critical "link between Europe and Asia" that allowed for continuous rail travel from the tip of the Korean Peninsula to Europe through Manchuria and Siberia, as well as a monument to the accomplishments of their burgeoning continental empire.[42] At the same time it was decried by anti-colonial nationalists as another means of perpetuating Japanese exploitation and violence in the region.[43]

Railways were integral to the projection of Japanese imperial power into Korea and southern Manchuria.[44] Colonial railways readily served the dyad of Japanese commercial and military interests Peter Duus has described as "the abacus and the sword," though it was ultimately the "sword" that provided the greatest impetus for the construction of steel railway lines over the Yalu.[45] Japanese railway construction in Korea began in 1903 with work on a rail line between Pusan on the southern coast and the Korean capital of Seoul. Spurred by the wartime need to quickly transport troops and supplies to the warfront, beginning in 1904 the Japanese Imperial Army's Provincial Military Railroad Department oversaw the completion of this rail line as well as the construction of an additional route linking Seoul to the Yalu border. In Manchuria, Japanese engineers also built a light rail connecting Andong on the Chinese side of the Yalu with previously constructed Russian railway routes at Fengtian (Shenyang).[46]

Elite military planners in Japan saw a railroad route through Korea, across the Yalu River, and into Manchuria as imperative to Japan's national survival. These military planners included figures such as Yamagata Aritomo, the former samurai and Meiji oligarch who commanded the First Army troops that crossed the Yalu during the Sino-Japanese War, and Terauchi Masatake, an army general who later became the first governor-general of Korea. Following the Japanese military's close victory in the Russo-Japanese War, these strategists remained convinced that Russia was planning a revenge campaign. In a 1907 army manifesto circulated among elite government officials, Yamagata and others advocated a "northern advance" (*hokushin*) approach to national defense.[47] This plan called for the strengthening of Japanese positions in northern Manchuria in case of a Russian counterattack. Essential to this plan, they argued, was the completion of a unified railway line across Korea and Manchuria that could quickly transport troops to continental battlefields.[48]

Begun while the Russo-Japanese War was still raging, Japanese engineers' plans for a railroad bridge over the Yalu River continued in the following years as a matter of perceived military necessity. Surveys for the bridge site took place in June 1904, as summer reached the Yalu and the war's frontlines moved elsewhere. The location eventually chosen by military surveyors was several miles downstream of Jiuliancheng, the site where previous military bridges had been built and where Russian and Japanese artillery fire had reverberated just two months earlier.[49] Here the river converged into one main channel rather than the delta-like configuration of multiple channels and river islands that characterized the river near Ŭiju and Jiuliancheng. The decision to build the bridge here consequentially reshaped the social geography of the lower Yalu.

Japanese colonists following in the wake of railway construction built infrastructure to channel the river's surging flow, engorged especially during monsoonal summertime rains, away from newly built borderland boomtowns. On the Korean side of the river, the frontier town that sprung around the terminus of a new railway line to Seoul was dubbed Sinŭiju or "New Ŭiju." Built entirely on the Yalu's marshy floodplain, this new colonial city was made possible by also building a large embankment to shield the town against the Yalu's periodically rising water levels.[50] Although the levee's protection would prove less than perfect, Sinŭiju soon superseded Ŭiju as provincial capital and the economically most important city in surrounding North P'yŏngan Province.[51]

Directly across the river a new Japanese settlement was also forming in close proximity to the Chinese city of Andong, and like Sinŭiju, the Japanese settlement at Andong featured a large embankment to protect it against seasonal flooding. According to a 1931 Chinese-language Andong County gazetteer, Japanese military authorities coerced Andong city officials into allowing the sale of land near the riverbank to house the settlement. Chinese farmers initially refused to yield their land, until they were coerced to do so at gunpoint by Japanese soldiers.[52] Japanese accounts of the settlement's creation told an entirely different story of grateful Chinese authorities "granting" the Japanese military land after Japanese improved the city's roads.[53] Regardless of the settlement's disputed origins, it would acquire important status as a rail terminus. Following the end of the Russo-Japanese War and the withdrawal of occupying Japanese military forces, treaties with the Qing government cemented this settlement's status as a treaty port and zone of Japanese extraterritorial privilege in China. Its Japanese population also grew rapidly—from 850 immediately before the Russo-Japanese War to 5,922 by September 1906.[54] The growth of colonial settlements at Sinŭiju and Andong added a new element to the already volatile, multiethnic mix of peoples at the Yalu River border.

It was between these newly formed colonial enclaves at Sinŭiju and Andong that bridge construction was to take place. As railway projects created new nodes and lines of Japanese imperial power, preparations were made for a railroad bridge that linked them over the Yalu River's shifting liquid surface. Beginning in February 1905, military engineers undertook systematic surveys of the river's depth and discharge.[55]

Surveys of the Yalu River for railway bridge construction confirmed what had already been sensed over the course of two previous military crossings, namely the seasonal volatility of the river's flow and shifts in the riverbed. In April 1905 engineers conducted boring tests at five different points along the riverbed. The use of a boring machine on the riverbank posed little difficulty, but as engineers moved into the middle of the river, the depth of the water and strength of the current forced them to use two Japanese cargo boats tied together to stabilize the machine. These tests determined that a rock stratum, which had to be reached to provide stability for the bridge's foundations, lay 72–85 feet below shifting successive layers of water, sand, and gravel.[56]

Other tests to measure tidal action, temperature variation, and levels of previous floods further highlighted the climatic and physical obstacles to bridge construction. As Japanese engineers recorded, the temperature variation between winter and summer along the Yalu could be as great as 140–150 degrees Fahrenheit. The differences in river height during high and low tides was also determined to be between twelve and seventeen feet, a figure determined only after tidal markers installed by the Japanese were initially destroyed by river ice in December 1905 and subsequently reinstalled.[57] The freezing of the river for three or four months of the year was a regular occurrence, closing the river to waterborne traffic and opening it instead to horse and ox-drawn sleds and pedestrian traffic. But even in this time of seeming fixedness of the river's surface, surveyors recorded the maximum daily movement of the river's icy surface at 7.2 feet.[58] Ice was very much a mobile part of the border's liquid geographies.

After these initial surveys, plans for the Yalu River Railway Bridge submitted by the Japanese Army to the Minister of State in July 1905 called for six 300-foot-long sections and six 200-foot-long sections. These sections would be supported by twelve masonry and concrete piers for a combined length of approximately 3,000 feet. The planned budget for this bridge was approximately 2.33 million yen, a hardly insignificant sum when imperial coffers were already strained by expensive overseas military campaigns.[59] Yet the alacrity with which the Japanese cabinet approved these plans in October 1905 illustrates Japan's deeply held fears of another Russian military invasion.[60] Blueprints for the bridge's design, completed between 1905 and 1906, drew on international as well as Japanese expertise. For design of the bridge's steel trusses, the Japanese protectorate government in Korea solicited the help of a Philadelphia-based American railway engineer.[61] Plans for the bridge also included eight-foot-wide pedestrian pathways on both sides of the steel trusses, which were explicitly designed to accommodate artillery during wartime.[62]

Despite engineers' careful anticipation of the Yalu River's environmental variability, their plans failed to account for the turbulent international politics of the border. In 1903, one year before the outbreak of the Russo-Japanese War, American officials in Beijing concluded a treaty with the Qing court that authorized the opening of Andong as a foreign treaty port.[63] Due to the war's outbreak, the first American consul in Andong, Charles J. Arnall, did not actually assume his post until 1906. Arnall was a committed advocate for the American principle of "Open Door" access to trade in China, which soon led him into conflict with Japanese authorities over their plans to build a railroad bridge spanning the Yalu River.[64] Arnall feared that the fixed nature of the bridge downstream from Andong would sever the city's access to the sea. This would harm the economic fortunes of the newly opened treaty port, or worse, leave its foreign trade entirely in Japanese hands. British diplomats also shared Arnall's fears about the deleterious impact of bridge construction, as they had a stake in ensuring that Chinese importers of British goods had ready access to the newly opened treaty port.

Anglo-American protests over Japanese plans for the Yalu River Railway Bridge show competing logics regarding the region's liquid geographies and managing cross-border flows of peoples and goods. For American and British diplomats, the river's accessibility to large ocean-going vessels was of greatest perceived value, whereas Japanese prioritized intersecting the river with railways to link Japanese colonial projects in Korea and Manchuria (the bridge would also not hurt the lucrative Japanese-controlled timber industry, as timber rafts could still travel downstream under the bridge). Anglo-American diplomats' ultimate suggestion to Japanese authorities was to alter plans for the bridge to include a section that would swing open to river traffic.[65] This opening section of the bridge would provide a literal "open door" to the upper Yalu, allowing ships to periodically pass through while preserving the functionality of the bridge as a means of rail transport. Japanese officials were initially reluctant to accommodate Anglo-American requests on the issue. American officials criticized Japanese diplomats' perceived capriciousness, quoting them as alternatively stating "on the one hand, that there was not enough upstream traffic to warrant the extra expenditure on a draw-bridge and, on the other, 'that the passage of junks would require it to be open too much of the time.'"[66]

Japanese engineers eventually acquiesced to Anglo-American diplomatic pressure on the bridge issue, modifying existing blueprints in November 1908 to include an opening section (see figure 2.3).[67] American officials cited begrudging Japanese diplomats as believing that "a fixed bridge would not seriously interfere with any major amount of navigation on the river and that they were

FIGURE 2.3. Japanese postcard depicting the completed Yalu River Railway Bridge with opening section.

Image courtesy of Skillman Library at Lafayette College Digital Scholarship Services, East Asia Image Collection, https://ldr.lafayette.edu/concern/images/jw827c61n.

giving in to a foolish request on the part of the foreigners merely to save an argument."[68] In the terse wording of a contemporary Japanese cabinet document, the changes were made for "diplomatic considerations" (*gaikō jō no jijō*).[69] This would not be the first time that diplomatic conflict followed in the wake of Yalu bridge construction, as a dispute later broke out between Japan and the Qing government over the bridge and river sovereignty.[70]

Fresh reminders of the challenges of the river environment, including seasonal flooding, came once construction of the Yalu River Railway Bridge officially began in August 1909. With modified blueprints in hand, Japanese engineers from the Railroad Bureau of the Japanese protectorate government in Korea officially supervised the project. One of these engineers was a young Tokyo University graduate named Koike Shin'ichi, whose detailed diary of his time on the project provides a rare, individualized window onto the construction process. As described in Koike's journal, the lead-up to the start of construction was hardly smooth. Engineers encountered repeated challenges from the wind and river waves, which hampered depth surveys.[71] There was also the flooding characteristic of the monsoonal Yalu summer. Just a few days before construction was set to start, Koike recorded that everything was "in commotion" (*oosawagi*) as rising waters threatened the construction site, and even after construction began markers on the Chinese bank had to be replaced due to flooding.[72] In addition to these larger environmental challenges to the bridge project, Koike's diary mentions personal grievances with "stinky" Chinese food and ungrateful bosses, though Koike was relatively well-off in comparison to most of the bridge site workers, as will soon be discussed.[73]

Going below the River's Surface

Engineers liked Koike supervised the Yalu bridge project, but the actual task of assembling the bridge fell to the thousands of Chinese, Korean, and Japanese workers who came to know the seasonal variability of the Yalu River environment intimately through their own sweat and labor.[74] On August 1, 1909, workers began moving materials to a selected site along the Korean side of the riverbank. But work on the first set of bridge foundations could not start until August 20 due to previously mentioned seasonal flooding. Once the rain-engorged waters receded, construction commenced on the first six foundation piers ("pier" here referring to a support for the end of adjacent spans in the context of bridge construction).[75]

Preparation of bridge foundations relied on the use of a new technology for Japanese engineers: pneumatic caissons. These were sealed, watertight retaining structures used to penetrate below the Yalu River's muddy riverbed and were entered by means of a pressurized air lock. First pioneered by early nineteenth-century French civil engineers, the use of pneumatic caissons was ubiquitous in many of the great bridge engineering projects of the nineteenth century, including the famous Brooklyn Bridge completed in 1883. The Yalu River bridge project represented only the second time that Japanese engineers had ever used fixed pneumatic caissons for bridge construction. Their first attempt was during the building of a smaller railroad bridge over the Ch'ŏngchŏn River in Korea, an experience that was seen as an important trial run for the subsequent Yalu River project.[76] As a result of the novelty of this particular technology, Japanese engineers turned once again, as they had in the case of the design of the bridge's steel trusses, to foreign expertise. This time the outside assistance came not from a Western source but from a Chinese contractor named Yang Guodong, who oversaw the procurement of laborers to work on these caissons.[77] While pneumatic caisson technology was novel in the context of Japanese civil engineering, Chinese engineering projects had been employing such technology for over a decade.[78] According to Japanese engineers' reports of the Yalu River Railway Bridge construction, among the previous examples of pneumatic caisson use they consulted was the 1907–1908 construction of the Liao River Railway Bridge by the Sino-British Imperial Railways of North China.[79] It was likely in light of this experience that Japanese engineers relied on Yang's help, a presence that subverted later Japanese depictions of the bridge as a purely Japanese technical accomplishment.[80]

Bridge construction reports give detailed accounts of the Chinese workers who descended into the airtight caissons and labored under the shifting, muddy banks of the river (see figure 2.4). As reports related, two "gangs" of 8–20 laborers worked together in one caisson, filling large buckets with mud and sand that was then lifted through an airtight lock back up to the surface of the water. These gangs alternated eight-hour shifts that rotated at 6:00 a.m., 2:00 p.m., and 10:00 p.m., working an average of twelve excruciating hours a day, shoveling and lifting soil.[81] Once enough soil within the caisson had been excavated, it was then filled with concrete to provide foundational strength for the bridge pier.[82]

A pervasive orientalism in the language of surviving Japanese reports portrays caisson workers as anthropomorphic machines whose labor power needed to be tempered by Japanese overseers' superior methods of management and concern for hygiene. In his detailed discussion of Japanese imperial exploitation of Chinese coolie labor, Mark Driscoll notes the rampant and inherently self-serving personification of Chinese laborers as "superhumanly strong workers, subhumanly stupid individuals, and doglike in their willingness to obey Japanese colonizers and their Chinese bosses alike."[83] Similar stereotypes also permeate

本圖ハ水面下四十呎ノ江底ニ於ケル潜水面内作業ノ實況ナリ

FIGURE 2.4. Photograph from an official bridge construction report. According to the original caption, "This picture shows caisson work being conducted forty feet below the surface of the water."

Source: Chōsen Sōtokufu Tetsudōkyoku, Ōryokkō kyōryō kōji hōkoku (Keijō [Seoul]: Chōsen Sōtokufu, 1912), 118.

reports of Yalu River bridge construction. Regarding the selection of caisson laborers, Japanese reports stated that they were a "special class" that was "accustomed" to the hard work within the caisson. The head coolie was "carefully selected, as his ability had a great influence on the progress of the work."[84]

A perennial concern for overseers was a condition they called "caisson disease," which resulted from variations in air pressure between the surface of the river and inside the caisson. Typical symptoms included ear pain, difficulty hearing, and increased fatigue.[85] To guard against this, Japanese overseers regulated the types of workers employed in the caissons. They were to be less than twenty-five years old, as younger bodies were said to be more "elastic" and thus allowed for better blood circulation in the pressurized environment of the caisson. When outbreaks of "caisson disease" still occurred, Japanese overseers blamed them on the workers themselves rather than their working conditions. "Chinese coolies," reports concluded, were "indifferent to the concept of hygiene (*eisei*) and cared little about their health, being the kind of race that refuses to acknowledge anything else in the face of money."[86] More likely, Japanese stipulations for caisson laborers, which included prohibitions against being "weak or fatigued" in addition to twelve-hour work days, incentivized these workers to simply ignore symptoms of discomfort resulting from air pressure until they became serious.[87]

The private sources of Japanese engineers indicate the very real physical dangers that accompanied caisson work. In an October 26, 1909, diary entry, engineer Koike Shin'ichi described leading two Japanese customs officials on a tour of the bridge construction site. Koike's curious guests expressed interest in entering one of the caissons to see ongoing foundation work. Upon entering the air lock, however, the visiting officials complained about ear pain caused by the change in air pressure. Finally, after one of the officials began "turning pale white," their descent into the caisson was quickly abandoned.[88]

The ultimate reward for Chinese laborers engaged in this dangerous work, one that Japanese customs officials were unable to withstand for even a few seconds, was a ten-hour wage of 0.55 yen, only slightly greater than the rate paid for normal unskilled laborers on the construction site.[89] In addition, discipline was enforced by the seven overseers and an interpreter who regularly alternated roles in directly supervising the excavation work within the caisson.[90] While only a minority of workers employed on the Yalu bridge construction site shared the experience of working below the river's surface in narrow iron chambers, the back-breaking and poorly remunerated nature of their work can be said to be typical of the majority of laborers on the site.

Seasons of Bridge Construction and the Bridge's Completion

Work stoppages for the wintertime icebound season and summertime flooding were a perennial feature of bridge construction. After the completion of the foundations for the first six piers in December 1909 by means of pneumatic caissons, the freezing of the river halted bridge construction.[91] As engineers later noted, while completion of the Yalu River Railway Bridge would technically take slightly over two years, the climate allowed for active construction to occur only sixteen months of this period.[92] Although the completed railroad bridge provided year-round transport across the river, its construction was firmly tied to the traditional seasonal cycles of life and activity along the river.

At the same time that winter obstructed bridge construction, diplomatic tensions were once again mounting over Japanese authorities' boundary-crossing intentions. Much like earlier Anglo-American protests, this Sino-Japanese conflict saw competing empires displaying competing logics when it came to bridge construction and the border's liquid geographies. Qing authorities expressed vocal concern over what they deemed an obvious threat to their sovereignty over the river's northern bank. As a telegraph sent to the governor-general of the Three Eastern Provinces expressed, bridge construction was a matter that "sorely affected" Qing border defense, especially as the river had traditionally been a natural "moat" between China and Korea.[93]

The last thing Qing rulers wanted was for the only all-weather passage for the flow of people and goods across the river to be under unilateral Japanese control. Soon after construction began in August 1909, the Qing court sent a petition asking that construction be stopped until a formal diplomatic agreement could be reached between the two countries. Qing officials also requested that Japanese authorities immediately remove a survey marker that had been erected on the Chinese side of the Yalu.[94] Japanese officials responded by claiming that bridge construction was permitted under earlier unequal treaties. Qing officials were unconvinced, and an initial round of negotiations fell through after both sides were unable to reach an agreement.[95] Finally, in March 1910, just as the ice over the frozen Yalu was beginning to thaw and break loose, Qing and Japanese diplomats reached an agreement that allowed for bridge construction to continue. As part of the terms specified by the agreement, customs inspections for incoming rail traffic were to be conducted on both the Chinese and Korean sides of the Yalu. In addition, the Qing government was given the option of purchasing the side of the bridge in the Chinese half of the river in fifteen years along with the rest of the Fengtian-Andong line (though, quite tellingly, Japanese control of the bridge would never actually be ceded until after 1945).[96]

Construction resumed in spring 1910, following the thaw in Sino-Japanese diplomatic tensions and Yalu River ice, but the Yalu's seasonal variations continued to determine the pace of the construction work. Excavation of each of the twelve foundation piers in the middle of the riverbed proceeded until November 1910, with pauses for a few months during the summer flooding season.[97] During this process, materials were moved by hand trolley, junk, and tow boat to each of the floating "caisson islands" of wood scaffolding erected during the process of foundation excavation.[98] Wintertime brought another cessation in construction, during which preparations began for erection of the large steel trusses, imported from the United States, that provided the main framework for the bridge. Truss installation entailed the creation of large wooden frameworks that could be used to hold each 200-foot or 300-foot span in place until construction had advanced enough for it to support itself. The material of choice for these timber frameworks was pine trees harvested from the dense forests of the upper

Yalu River basin.[99] Standing on these timber frameworks, laborers lifted the giant steel beams into place for the bridge trusses and riveted them together. Riveting gangs were typically composed of small groups of Japanese and Korean blacksmiths who used a pneumatic riveter also imported from the United States as well as a larger number of temporarily employed Chinese and Korean laborers.[100]

Whether or not the workers laboring on the bridge had any awareness of the larger ecological consequences of their actions, the harvesting of timber from the upper Yalu River basin to build their frameworks and scaffolds was inextricably linked to the summer floods that threatened to wash away these same temporary structures. The most dramatic of these floods occurred on July 19, 1911, when intense rains caused the river level to rise seventeen feet and swept away one of the steel trusses into the river. Although the wooden framework was quickly rebuilt and parts of the steel truss recovered downstream, other steel parts had to be ordered from Japan to rebuild the washed-out section.[101] Engineering reports portrayed these floods as unavoidable natural features of the riverine environment, but as observers in the region such as the compilers of Chinese local gazetteers later noted, they had undoubted anthropogenic characteristics. Deforestation in the upper Yalu River basin caused increased amounts of eroded soil and rainfall to drain into the river, exacerbating the effect of floods downstream.[102] As the case of flooding demonstrates, Yalu bridge construction and forestry were integrated together in a system of resource extraction that remade the natural ecology of the river basin at the same time bridge construction was reconfiguring the region's social and commercial geographies.

Completion of the Yalu River Railway Bridge entailed significant financial costs as well as labor and even loss of life. Technically speaking, the project was accomplished significantly under budget—a feat that Japanese reports claimed, in self-congratulatory tone, reflected "the excellent plans made by the engineers concerned" (although unspoken factors such as exploitative colonial labor also played a substantial role in achieving these savings).[103] When compared to other railroad bridges built in colonial Korea, however, the Yalu River project was not cheap. Such an observation bears true even when accounting for the Yalu's status as the largest river on the peninsula. For example, the Japanese-built railroad bridge over the Ch'ŏngch'ŏn River stretched a total of 2,582 feet, or 82 percent of the total length of the Yalu bridge, but only cost 52 percent as much, at 894,738 yen.[104] Engineers attributed the greater cost of the Yalu bridge to the swinging section, a concession to Anglo-American diplomatic pressure, as well as the pedestrian pathways abutting the bridge, a concession to the concerns of Japanese military strategists.[105] There were also human costs of bridge construction, including the death of a laborer who was struck in the head by a falling timber beam while disassembling the framework on one of the steel trusses.[106]

Japanese promoters of the bridge in Korea marked its completion with a grandiose "opening ceremony" (*kaitsūshiki*) that brought colonial dignitaries to the frontier railroad town of Sinŭiju on the Korean side of the river. Presiding over the ceremony was Terauchi Masatake, then serving as the first governor-general of the Japanese colony of Korea. Terauchi's prominent presence at the ceremony reflected not only his personal investment in this strategic lifeline to Manchuria but also the Japanese annexation of Korea just one year prior. Bridge building had begun in 1909 under the auspices of the Japanese protectorate government in Korea and the ostensible sovereignty of the Korean government. According to one report, the Korean monarch even visited the construction site in January 1910 to supervise ongoing efforts.[107] But the reality even during this period was that the Yalu River Railway Bridge was a thoroughly Japanese initiative, and with the pretense of Korean sovereignty over the peninsula obliterated by 1911, Japanese attendees at the event in Sinŭiju were hailing it as a landmark of Japanese imperial engineering. Speeches at the opening ceremony by Terauchi, chief bridge engineer Yamada Kamechi, and chief of the Railway Bureau of the Government-General of Korea Ōya Gondaira were followed by the distribution of prizes to the main contractors and cheers of "banzai" to the Meiji emperor.[108] Providing additional entertainment to the mostly male assemblage were fifty Korean female entertainers, or *kisaeng*, specially sent from Seoul by rail for the occasion.[109]

Obstacles to the bridge's construction were acknowledged in triumphant reports that buttressed growing Japanese nationalism but also downplayed the very real costs of trying to overcome the seasonally variable river. In the words of one overview published and translated into English by the Railway Bureau of the Government-General of Korea, "The successful completion of the bridge, the mission of which is to assist in facilitating communication between Europe and Asia, has amply demonstrated our technical ability to the world." As the publication of this translated report demonstrates, pride over the bridge's completion was proclaimed to a global as well as regional audience. This report noted the environmental challenges of the river that Japanese engineers had overcome: "great depth, strong tidal flows, terrible floods, and ice." But it also purposefully masked the transnational expertise, technology, and labor that went into bridge construction. Construction of the Yalu River Railway Bridge would have been impossible without exploited laborers that dealt most directly with the seasonally changing river environment, or the importation of Western technology and bridge design expertise.[110]

The spanning of the Yalu River with a permanent railroad bridge also inevitably affected the international politics of the border and its liquid geographies. With evident pride, engineer Koike Shin'ichi remarked in his journal how the bridge had "dismantled" the old Sino-Korean boundary.[111] A Japanese settler magazine in Korea proclaimed that the bridge metaphorically "obliterated" the "long channel" that historically separated the two regions. These sources spoke to boosters' ambition of the Yalu River no longer posing a practical boundary to Japanese expansionism.[112] But the political boundary at the Yalu did not actually disappear, as subsequent Sino-Japanese negotiations over bridge traffic show. Just two days after the opening ceremony, Japanese and Chinese diplomats inked the last of a series of important agreements concerning the transit of goods across the bridge. The treaty allowed for the inspection of goods by customs officials on both sides of the river while reaffirming Chinese sovereignty over the western half of the river.[113] In theory the Yalu River was a space of bilateral negotiation, but as later chapters show, Japanese colonizers aggressively and unilaterally tried to channel liquid cross-border flows of people and goods for their own benefit.

The Yalu River Railway Bridge marked the culmination of repeated Japanese military efforts to bridge the fluid Sino-Korean boundary that stretched from 1894 until 1911, after Japan's formal annexation of Korea. The steel passage across the river became a stable, all-weather means of transport across an environment that otherwise unpredictably swelled and receded, froze and unfroze with the seasons. Unlike previous military bridges that floated precariously at the water's surface, the railroad bridge transported travelers above the river, offering them an elevated view of the landscape contested by successive ranks of Chinese, Russian, and Japanese engineers, soldiers, and laborers. Featured on Japanese postcards, travel books, and photograph collections of Korea and Manchuria, it also became one of the most prominent aesthetic symbols of the Japanese presence along this frontier edge of empire.[114] Such genteel souvenirs belied the violence and labor necessary for erecting this overpass.

Threads of steel, cement, and commerce wove the Yalu River firmly into the fabric of Japan's overseas empire. Following the bridge's completion, the number of people and amount of goods that traveled by rail across the Yalu increased exponentially. According to Japanese reports, the value of cross-border trade entering Sinŭiju more than doubled in two years, from 1.89 million yen in 1911 to 4.04 million yen by 1913.[115] Increased trade and traffic along the Korean-Manchurian rail route was fostered and incentivized by imperial policies. A 1913 agreement between the Government-General of Korea and the fledgling Republic of China led to the reduction of customs rates on goods traveling by rail between Korea and Manchuria by nearly one-third.[116] This agreement was vigorously promoted by Governor-General Terauchi, who campaigned for uniting the formal Japanese colony of Korea with Japanese economic interests in

Manchuria.[117] In 1910 a single train made an average of 7.4 one-way journeys between Seoul and Sinŭiju each day, but by 1917, there were on average 12.3 daily trips.[118]

Yet, as important as the railroad bridge was to regional trade and colonial ambition, it represented only one small channel of imperial control amid a dense network of seasonally contingent human and nonhuman mobilities, or liquid geographies, that comprised the Yalu borderland and border water. Boat traffic continued to be an important means of transport across a river whose water levels variably swelled and lowered. Moreover, with the freezing over of the river each winter, sledges, carts, and pedestrians could also engage in what colonial police viewed as a subversive "freedom" of movement on the river's surface.[119] Smuggling also flourished along the five-hundred-mile border. As police reports noted, many smugglers simply avoided the heavily guarded railroad bridge between Andong and Sinŭiju, plying their trade instead along less monitored parts of the river.[120] Following the Japanese annexation of Korea in 1910, opponents of the new colonial regime also fled en masse to Manchuria, where they made periodic cross-border raids on Japanese outposts in Korea.

As will be analyzed in the next two chapters, Japanese efforts to police anti-Japanese guerrillas and smugglers reinforced the importance of the Yalu River border as boundary long after boosters claimed the bridge had "obliterated" it. Rather than actually "obliterating" the border, imperial authorities tried to make it into a selectively permeable barrier that would allow some goods and peoples to pass in seemingly boundary-less fashion while blocking others. But these efforts were not always successful, as they still needed to grapple with the seasonally changing mobilities of the human and nonhuman environment.

3

SEASONS OF YALU RIVER BORDER POLICING

The freezing Yalu River provoked an annual crisis for officials on the Chinese-Korean border. To some border authorities, wintertime surveillance constituted the "real work of border patrol," especially as the former "moat" around Korea became a pathway for anti-Japanese rebels.[1] Guerrilla leader and later president of North Korea Kim Il-sung recounted Japanese colonial police so desperate to block guerrillas' advances that they "dragged people out to noisily break the ice on the Yalu every night."[2] Exaggerated as Kim's story may be, administrators' anxieties about the frozen Yalu and the heightened mobility it supposedly allowed on the river's surface were real. Prior to the Japanese occupation of Manchuria in 1931, Chinese border officials on the Yalu's northern bank also worried that the frozen river "posed no obstacle" to Korean independence activists and, more menacingly, border-trespassing Japanese police.[3] Anxieties of seasonal border-making also extended beyond winter. As one Japanese official explained, "Spring, summer, fall, and winter, there is not a single day where one can stretch out and rest."[4]

As previous chapters have shown, from an early point Japanese officials endeavored to make the seasonally changing river border permeable to peoples and goods that buttressed imperial aims, whether through the attempted monopolizing of access to river-borne natural resources during the protectorate period (1905–1910) or completion of the Yalu River Railway Bridge in 1911. But permeability was a double-edged sword. For Japanese border agents, channeling the Yalu's liquid geographies also entailed containing the fluid mobilities of actors deemed antithetical to imperial aims. This included the policing of smugglers and illicit commodities (covered in chapter 4) and the surveillance of anti-Japanese activists.

For decades after the Japanese annexation of Korea in 1910, the policing of so-called bandits (a broad umbrella term including both traditional brigands and anti-Japanese guerrillas) was inexorably shaped by the seasonal rhythms of the Yalu River borderland. Scholars like Matsuda Toshihiko and Erik Esselstrom have helpfully noted the general importance of the Sino-Korean boundary to imperial policing, yet these previous studies pay little attention to the physical landscapes of border surveillance.[5] Even if the ice and cold of Yalu winters or the heat and floods of its summers are absent from these histories, they are everywhere in the historical writings left by border officials, anti-Japanese rebels, ordinary border residents, and other period reports. These records show that the cyclical thawing, flooding, and freezing of the river fundamentally framed the cross-border mobilities of both border agents and those who sought to evade them. The seasonal presence (or lack thereof) of plant cover, food supplies, and snow on the mountainous and forested banks of the upper Yalu also had transformative impacts on the guerrilla war waged between colonial officials and anti-Japanese activists.

The following narrative moves both chronologically from approximately 1910 until the mid-1930s and seasonally from spring to winter. It begins by highlighting how border agents responded to the arrival of spring and the thawing of the frozen river, a period known locally as the "thawing season" (K: *haebinggi*, C: *jiedongqi*, J: *kaihyōki*). Spring promised initial relief to border officials as large chunks of liberated ice impeded border crossings. Yet the opening of the river to waterborne traffic soon necessitated twenty-four-hour surveillance of the numerous timber rafts, "propeller boats," and other vessels that plied their way up and down the river's course. The flowing river proved an unreliable barrier against armed political dissidents, Manchurian "mounted bandits" (K: *majŏk*, C: *mazei*, J: *bazoku*), and others who chipped away at competing Sino-Japanese claims to the border region. By summertime, heavy monsoonal rains transformed the river into a treacherous torrent, while at the same time the abundant foliage of the "flourishing season" (K: *pŏnmugi*, C: *fanmaoqi*, J: *hanmoki*) provided extensive cover for anti-Japanese forces on the river's banks. The pursuit of anti-Japanese rebels, however, also presented an opportunity for Japanese police to expand their influence across the border in ways that frustrated local Chinese officials.

The chapter's sections on the springtime thawing season and summertime flourishing season focus primarily on events and sources from the 1910s and 1920s. Although border attacks occurred all throughout the year, it was the spring through fall months, especially summer, that became identified by border officials as the time of greatest seasonal threat during this period. These seasonal dynamics changed, however, as a result of the September 18, 1931, Manchurian Incident and Japanese occupation of Northeast China. Events after 1931 led border officials to place greater emphasis on the threats of the "icebound season" (K: *kyŏlbinggi*, C: *jiedongqi*, J: *keppyōki*), when the frozen Yalu afforded a readily accessible pathway for reinvigorated anti-Japanese resistance. As analyzed later in the chapter, the early-middle 1930s saw multiple border attacks by guerrillas and retaliatory "bandit suppression" campaigns by officials during this season. Colonial Korean authorities both cooperated and clashed with Manchukuo officials over how to police the seasonally changing intraimperial boundary. And even as Japanese police and military officials themselves used the frozen river and snowy riverbanks to track down rebels, their writings repeatedly highlighted anxieties about the particular dangers of the icy Yalu corridor.

Spring and the Thawing of the Yalu Ice

Springtime along the colonial Yalu River was typically a time of relief for Japanese border officials as warming temperatures caused the Yalu's thick ice to dissipate. The exact timing of the "thawing season" varied by year and by region. In Yongamp'o, located at the mouth of the river near the Yellow Sea, the ice began melting as early as mid-March, whereas upstream it might not thaw until late April.[6] As described by Japanese policeman Yoshimura Yoshizō, the joys of the "blissful spring" (*ureshii haru*) could only be known by people who lived in the region.[7] As another border policeman noted, the most cheerful time for border patrol was not New Year's (*shōgatsu*) or *Obon*, the typical days of greatest festivity in the Japanese calendar. Rather, it was the brief, "festival-like" three- or four-day period at the beginning of the thaw when floating chunks of ice stopped the movements of anti-Japanese guerrillas and smugglers across the border.[8]

Colonial officials did not always greet the coming of spring in such romantic terms. This was especially the case in 1919 following Korea's March First Independence Movement and the anti-Japanese May Fourth Movement in China. After Japanese officials' brutal suppression of Korean "Righteous Army" (*ŭibyŏng*) independence fighters during the protectorate period (1905–1910), an illusory peace seemed to prevail over the Korean side of the Yalu River. Chinese "mounted bandits" roamed on the Manchurian side of the border, where a vacuum of leadership after the 1912 collapse of the Qing empire provided fertile conditions for their activities.[9] But Japanese military police (*kenpei*) largely kept this violence from spilling over into Korea. The strategies used to successfully fight "mounted bandits," as well as eradicate an incipient Korean resistance movement, included the surveillance of Korean migrant communities in Manchuria. Colonial rulers in Korea claimed imperial subjecthood for Korean migrants as a way of stretching Japan's territorial ambitions and trying to police the growing Korean nationalist movement in exile.[10] Such strong-armed tactics only exacerbated, however, preexisting Korean discontent with Japanese rule along the border and elsewhere.[11]

Simmering Korean dissatisfaction with the brutality of Japanese colonial rule led to the 1919 outbreak of the March First Korean Independence Movement. Now recognized as a watershed moment in the emergence of Korean anticolonial nationalism, the movement began as a series of nonviolent protests in the colonial capital of Seoul. By the end of the month, the protests had enveloped the entire peninsula and beyond. Seasonal metaphors permeated the movement's discourse, with a "declaration of independence" drafted by leading Korean activists declaring that "a new spring has arrived prompting the myriad forms of life to come to life again. The past was a time of freezing ice and snow, stifling the breath of life; the present is a time of mild breezes and warm sunshine, reinvigorating the spirit."[12] Japanese authorities unnerved by the sight of over a million Koreans taking to the streets and shouting pro-independence slogans unleashed a brutal wave of violence that resulted in thousands of deaths and even more arrests.[13] In response to Japanese suppression, scores of Korean nationalists fled north of the Yalu and joined forces with the Korean resistance movement in southern Manchuria to begin armed cross-border raids against Japanese outposts.[14]

The Spring of 1919 also saw the May Fourth Movement in China grow out of a series of student protests against Japanese imperial expansion into a widespread social and cultural movement. As anti-Japanese sentiment rose throughout the country, Chinese authorities began sympathizing with Korean independence movements in Manchuria and elsewhere.[15]

This burst of anti-Japanese sentiment and borderland violence unnerved Japanese authorities, who began committing increased manpower and resources to policing the Yalu border.[16] It also coincided with the thawing of the Yalu River, marking the beginning of what came to be a distinctive seasonal cycle of border security. An April 6, 1920, telegram sent to top Japanese military officials warned that with the unfreezing of the Yalu, Korean independence groups would likely attempt to smuggle weapons into the Chinese border city of Andong. The document thus called for increased surveillance of river traffic.[17] Japanese naval ships were also dispatched to the mouth of the Yalu to monitor for signs of "rebellious Korean" activity.[18]

The intensity of Japanese attempts to suppress the armed Korean independence movement alarmed observers on the Chinese bank of the Yalu. By this time Manchuria was under the control of Zhang Zuolin, a warlord of humble bandit origins who began ruling the region after an initial period of unrest following the collapse of the Qing dynasty in 1912. In his interactions with the Japanese, Zhang sought technical and military support for his Fengtian clique in exchange for protecting Japan's extensive Manchurian railway concessions. At the same time, Zhang's regime was determined to hold further Japanese expansion at bay.[19] Officials in the Yalu-bordering counties of Andong, Kuandian, Ji'an, Linjiang, and Changbai had long been urged to "exercise caution" when dealing with local Korean migrants, Japanese settlers, and Japanese officials on the Yalu's opposite bank.[20] But such calls took on greater urgency in the wake of the March First Movement, as Japanese naval ships moved with impunity near Andong and Japanese police began crossing the river at will to pursue alleged Korean independence fighters.[21]

As accumulated ice slowly retreated from the Yalu's surface, the surveillance of boat traffic became a prominent concern for Chinese and Japanese border officials alike. Period sources spoke unfavorably of the river's accessibility to waterborne traffic due to its shallow flow and numerous rapids.[22] Despite these limitations, the Yalu's position as a strategic conduit between Korea and Manchuria encouraged a thriving river trade. Means of river transport included junks, sampans, canoes, sailboats, timber rafts, and "propeller boats."[23] Responsibility for policing river traffic on the Chinese side of the border was split between the Yalu-Hun River Waterfront Police, an agency created by the Qing in 1909 to monitor the Yalu and its tributary the Hun River, and officials from various border counties. With spring's arrival, these officials relayed to superiors detailed information about ice-melting patterns and the estimated starting date for waterborne traffic.[24] Japanese authorities circulated similar information on the Korean side of the river, where the day-to-day work of border surveillance fell primarily to police units from the provinces of North P'yŏngan and South Hamgyŏng.[25]

Timber rafts and "propeller boats" were two particularly distinctive forms of river transport that also served as ready targets for "bandit" groups and anti-Japanese dissidents.[26] Floated downstream from the richly forested upper Yalu, these log rafts were a perennial feature of the Yalu cultural landscape.[27] Popular songs like the Japanese "Ōryokkō bushi" (Yalu River melody) romanticized the springtime journeys of raftsmen in the wake of the Yalu's melting ice.[28] Yet the song's peaceful nature belied the actual dangers of timber rafting. As discussed in chapter 1, Japanese rafters were targeted during the protectorate period by disgruntled Chinese timbermen. And as reminders of Japan's colonial presence along the border, raft pilots remained targets years later as raids by anti-Japanese dissidents and bandits rocked the border region. On June 7, 1924, for example, a Japanese rafter named Matsumi Kumajirō was shot and killed by six "bandits" on the Yalu River near Ch'osan County.[29] Non-Japanese raftsmen occasionally fell victim to border violence as well, as was the case on May 29, 1928, when four Korean raftsmen were shot and killed by Chinese "mounted bandits" near the upper Yalu city of Hyesanjin.[30]

While timber rafts represented one precarious aspect of Yalu River transportation, another was the "propeller boat" (*puropera fune*). Propeller boats were shallow-bottomed passenger boats equipped with airplane-like propellers that sat above the water to help navigate the Yalu's shallow depths.[31] The use of propeller boats began on the Korean side of the river in 1922 as a joint venture between the Korean colonial government and Sinŭiju-based Japanese timber entrepreneur Tada Eikichi.[32] In exchange for government-general subsidies, the propeller boats, operated by Tada's Yalu River Transport Company (Ōryokkō Yusen Kōshi), were used to deliver mail and provide regular passenger service along an officially designated route that stretched from Sinŭiju to Singalp'a at the Yalu's upper reaches.[33]

Propeller boats provided the quickest and most reliable means of transport on the river until the completion of railroad routes along the upper Yalu in the late 1930s. This made them indispensable to border administration and development but also convenient targets for "bandit" attacks. On May 25, 1928, "bandits" dressed like Chinese officials raided a propeller boat near the Korean county of Chasŏng, killing two passengers and kidnapping a military officer, Lieutenant Wakabayashi, who was also on board.[34] A combined force of border policemen and Japanese troops from as far afield as the colonial capital of Keijō failed to recover the kidnapped officer. They did, however, incite protests from local Chinese authorities, who themselves mobilized thousands of troops and offered a reward of 200,000 *yuan* for information about Wakabayashi's whereabouts before he was ultimately found dead.[35]

Propeller boats' susceptibility to attack became especially clear with the attempted assassination of Governor-General of Korea Saitō Makoto in spring 1924. On May 19, a group of Korean independence fighters fired on Saitō and an accompanying party of colonial bureaucrats, border policemen, and newspaper journalists as they traveled upstream via propeller boat as part of a "border inspection tour."[36] The rebels' bullets grazed the earlobes of two Japanese policemen, causing them to topple into the river, while other policemen began firing off a volley of return fire in the direction of the Chinese riverbank. The attackers, thought by police at the time to be about ten in number, immediately fled before they could be positively identified by pursuing Japanese officials.[37] In the wake of the attack, Japanese colonial authorities telegraphed Chinese governor of Dongbiandao Wang Shuncun to demand increased security on the remainder of the governor-general's intended route.[38] Wang issued an official apology for the attack, but Wang Yubin (not related), chief of the Chinese county of Ji'an where the attack had allegedly taken place, claimed that Japanese authorities had fabricated the whole event in order to trespass into Chinese territory.[39] For many Chinese observers, the cross-border mobility of Japanese imperialists posed a far greater threat to local stability than Korean dissidents.

As the Yalu ice retreated, local Chinese bandits and Korean guerrillas not only attacked river boat traffic but also crossed the river to raid Japanese police and forestry stations as well as threaten wealthy landlords and alleged pro-Japanese collaborators.[40] Officials in colonial Korea recorded some 1,652 "incidents" of border violence in 1920 alone.[41] Bandits and anti-Japanese fighters often used small junks or simple dugout canoes to cross the border under the cover of nighttime darkness.[42] These groups also commandeered other river-going vessels. As an American missionary traveling along the Yalu in 1926 noted, colonial officials required all river-going traffic to dock at night near border police stations out of fear that Korean independence fighters "might seize the boat[s] and use [them] to transport men or ammunition from the Chinese side."[43]

To guard against cross-border attacks, Japanese placed police stations and substations at nearly every *ri* (approximately 2.4 miles) along the Sino-Korean border, with four to ten policemen stationed at each of these outposts.[44] By 1923 the total number of police officials along the Sino-Korean border was 2,344, two-thirds of whom were ethnically Japanese and the remaining one-third Korean, and border police numbers only continued to grow as efforts to crack down on anti-Japanese resistance escalated.[45] While these remote frontier stations were typically built from preexisting Korean-style structures (see figure 3.1), they were also fortified with fences, ditches, and sometimes watchtowers built with forcibly mobilized local labor. Additional fences were also sometimes built at ferry crossings and key checkpoints along the border.[46] Traveling on the Yalu in 1933, German geographer Hermann Lautensach described border police stations as resembling "small fortresses."[47] Underscoring the militarized nature of the border, Japanese troops stationed near the border "frontline" also provided key support for border surveillance operations in addition to regular police units.[48] The intended effect was to project an image of control over the militarized border landscape, though this display of strength belied the challenges of containing fluid human mobilities across an approximately 800-kilometer-long river.

Summertime Violence, Floods, and the "Flourishing Season"

As seen by officials, the need for multiple lines of well-staffed border police was especially keen during the warm summer months.[49] Officials referred to this

FIGURE 3.1. Colonial Korean border police outpost near the upper Yalu River, 1923.

Source: Keisanchin Keisatsusho, Ōryokkō jōryū chihō shashinchō *(Osaka: Kuwata Kōjō, 1924).* Image courtesy of the Albert and Shirley Small Special Collections Library at the University of Virginia.

period as the "flourishing season"—a time when vegetation cover along the Yalu River was at its fullest and food supplies were most readily available.[50] The accessibility of food and hiding places was especially important for anti-Japanese fighters, who lived a precarious existence between periodic raids and avoiding capture and death at the hands of Japanese authorities. One former Korean resident of the Yalu region sympathetically recalled the ragged appearance of guerrilla fighters who visited his home as a child:

> Their appearance ... was completely different from what I had imagined. ... Wearing oxcart overalls and with their hair tied up with cotton towels, they looked completely like countryside farmers. I expected that independence fighters, even if their clothes were not that fancy, would at least have a pistol strapped to their waist, but they did not even have an old-style hunting rifle let alone a pistol.[51]

Such poverty regularly compelled anti-Japanese guerrillas to rely on help from local communities along the border. Korean villagers sometimes aided guerrillas of their own volition, providing food and shelter or information about local police movements.[52] Yet cooperation with anti-Japanese guerrillas came with severe risks. In August 1924, for example, colonial police surrounded the homes of villagers accused of harboring insurgents in Hwach'ang township, North P'yŏngan Province, and set them on fire, killing most of the occupants inside.[53]

In addition to such human violence, another unique challenge of summertime border security was the monsoonal rains that brought heavy floods to the region. The summer months of June through August saw higher levels of precipitation than any other time of the year.[54] The flooding during this annual rainy season, exacerbated by heavy logging and deforestation along the upper Yalu, posed unique obstacles to border security.[55] Riverside patrols assumed an added layer of risk as roads used to navigate between watch points were frequently washed out. If one was not careful, wrote Japanese police officer Mizuno Takusaburō, they would find themselves swept away into the river's roaring current, where it was "doubtful that one could stay afloat forever."[56] Such warnings about the volatility of the summertime river were based on actual experience. After repeated heavy rains in August 1928, three military police were crossing a bridge over a small Yalu tributary not far from the border when the bridge was swept away, drowning one of them in the process.[57] In an earlier incident on August 27, 1921, four policemen were riding a raft while patrolling the Yalu near Huch'ang when the raft overturned, drowning one of the policemen who was unable to swim his way out.[58]

Floods could destroy outposts on both sides of the river with unmatchable force. This was discovered by Chinese officials from the Yalu-Hun River Waterfront Police in 1923, when summertime flooding destroyed two of their riverfront patrol stations.[59] Of course, anti-Japanese guerrillas and residents of local border communities were just as vulnerable to the dangers of Yalu flooding as Chinese and Japanese policemen. But in the pages of popular newspapers and police memoirs, guerrillas and "bandits" seemed impervious to such natural disasters. An August 26, 1923, article in the Tianjin-based Chinese newspaper *Yishi bao* described Korean guerrillas carrying out raids amid the chaos of massive flooding that year.[60]

Summertime, especially late summer, was also prime harvesting time for another destabilizing fixture of the Sino-Korean border region—opium. As a cash crop, opium helped many communities along the border survive. This was especially true for impoverished Korean migrant villages in the remote Changbai region along the Chinese side of the upper Yalu. But illicit opium cultivation also contributed to the instability of the border region, especially when opium harvesters became the targets of local "mounted bandit" groups.[61] Separate articles in the August 20 and August 23, 1928, editions of the *Tonga ilbo* (East Asia Daily) describe bandits raiding Korean migrant villages in Changbai and kidnapping villagers as well as absconding with copious supplies of stolen opium. Attacks specifically timed to the "opium harvesting season" left local villagers in their wake "greatly disturbed."[62] Locally stationed Chinese soldiers managed to secure the release of fifty kidnapped villagers and kill a bandit informant, though the fate of the bandits themselves was left unclear.[63]

A more mundane but no less noticeable feature of summertime Yalu border security was the intense heat and humidity. The range between lowest winter and highest summer temperatures in Chunggangjin on the Korean side of the upper Yalu River was a dramatic 81.6 degrees Celsius.[64] It is little surprise, then, that Japanese colonial media such as the popular "Northern Korea Border Patrol Song," written in 1928, mentioned "boiling" summer temperatures reaching nearly 40 degrees Celsius along with the frozen river and winter nights of less than -40 degrees Celsius.[65] Writing about his experience standing watch over summertime ferries, police officer Mizuno complained about the sweat that "drenched my whole body" as he stood on the shade-less river bank. One could not escape the heat by drinking from the river, however, lest the dirty water induce multiple harried trips to the toilet.[66]

Police records attest to the potent combination of environmental and human factors that made summertime a dangerous period for Yalu River border security. Records of border raids and other high-profile incidents between 1920 and 1927 published by the Police Affairs Bureau of the Government-General of Korea shows that approximately 43 percent, or nearly half of the total border incidents for the year, occurred during the four-month period between June and September (see figure 3.2). August in particular was dangerous, with nearly 13 percent of attacks taking place during this month alone.[67] Records of North P'yŏngan Province police fatalities from 1910 to 1936 also show August to be the deadliest month for those stationed on the border, with nearly a quarter of total fatalities (see figure 3.3).[68]

Such statistical observations are borne out in individual media accounts of summertime border violence. Throughout the early 1920s, newspapers in Korea, Japan, and China carried numerous reports of Korean guerrillas crossing the flowing Yalu to raise funds, "punish" wealthy Korean landlords and Japanese collaborators, distribute anti-Japanese pamphlets, and attack Japanese police or forestry stations.[69] Guerrilla activity also occurred along the nearby Tumen River, though the occupation of Kando by Japanese police and military officials in October 1920 compelled most armed Japanese resistance groups to shift their focus to the Yalu and the northwestern Korean provinces of North P'yŏngan and South Hamgyŏng, where the Japanese presence was far less concentrated and

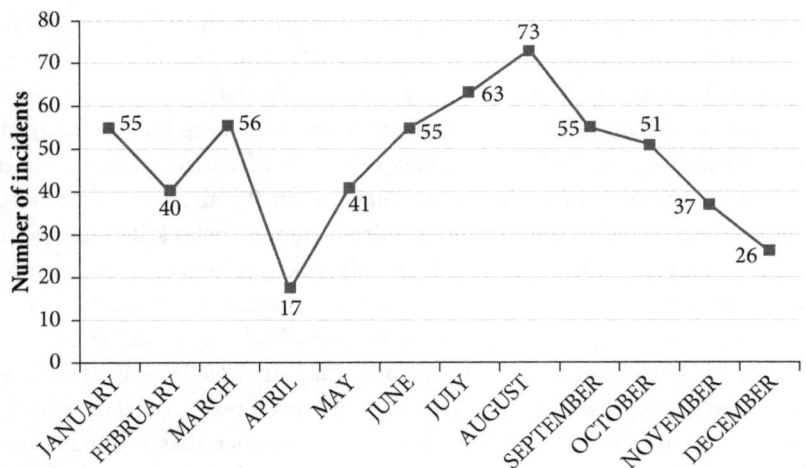

FIGURE 3.2. Line chart, organized by month, showing the number of incidents along the Yalu River border recorded by colonial Korean police authorities between 1920 and 1927. Note the highest number of incidents in July and August.

Source: *Chōsen Sōtokufu Keimukyoku, Kōtō keisatsu kankei nenpyō.*

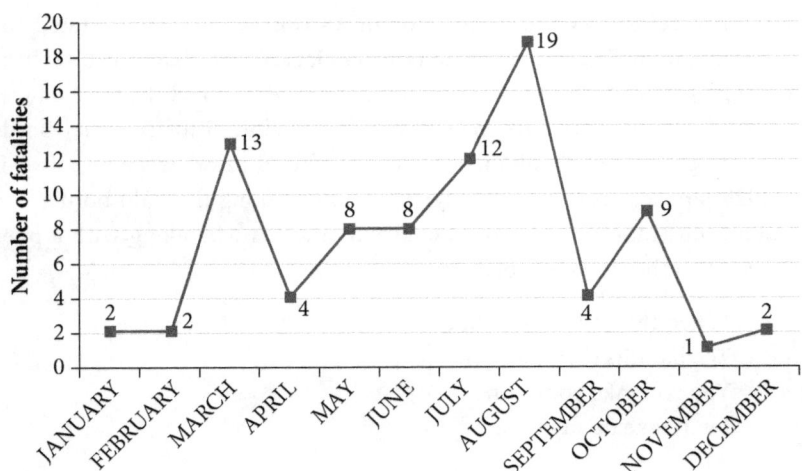

FIGURE 3.3. Line chart, organized by month, showing the number of fatalities among border police in the colonial Korean border province of North P'yŏngan between 1910 and 1936.

Source: Kosako Shintarō, *Kokkyō no hana* (Shingishū [Sinŭiju]: Shingishū Insatsu Kabushiki Kaisha, 1936), 5–18.

the geography more remote.⁷⁰ By 1924–1925, as one border official later recollected, summertime attacks seemed to be occurring "on a daily basis."⁷¹ On August 7, 1924, a group of Korean independence fighters set fire to a Forest Management Bureau office near Huch'ang before retreating into a nearby forest. Just two days later, five Japanese police officers were returning from the opening of a gold-mining office in Ch'angsŏng, North P'yŏngan Province, when they were ambushed by Korean independence fighters, who killed four of the policemen and seriously injured the fifth.⁷² The unexpected nature of this attack was similar to that of another raid a year later. On August 28, 1925, anti-Japanese guerrillas raided Yangsan in the border county of Sakchu, shooting two local Koreans and burning down their homes after they attempted to report the guerrillas' presence to nearby police. The next day seven police officials from the Yangsan station formed a search group to pursue the guerrillas, leaving just one officer behind to guard the police station. Later that day the guerrilla fighters attacked the station, killing the wife of one police officer and the wife and adopted daughter of another.⁷³

The dramatic deaths of Japanese police wives during the Yangsan attack captivated the Japanese popular imagination in reports reiterating the seasonal dangers of the Yalu River border. A 1929 article in the popular magazine *Kingu*, for example, narrated the life of one victim, Kiyoko, who worked as a textile factory worker before marrying and moving to Korea. The article stated that Kiyoko had originally been invited to return to Japan immediately before the attack, but had stoically refused to do so until after the summer, the most dangerous time for border security, had passed.⁷⁴ The linking of seasonal border violence to police wives' valiant sacrifice was found in other sources as well. One 1929 Japanese collection of vignettes on life along the Yalu border contained an illustration of a border policeman and his wife along with a poem narrated from the wife's perspective:

> When the green leaves flourish
> The bandits thrive as well
> You will take your gun
> I will take up my sword
> Ah . . .
> In life or death, our fates are intertwined.

This poem's seasonal reference to "flourishing green leaves" reinforced the dangers of the "flourishing season" while valorizing the masculine virtue of colonial policemen.⁷⁵ But ethnically Japanese border police wives were far from the only female victims of summertime border violence. The merciless "bandit suppression" tactics of colonial police themselves inflicted untold hardship on local

Korean and Chinese women. In August 1924, for example, the Korean nationalist newspaper *Tonga ilbo* ran a series of articles accusing Japanese and ethnically Korean policemen in Kanggye County, North P'yŏngan Province, of raping local Korean women under the pretense of conducting "investigations." The same women were then threatened by police after they tried to report these crimes.[76]

Responses to the seasonal violence that rocked the Yalu region during the early 1920s reached beyond the domestic to the diplomatic, contributing to mounting cross-border tensions between Japanese and Chinese officials. Chinese diplomats stationed in Sinŭiju complained how every spring and summer anti-Japanese rebels "exploited the lush and dense mountain forests" to make cross-border raids, which Japanese police then used as an excuse to "suppress Korean dissidents" and trespass onto Chinese soil.[77] At first, the attitude of Chinese observers toward anti-Japanese activists was sympathetic, in large part due to their own concerns about Japan's expansion into Manchuria and the rise of anti-Japanese nationalism in the wake of the May Fourth Movement.[78] Within a few years, however, attitudes shifted as the number of Korean migrants grew and Chinese officials became increasingly worried about Japanese suppression of the Korean independence movement becoming a pretense for further expansion into Manchuria.

In June 1925 an accord was finally struck between Mitsuya Miyamatsu, head of the Government-General of Korea's Police Affairs Bureau, and Yu Zhen, police chief of Zhang Zuolin's Fengtian regime. Known later as the "Mitsuya Agreement," this 1925 agreement promised that Chinese officials would arrest dissident Koreans and turn them over to authorities in colonial Korea. Most importantly for Chinese negotiators, a clause was also included stating that both sides would refrain from crossing the river into each other's territory.[79] The commencement of greater Sino-Japanese cooperation on the policing of "rebellious Koreans" had devastating consequences for anti-Japanese guerrillas along the border. Guerrilla groups were already reeling from years of Japanese suppression as well as fierce factional politics and infighting that split the anti-Japanese insurgency.[80] As a result, the total number of border "incidents" dropped precipitously from 270 in 1925 to 69 in 1926, becoming almost nonexistent by the end of the decade.[81]

Despite the successful blow to Korean guerrillas dealt by the Mitsuya Agreement, Sino-Japanese tensions over the policing of the river border continued, often coming to a head during the warm and humid Yalu summer. On July 9, 1925, Chinese officials from the Yalu-Hun River Waterfront Police began building an outpost on a river island near the upper Yalu county of Changbai to help patrol a nearby ferry crossing. Japanese policemen on the Korean side protested this construction by claiming that the island was actually Korean territory.

Chinese officials refused to tear down the half-completed building, defending their actions by saying that they were unaware of the island's disputed status. Ultimately the Japanese police chief in Hyesanjin took matters into his own hands by ordering the unilateral destruction of the wooden outpost.[82]

In such ways Chinese border officials' plans for "summer defense" (*xia fang*) were continuously frustrated by a determined Japanese police presence on the opposite side of the border. One detailed plan for "summer defense" in Andong described the city as "an important confluence point between land and water" and suggested mobilizing manpower from a variety of local administrative offices, including the Yalu-Hun River Waterfront Police and Andong city police, to police the region.[83] In a 1930 report, Yalu-Hun River Waterfront Police chief Luan Yunkuai gave additional suggestions for combating Japanese police who used "bandit" border crossings as an excuse to "destroy the public order" on the Chinese side of the river. These included increasing the overall number of Chinese border police, connecting remote police stations with telephone wires, and undertaking regular patrols of the river using propeller boats.[84]

Measures undertaken by Chinese officials to reassert their border sovereignty worked to limit Japanese control over the Yalu border, but only for a time. Eventually, events on the eve of the autumn equinox of 1931 would irrevocably alter the preexisting regional balance of power.

The Brief Yalu Autumn

After long summers of searing temperatures, high humidity, riverside raids, and heated diplomatic tensions, the general consensus among Japanese border police about the Yalu autumn was that it was far too brief. "It is usually said that a single falling leaf heralds the coming of autumn," remarked police officer Yamada Ainosuke, "but in the northern borders of Korea that does not apply. If a single leaf falls, then winter is known to be coming."[85] Such observations were not divorced from reality. According to data collected by a Government-General of Korea weather observation station in Chunggangjin along the upper Yalu, average maximum temperatures during the period 1925–1930 were 22.5 degrees Celsius in September versus 2.7 degrees Celsius in November, when ice often first started to appear on the river's surface.[86] As a result of the season's brevity, discussion of autumn among border officials tended to focus on preparation for the upcoming "icebound season," including the strengthening of police station fortifications.[87]

For others, the Yalu autumn (however brief) presented another possible window for furtive border crossings. In the late autumn of 1919, Korean revolutionary activist Yi Tusan decided to leave Korea and flee for the Chinese metropolis of

Shanghai, where many Korean independence activists were gathering in the wake of the failed March First independence protests. In a later memoir Yi recalled taking a train from southern Korea to the Yalu River border. Fearing the heavy police presence in Sinŭiju, Yi and a fellow traveler disembarked from a small rural station outside the border city and proceeded to travel in disguise through the tall autumn grass to the river border. Night was approaching once they reached the Yalu and attempted to cross it by boat, only to be greeted by gunshots from the Korean side of the border as they crossed over.[88] Whether the gunshots actually occurred or were a later embellishment, Yi was probably right to avoid the train. From 1919 to 1922 all Korean travelers across the border were required to show border agents a "travel certification" (*ryokō shōmei*) signed by Japanese police in their hometown. It would have been impossible for an independence activist like Yi to secure such papers.[89] Measures instituted even after the abolition of this "travel certification" requirement were similarly repressive, including full-body searches and interrogations of border crossers.[90] But Yi and other anti-Japanese activists continued to find ways to successfully penetrate border defenses.

On the eve of the autumn equinox of 1931, however, a key set of events occurred that radically altered the Yalu's political landscape. At 10:00 a.m. on September 18, 1931, Japanese military officers with the Kwantung Army staged a railway explosion outside the Manchurian capital of Mukden (Fengtian), which they then used as a pretext to occupy the city and begin their planned conquest of Northeast China. Less than twenty-four hours later, Japanese military garrisons had already occupied Andong as well as other major cities in southern Manchuria.[91] Military units stationed in Korea also hastily crossed the Sino-Korean border to help with the invasion and subsequent occupation, which would be cemented months later with the creation of the Japanese puppet state of Manchukuo.[92]

In response to the Japanese takeover of Manchuria, later known as the "Manchurian Incident," the Yalu River frontier once again erupted into what one Japanese policeman called a "state of war" (*senji jōtai*).[93] Within China, Zhang Xueliang's support of Chinese Nationalist leader Chiang Kai-shek's decision to not resist the Japanese invasion sparked popular outrage and support for various Manchurian rebel groups.[94] Such groups included multiethnic Chinese and Korean Communist-led militias such as the Northeast People's Revolutionary Army (formed in 1933), which three years later became the Northeast United Anti-Japanese Army.[95] Older outlaw groups such as the Shandong-based "Big Sword Society" also utilized the political upheaval to expand their activities while occasionally allying with Communists and other guerrilla groups.[96]

The chaos of this border violence came to be closely entwined with the Yalu's wintertime topography. Since the 1920s, cross-border media reports on wintertime border security had emphasized the extreme measures undertaken to police the

Yalu ice. For instance, in January 1922, a notice published in the Korean-language newspaper *Tonga ilbo* informed its readers that anyone traveling on the frozen river's surface outside permitted daylight hours would be shot immediately.[97] But at the same time, official and popular discussion of Yalu border security also devoted significant attention to the spring "thawing season" and raids during the summer "flourishing season." It was not until after the 1931 Manchurian Incident that a proliferation of high-profile attacks, among other factors, caused official anxieties to focus overwhelmingly on the winter.

Wintertime Policing and Violence along the Freezing Yalu

The appearance of floating ice heralded the imminent icebound season, which covered the Yalu's surface in a thick layer of ice for almost one-third of the year.[98] The river's freezing carried multiple meanings and uses to those who lived along its banks. As detailed in chapter 1, for those Chinese, Japanese, and Korean workers in the Yalu timber industry, winter allowed newly felled timber to be easily transported by sledge over the now-frozen earth to the river, where it was stacked to be floated downstream in the spring. The frozen river was also a valuable source of fresh ice, which local residents cut and stored for use in the warm summer months.[99] For many, moreover, the frozen Yalu brought new recreational opportunities. Ice skating was a popular sport in the frigid climes of northern Korea and southern Manchuria, where large sections of the river near the cities of Andong and Sinŭiju were converted into outdoor skating rinks and skating competitions were held with some regularity. As former Japanese and Korean residents of Sinŭiju later remembered, the region produced champion speed skaters recognized throughout the empire.[100]

For border police on guard against cross-border "invasion," however, the frozen river was less a place for recreation or commerce than a dangerous threat to their work. According to an internal document of the North P'yŏngan Province Police Affairs Bureau, the Yalu River served as a strategic "moat" around Korea during the spring, summer, and autumn months. But with the coming of winter this natural fortification disappeared (see figure 3.4). A subversive "freedom" of access was now allowed on the river's icy surface, which became a convenient corridor for smugglers, "bandits," and other groups whose activities threatened imperial control.[101]

Winter was a double-edged sword for Japanese border officials in the aftermath of the 1931 Manchurian invasion. So-called bandit suppression campaigns in Manchukuo aimed at crushing guerrilla resistance were often carried out in the winter, when, as one former Japanese soldier recalled in an oral account, the fresh

FIGURE 3.4. Image of wintertime border policing from a commemorative photo album. The original caption reads "inspection of travelers on the ice," while the sign in the photograph shows "regulations for traveling on the ice," including a proscription against nighttime border crossings.

Source: Heian Hokudō Keisatsubu, Kokkyō no mamori (Shingishū [Sinŭiju]: Heian Hokudō Keisatsubu, 1933), 27.

snow exposed the footprints of retreating guerrillas.[102] At the same time, colonial police in Korea feared that retreating Manchurian guerrillas in desperate need of supplies would exploit the frozen river's accessibility to make raids into Korea.[103] As ethnically Korean border policeman Ch'oe Kiju wrote in 1933, so-called bandits incited by the Manchurian Incident "would not miss the chance to run amok with the coming of the icebound-season."[104] Whereas summer was the statistically most deadly time for colonial Korean border security in the 1920s, the years 1932–1933 saw over half of so-called bandit invasions into the Korean border province of North P'yŏngan occur during the winter months of December–March.[105]

Concerns about frozen river crossings were most prominent among officials in colonial Korea. A concentrated police presence and decades of authoritarian colonial rule in Korea made the threat of "bandits" crossing into Manchukuo from Korea virtually nonexistent.[106] By contrast, the mountainous and heavily forested frontier of southern Manchuria, with rampant rural poverty on both sides of the border, had long provided favorable conditions for bandit and dissident activity. Colonial officials' amplified concerns about the Yalu winter manifested themselves in a variety of settings. Documents sent by the Government-General of Korea to the Ministry of Colonial Affairs in Tokyo cited the specific dangers of the frozen Yalu and the increased "freedom" of movement on its surface in a plea for more financial resources and manpower.[107] The tenor of official police publications also shifted to reflect greater fears about the wintertime Yalu. A 1925 edition of the *Overview of Police Operations in Korea* (*Chōsen keisatsu gaiyō*), published annually by the Government-General of Korea, noted that border attacks generally decreased during the winter season.[108] But beginning with the 1931 edition, mentions of the "icebound season" highlighted it as "the most important time for police surveillance," a theme repeated thereafter.[109]

While the frozen Yalu had long been a staging ground for illicit cross-border activity, three episodes illustrate the factors that led officials to consider winter particularly dangerous after the Manchurian Incident: the "T'osŏng Incident" of 1934, the "Tonghŭng Incident" of 1935, and a raid on Taegil in March 1936 (see figure 3.5). Just before midnight on January 22, 1934, approximately 140 anti-Japanese guerrillas launched a raid on a Japanese police box in the village of T'osŏng near the Yalu River. To escape detection, the group split up into smaller contingents of three to five people to reduce the crunching under their shoes as they traversed the snow piled up on the river's ice. They were first noticed by two local Korean villagers conducting night-time river patrols as members of a police-organized "self-defense corps." By the time these villagers could contact a Japanese officer on patrol, the guerrillas had already reached the eastern entrance of the village. Hurriedly grabbing machine guns, the five officers stationed at the police box engaged with the guerrillas in a battle that ultimately left six villagers and one guerrilla dead before the anti-Japanese force fled back across the river into Manchuria.[110]

On February 13 of the next year, ethnically Korean Communist leader Yi Honggwang led approximately two hundred members of the Northeast People's Revolutionary Army across the frozen Yalu to attack the Korean village of Tonghŭng. Records of female "comrades" in Yi's band also shows how women were implicated in the seasonal politics of this border as more than just victims of border violence.[111] According to one Chinese source, Yi's attack began with a rallying speech about "striking down the enemy" and "winning back our homeland."[112] The guerrillas did not retreat until after burning several houses, kidnapping villagers, and engaging in an intense gunfight with colonial police that lasted nearly two hours.[113] The wintertime attack on Tonghŭng prompted speculation in the Korean-language media of a second raid by Communist-led forces. Such an attack did indeed occur during the winter of 1935–1936. Some 150 anti-Japanese guerrillas crossed the frozen Yalu before dawn on March 25 to raid a police substation at Taegil, shooting and killing two policemen and taking all of the weapons in the station's armory.[114]

FIGURE 3.5. Map of major icebound season "bandit" raids along the Yalu River, 1934–1936.

One way border officials responded to dramatic wintertime raids was by deploying technologies such as airplanes and telephone wires—all-weather tools also useful in other seasons of border surveillance. Airplanes were first used for border security in February 1935 after the North P'yŏngan Province Police Affairs Bureau purchased two Salmson 2–type biplanes for reconnaissance purposes. As a contemporary newspaper noted, the use of aircraft for policing was a first not only in Korea but in the entire Japanese Empire.[115] Airplanes afforded a previously inaccessible birds-eye view of the region, allowing border officials to trace the movements of "bandits" and smugglers and spot their "hideouts" more effectively. Telephone technology further diminished the Yalu River border's spatial challenges. The installation of telephone wires to connect remote police outposts on the Yalu was a priority of officials throughout the 1930s, and villagers living in riverside communities were often forcibly mobilized to help build telephone poles.[116] As Daqing Yang has previously shown, the expansion of Japan's telecommunications network was essential for maintaining control in Korea and elsewhere in the empire.[117] But as quickly as border officials installed these wires to strengthen their regulatory reach over the river, anti-Japanese activists cut them down. When guerrillas attacked the Taegil substation on March 25, 1936, they first snipped the station's telephone wires before crossing the frozen river.[118] Kim Il-sung's autobiography also describes how guerrillas appropriated telephone parts for other purposes, including extracting the sulfur from telephone insulators for use in gunpowder production.[119]

While the use of technologies such as telephones and airplanes was critical to the border security apparatus, the actual day-to-day work of wintertime river patrol still relied on a massive mobilization of human labor. Police officers in colonial Korea often moved from nearby locations in the northern provinces to other stations and substations on the river "frontline" (*daiissen*) each winter. As figure 3.6 demonstrates, for most years during the period 1931–1940, the number of police on the border consistently rose in the winter months.[120]

In addition to buttressing their own numbers, colonial police forcibly mobilized local civilian populations to carry out wintertime riverside patrol. In villages along the Korean side of the Yalu River, colonial authorities began mobilizing local residents—primarily young men—to form rural "self-defense corps" " (J: *jikeidan*, K: *chagyŏngdan*) since soon after the outbreak of the March First Movement.[121] By February 1938 the total membership in "self-defense corps" had grown to 16,932, more than seven times the number of full-time colonial police on the Korean side of the Manchurian-Korean border in March of the same year (2,407).[122] Members of the "self-defense corps" were expected to carry out basic river patrol duties under the supervision of local police and were armed only with clubs while rotating hourly patrol shifts of the frozen border river until sunrise.[123]

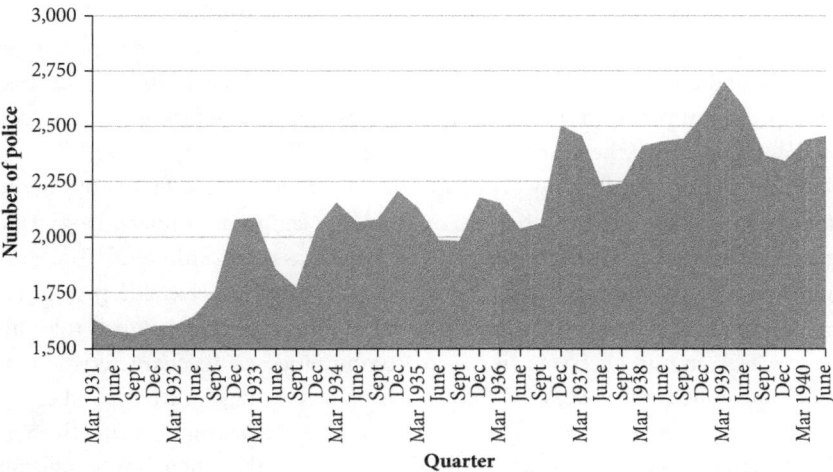

FIGURE 3.6. The number of border police stationed along the Korean side of the Manchurian-Korean border, 1931–1940. Note the obvious peaks around the winter months of December and March and lower numbers around June and September. Numbers are unfortunately missing for December 1937.

Sources: Chōsen Sōtokufu Keimukyoku, "Kokkyō Dai ichi, nisen keisatsu haichihyō, Shi Shōwa go-nen ji Shōwajūichi-nen (1930–1936)," National Archives of Korea; Chōsen Sōtokufu Keimukyoku, Kokkyō Dai issen, "Dai nisen keisatsukan haichi kankei," Shi Shōwa jūni-nen ji Shōwa jūshichi-nen (1937–1942)," National Archives of Korea.

The memoir of one Korean corpsman who grew up in the border county of Sakchu recalled how "one to two village residents were called up every evening to keep guard during the night under the banner of 'border security.' If the sound of a barking dog or something similar was heard across the frozen ice . . . we had to stare and watch with an intensity that pierced the frozen darkness."[124] Self-defense corps members often paid a heavy price for their connection to colonial authority, such as during the March 1936 Taegil raid when one "self-defense corps" member, a Korean villager named Pak Killok, was killed by a guerrilla bullet.[125]

Manchukuo officials also mobilized local populations against "bandits" on the other side of the Yalu River border. These efforts included organizing locals into "self-defense groups" (J: *jieidan*, C: *ziweituan*) that resembled those in Korea (except the fact that they were allowed to actually carry firearms). Manchukuo authorities also implemented a *baojia* (J: *hokō*) system of collective responsibility for local security that was based on traditional Chinese precedents as well as Japanese pacification policy in colonial Taiwan.[126] Under this policy, allegations of colluding with guerrilla fighters could lead to violent reprisals not only against individuals but against entire communities. To further discourage local support of anti-Japanese guerrilla movements, Manchukuo officials wrested peasants from their land and gathered them into closely guarded "collective hamlets" (J: *shūdan buraku*), where they were forced to display identification papers upon entering and leaving. This policy inflicted unprecedented hardship as deadly disease spread rampantly in the cramped collective villages and farmers were forced to abandon much of their farmland in the name of "bandit suppression."[127]

Humans were not the only organisms mobilized in the fight for control of the Yalu River border, nor were they the only ones to endure its winters. Dogs were raised at border police and customs stations for use as patrol animals.[128] These canines accompanied border police and custom officers on riverside patrols for smugglers and "bandits," with their ferocity in fulfilling their assigned roles inspiring fear among observers in border communities. With characteristic bravado, one police officer declared that all it took was a single dog bark and cry of "who are you!" (*nuguyo*) in Korean to stop many guerrillas from making the border crossing.[129] Yet when faced with the depths of the Yalu winter, border officials wrote sympathetically of their station dogs "refusing to eat" until they had been sufficiently warmed, the cold nights draining them until "they had little energy to bark."[130]

Carrier pigeons were another animal both essential to Yalu River border patrol and susceptible to its climatic extremes. Carrier pigeons were widely used to relay messages between police substations in remote locations such as river islands. They were also used by border police for cross-border "searches" (*naisa*) and "bandit suppression" in the Manchurian frontier.[131] Accounts published by border officials contain numerous expressions of gratitude to these birds, and border police stations were often equipped with pigeon shacks in the event that their services were needed. Used most often during the summer months, the release of pigeons was often stopped in the winter due to climatic concerns. Care had to be taken that pigeons did not freeze to death during the most severe of Yalu winter nights, when temperatures would drop to -40 degrees Celsius or lower.[132] In a 1936 article for the metropolitan newsmagazine *Asahi gurafu*, border policeman Noritake Kazuo included a list of animals—120 dogs, 194 chickens, 2 ducks, and 4 pigs and cows—that froze to death in the area supervised by the Tonghŭng border police station in the winter of 1935–1936.[133] Such figures confirm Aaron Skabelund's observation that Japanese imperial expansion, including Yalu border security, truly entailed the mobilization of "all creatures great and small."[134]

As in years past, government-general officials' success in patrolling the Yalu River during the 1930s often hinged on successful cooperation with authorities on the "opposite bank" (*taigan*). While such cooperation was significantly easier following the Japanese takeover of Manchuria, bureaucratic rivalries and differing priorities between colonial governments in Korea and Manchuria meant that it was by no means automatic. After the hasty participation of the Korea-based Chōsen Army in the Manchurian Incident, the first official meeting about border security between the Government-General of Korea and the newly created Manchukuo government did not take place until January 15, 1933, nearly a year and a half later.[135] Manchukuo authorities also complained about colonial Korean policemen's border trespassing in a manner similar to their Chinese predecessors. Such disputes were cited in a 1937 agreement between police officials in North P'yŏngan Province, which noted the "friction and discord" caused by "lack of contact" between authorities on opposing sides of the river. This same agreement also described the icebound season as the most urgent time for cross-border cooperation, showing how conflicts over border policing were linked to entrenched seasonal anxieties.[136]

Suppression of guerrilla groups in their hideouts north of the Yalu ultimately mattered far more to Manchukuo authorities than the policing of the river itself. This was made evident in December 1934, when the Manchukuo government decided to remove some 200 policemen from the Yalu-Hun River Waterfront Police in the middle of the icebound season, cutting the overall size of the force in half.[137] For authorities in colonial Korea, this decision seemed to confirm that they bore the brunt of Yalu border security. When asked by a newspaper reporter about the potential effects of this move, an official from North P'yŏngan Province replied that while "it was difficult to say it would not affect their operations, we in North P'yŏngan haven't really been able to rely on them for much help [in the past]."[138]

Even with these tensions, during the river's icebound season Japanese military and police officials from both sides of the border continued to launch coordinated and brutal counter-insurgency campaigns against Manchurian guerrillas. Winter was the typical season for "bandit suppression" campaigns, which mobilized thousands of troops and policemen from across Manchukuo and Korea and often destroyed whole villages accused of harboring rebels. The choice of winter for counterinsurgency campaigns was motivated by a number of factors, including the scarcity of supplies for anti-Japanese guerrillas, which was hoped to induce their quick surrender, and the ability to track insurgents' footprints in the freshly fallen snow. In a 2009 interview recalling his participation in Yalu "bandit-suppression" campaigns, former Japanese soldier Takamura Eizō cited such explanations while declaring that summertime counterinsurgency "simply didn't work." Takamura also punctuated his recollections with exclamations about the border region's cold: "I was so shocked when I went by just how cold, so cold it was. Thirty below. God was it fierce!"[139]

The correspondence of Communist guerrilla leaders confirms that winter was indeed a time of considerable hardship. Even as border police writings described the icebound season as a prime moment for "bandit" attack, guerrilla leaders first had to convince their comrades that operating in the winter at all was a good idea. In a letter circulated to Communist guerrilla leaders throughout Northeast China, one Chinese commander argued that despite the extreme cold and a lack of material resources when compared to the summer, "we must oppose the tendency to say 'we cannot engage in guerrilla attacks during the winter.'"[140] Other guerrilla leaders' writings are also filled with concerns about a lack of warm clothes and other supplies necessary to pass the harsh Manchurian winter, a desperation that may have motivated them to carry out further raids.[141] In an interview allegedly given to a Korean villager captured by his guerrilla forces, Manchurian guerrilla leader and later North Korean president Kim Il-sung bemoaned the plight of his troops: "I'm a person with blood, with tears, with a soul, but here we are spending the cold winter wandering around like this."[142] Frostbite was unsurprisingly a major enemy of guerrilla groups in the region in addition to Japanese military and police patrols.[143]

Better-equipped and -funded than their guerrilla counterparts, Japanese border police nonetheless had their own complaints about the experience of the bitterly cold wintertime Yalu. In a 1936 commemorative album entitled *Border Security* (*Kokkyō keibi*), Japanese police chief Morinishi Takejirō described his experience weathering the coldest temperatures ever recorded on the Korean Peninsula, −43.6 Celsius (−46.48 Fahrenheit), at the Chunggangjin police station on January 12, 1931.[144] "It's impossible for me to describe in words the cold of −43.6 Celsius," wrote Morinishi. "Even though the fire of the *ondol*[145] is lit and the bottom of my futon is hot to the point of burning, the top of my futon is as cold as ice." Hair washed with warm water would immediately freeze, and if one were to run his fingers through his hair it would easily break off. The eating of raw fish or *sashimi* was done "with bellies flat against the ondol-heated floor," lest the essentially frozen fish be digested improperly.[146]

As a feminine antidote to portrayals of male border police suffering alone along the frigid, frozen Yalu, Japanese publications sympathetic to the border policing effort highlighted policemen's wives' responsibility for protecting the welcoming warmth of border officials' homes, both figuratively and literally. A police wife interviewed by a Japanese settler newspaper in Korea described caring for her husband's frostbite wounds after he returned from wintertime counterinsurgency campaigns, while in a 1934 article in the popular women's magazine *Shufu no tomo* (Housewife's friend) police wife Kuromitsu Yoshiko described the "tremendous" costs required to fuel the *ondol* underground heater of their home as one of their family's major expenses.[147] Noticeably absent from these accounts of imperial domesticity along the frozen Yalu were the voices of Korean wives of

FIGURE 3.7. Border police and family members.

Source: Heian Hokudō Keisatsubu, Kokkyō no mamori (Shingishū [Sinŭiju]: Heian Hokudō Keisatsubu, 1933), 52.

ethnically Korean border policeman. Korean-language media also hardly mentioned these women—preferring to focus instead, when possible, on the plight of those Korean women victimized by the colonial security regime. What does survive in the archive are haunting images like figure 3.7, a wintertime photograph from a 1933 border police photo album that shows a cold-looking Korean border police wife and her Japanese counterpart surrounded by thickly bundled male policemen stationed at one remote police outpost.

In a bid for sympathy and greater resources, border officials' experiences with the wintertime Yalu were narrated in special radio broadcasts,[148] a "Northern Korea border security" commemorative edition of the photo newsmagazine *Asahi gurafu*,[149] and even on the silver screen. Produced by major Tokyo film studio Toho Co. Ltd,, the 1943 film *Suicide Squad at the Watchtower* (*Bōrō no kesshitai*) was set in a remote Korean village on the upper reaches of the Yalu.[150] During the summer and fall the village is an idyllic place where residents live in relative peace under Japanese colonial rule. Suspense builds, however, as winter approaches and what sounds like rifle shots emanate from the river's direction. The sound is actually that of the Yalu River freezing over, which portends the coming of the "bandits" who live across the border.[151] The film thus reflected a well-entrenched vision of the Yalu as a riparian border where seasonal flows of ice were as dangerous as cross-border "bandits."[152]

The cross-border movements of anti-Japanese dissidents and Manchurian "mounted bandits" across the alternatively flowing or frozen Yalu River were a recurring feature of Sino-Korean border politics in the decades following the Japanese annexation of Korea. As an integral aspect of the imperial border's liquid geographies, the mobilities of these human actors interlocked with the seasonally changing movement of water, ice, and other nonhuman elements of the border to present both opportunity and obstacle to imperial border-making efforts.

For Japanese border agents trying to police the fluid mobilities of border crossers, the thawing of ice and resulting upsurge in riverboat traffic, the intense summertime heat, humidity, and river flooding, and cold, frozen pathways of winter each posed different considerations and resulted in an intensive mobilization of physical and human resources. As this chapter has shown, the significance attached to different seasons also evolved over time in response to different major political crises within the broader Manchuria-Korea region. Prior to the Japanese occupation of Manchuria, colonial Korean border police used the cross-border activities of Korean nationalists, which grew most intense during the summer "flourishing season," as an excuse to cross the Yalu River at will and weaken Chinese sovereignty in the process. But anti-Japanese guerrillas also succeeded in penetrating border defenses and threatening the overall stability of colonial rule along the border by launching numerous deadly raids against river traffic and local police outposts.

Following the Japanese occupation of Manchuria, the accessibility of the frozen river and ability to track guerrillas along snowy riverbanks made winter an ideal time for "bandit suppression." Yet the same iced-over Yalu was also a ready pathway for opponents of imperial rule, who made several large-scale attacks across the frozen river in the early to mid-1930s. This in combination with the Yalu's frigid temperatures also made border agents regard the "icebound season" with feelings of dread. Icy cross-border tensions also surfaced between colonial officials in Korea and Manchukuo, who sometimes viewed each other with suspicion even as they generally cooperated to further broader goals of imperial expansion. These intraimperial tensions over how best to police the dynamic liquid geographies of the Yalu boundary would manifest even more dramatically in the case of smuggling, the subject of the following chapter. Encouraging the mobility of capital and commodities across the Sino-Korean border was a perennial goal of Japanese border-making, but as was the case with other border mobilities, violent consequences ensued when these flows spilled outside officially-set channels.

4

ENVIRONMENTS OF YALU RIVER SMUGGLING

Violent encounters with customs officials were nothing new for Yalu River smugglers. But for even the most battle-hardened, the morning of August 4, 1936, was especially deadly. At around 10:00 a.m., Manchukuo customs officials in Andong received word that three sampans manned by nearly one hundred Korean smugglers were operating in nearby waters. Hours later, customs officials were in hot pursuit, chasing the bootleggers as they attempted to flee to safety on the Korean side of the river. As one of the Koreans' vessels escaped, the other two became locked in battle with customs officials' motorboats. Smugglers pelted customs officials with stones and beat them with clubs, while customs officers, according to one source, threatened smugglers with gunshots and knives. By the end, embattled smugglers leapt into the murky, rain-engorged waters of the summertime Yalu in a last-ditch attempt to escape. Twenty-five of them drowned. Popular Korean-language media responded to customs "cruelty" with outrage. Meanwhile colonial officials in Korea condemned Manchukuo customs officers' intrusion into their administrative territory, though the fluid boundary line between Korean and Manchurian sides of the river had always been near-impossible to define in practice.[1]

The movements of smugglers and flows of illicit commodities were a fundamental aspect of the Yalu River border's liquid geographies.[2] Following the Japanese annexation of Korea, most cross-border smuggling took place in a circumscribed riparian space adjacent to the Japanese railway concession in Andong.[3] Even within this limited stretch, smugglers moved among and between the competing administrative claims of the Japanese colonial government in

Korea, various regimes, both Chinese and Japanese-controlled, on the Chinese side of the river, and the South Manchuria Railway Company, which administered the Andong railway concession until its dissolution in 1937. Smuggling was shaped both by these fractured, competing, and ill-defined zones of political sovereignty and the seasonally changing environment of the river itself. Smugglers proved adept at navigating across the river by boat in the spring through autumn months, utilizing their knowledge of riverine topography and the fractured sovereignty of the river shore. Winter was no obstacle either, as official sources anxiously noted smugglers rushing to move goods across the frozen river.

Like the surveillance of political dissidents and "bandits" covered in the previous chapter, the policing of smugglers' mobilities across the seasonally changing river environment illustrated the strengths and limits of the colonial border regime. This chapter narrates how Japanese imperial officials in Korea and Manchuria attempted to channel and contain the liquid geographies of Yalu River smuggling in ways that benefited the regional expansion of Japanese power from the 1910s until the mid-1930s. Smuggling's grunt work was done primarily by impoverished ethnic Koreans in the border cities of Sinŭiju and Andong, who came to know the flowing or frozen environment of the Yalu River intimately through their labors. These smugglers also acted as inadvertent foot soldiers of Japanese economic expansion by engaging in frequent violent encounters with Chinese customs officials. In many cases Japanese colonial officials and Japanese merchants on both sides of the border stood to benefit from smuggling, especially pre-1931 when the movement of illicit goods from colonial Korea to Manchuria weakened Chinese sovereignty. But as much as smugglers' pursuit of profit and seasonally contingent cross-border mobilities could work in favor of Japanese expansion, they also displayed the limits of the imperial border regime, especially as they collided against competing agendas of different Japanese colonial regimes that emerged after the Japanese takeover of Manchuria in 1931.

Manchukuo officials clashed with their counterparts in Korea and the Andong railway concession over the smuggling issue. While scholars have discussed discursive efforts to establish Manchukuo's alleged autonomy and "sovereignty," few have analyzed how Manchukuo's distinct status in the empire was embodied through daily local practices like customs enforcement on the border with colonial Korea.[4] Manchukuo customs officials' increasingly aggressive efforts to bolster the economic stability of the newly created Japanese client state through customs tax collection brought them into direct conflict with Japanese officials in Andong and colonial Korea who had long benefited from smuggling. Smuggling enforcement was also an act of seasonal border-making, as wintertime was an especially active time for illicit trade, but the warmer months also saw dramatic confrontations between smugglers and Manchukuo customs agents on the watery surface of the Yalu. The alternatively watery and icy landscapes of Yalu smuggling were imagined in gendered terms that distinguished the sympathetic female smuggler from the organized "gang"-like activities of the male smuggler. With intensifying enforcement, the scale of these illicit economies finally began to retreat, though even these belated effects would prove illusory in the long term.

The Origins of Smuggling along the Colonial Yalu Border

Smuggling was a problem (or, depending on one's perspective, opportunity) as old as the border itself.[5] By the early twentieth century, illicit flows of cross-Yalu commerce took on new meaning as Japanese empire-builders tried to channel these liquid geographies for their own benefit.

The 1907 creation of a Japanese extraterritorial settlement and railway concession in Andong, immediately across the river from the new railroad city of Sinŭiju in protectorate-era Korea, provided an ideal legal haven for bootleggers' activities. As a result of treaties concluded between the Qing state and Japan in the wake of the Russo-Japanese War, the policing of the Japanese settlement in Andong was under the jurisdiction of the governor-general of the Kwantung Leased Territory in Dalian rather than Chinese officials.[6] The Chinese Maritime Customs Service, a foreign-managed product of Western gunboat imperialism that oversaw Chinese customs revenue collection, ostensibly maintained an official outpost near the Andong railway station.[7] This gave Chinese customs officials an administrative toehold in the settlement, but they were otherwise powerless to use weapons, issue citations, or perform their duties without the cooperation of concession police. Such an arrangement proved a perennial source of frustration for customs officials on the Chinese bank of the Yalu, who described the Japanese settlement in one 1916 report as the beating "heart" of Yalu smuggling operations.[8]

The illicit economy based around the Sinŭiju-Andong corridor expanded further after the completion of the Yalu River Railway Bridge in 1911. The bridge, which channeled flows of goods across the seasonally variable river, also encouraged a rising tide of illicit trade. Just as the scale of legal trade across this rail route grew, so did smugglers' activities. While stories of individual smugglers trafficking goods such as salt and currency splashed across newspaper headlines,[9] early records from the Chinese Maritime Customs Service in Andong show that corporate customs evasion by Japanese merchants operating for the newly opened South Manchuria Railway Company (SMRC) was just as, if not more, pervasive than other forms of smuggling. In 1914 a full 69.8 percent of customs violations recorded in Andong were by Japanese merchants, many of them contracted by the SMRC, who falsely reported the amount or value of their goods. Statistics such as this show that even after a special one-third reduction in customs rates on goods traveling over the Yalu via rail was negotiated between the Chinese and Japanese governments in 1913, attempts to defraud the Chinese customs remained rampant.[10] And while the pull of the China market resulted in most contraband traveling north across the Yalu, smuggled goods flowed the other way as well. A July 15, 1922, article in the Korean-language *Tonga ilbo* (East Asia Daily) reported that 125 cases of smuggling had been recorded in Sinŭiju so far that month, an increase of nearly 60 percent over the previous year's figures.[11]

Smugglers took advantage of the infrastructure built by Japanese imperialists to facilitate trade across the river, including the Yalu River Railway Bridge. As previously mentioned, transporting goods by rail and then misstating their amount or value was one common tactic for merchants seeking to fatten their profit margin at the expense of customs officials.[12] In addition, some individuals attempted to smuggle undeclared goods within passengers' luggage.[13] To combat this, Japanese and Chinese officials began joint inspections of travelers' goods at the Andong railway station soon after the railway bridge's completion.[14] The level of inspection was deep and invasive enough to cause inconvenience, if not outright embarrassment for ordinary travelers making the cross-border journey. In her 1928 account of an SMRC-sponsored journey through Manchuria, Japanese poet Yosano Akiko related how Japanese schoolchildren returning to Japan from a Manchurian sightseeing trip were forced to leave out their open bags for customs inspection, revealing to passers-by knapsacks stuffed with several cartons of Western and Chinese-made cigarettes. Unsure whether the cigarettes were intended as family souvenirs or placed there by a teacher eager to supplement his meager salary, Yosano nonetheless expressed disgust at a Japanese customs bureaucracy seemingly devoid of "empathy or human kindness."[15]

The railroad bridge also offered smuggling opportunities on the eight-foot-wide pedestrian pathways that abutted the railway tracks on either side. Every day a motley assortment of students, laborers, peddlers, and others jostled their way across the paths on rickshaws, bicycles, and by foot to their destinations on either side of the river.[16] During the spring through autumn months, foot traffic typically peaked immediately before and after times when the central portion of the bridge swung open to boat traffic and pedestrians were not allowed on the bridge. Taking advantage of these bottleneck periods, smugglers attempted to meld into the crowd and evade the suspicion of onlooking customs officials. In other cases, smugglers on rickshaws or bicycles would rush quickly across to the safety of accomplices elsewhere in Sinŭiju or Andong, or most violently, split into two groups, one of which would engage customs officials while the other group blasted past.[17] The most daring would even leap onto or from passing trains or catch goods thrown out of train windows.[18]

The only nonaquatic means of crossing the river most months of the year, the railroad bridge was a convenient enough target for smugglers, but the density of police and customs surveillance ultimately made it a less attractive venue for large-scale smuggling than the fluid surface of the Yalu itself. For much of its history smuggling on the colonial Yalu River border was primarily river borne, which made the rhythms of these contraband flows inextricably bound to the annual cycles of the river environment.

Seasonal Environments of Yalu River Smuggling and Smugglers' Identities

By the mid-1920s, smuggling on the Yalu River came to assume the specific environmental characteristics that would define its place in the regional economy for years to come. The spatial politics of the Yalu's illicit economy was, to use a Dickensian phrase, a "tale of two cities," Andong and Sinŭiju (figure 4.1). While the anti-Japanese guerrilla raids discussed in the previous chapter occurred all along the border, the bulk of Yalu smuggling occurred in a relatively circumscribed stretch of river adjacent to two particular sites: the Yalu River Railway Bridge and the district of Liudaogou in the Andong railway concession.

For goods traveling across the river from Sinŭiju to Andong, the main destination was a marshy corner of the Japanese concession known as Liudaogou. Liudaogou's propitious siting as a smuggling entrepôt was described in the following terms by a Western commissioner of the Chinese Maritime Customs Service:

> Liutaokou [sic] is a desolate expanse of foreshore situated in nearly the extreme corner of the Japanese settlement limits. Its facilities for smuggling are these: It is a very lonely spot, far from the town and from any probability of interference. It is cut off from approach by our patrols, except by a very long detour, by a broad creek which running obliquely into the main river just above Liutaokou, scours a deep channel right under the bank there permitting comparatively deep drought native boats to approach close to the shore. A village of the roughest type of Coreans [sic] adjoins this foreshore. Some of the houses are said to be godowns for storing the goods brought across from Shingishu [sic]. The railway yards with their warehouses are within easy reach. The Customs House is nearly two miles away."[19]

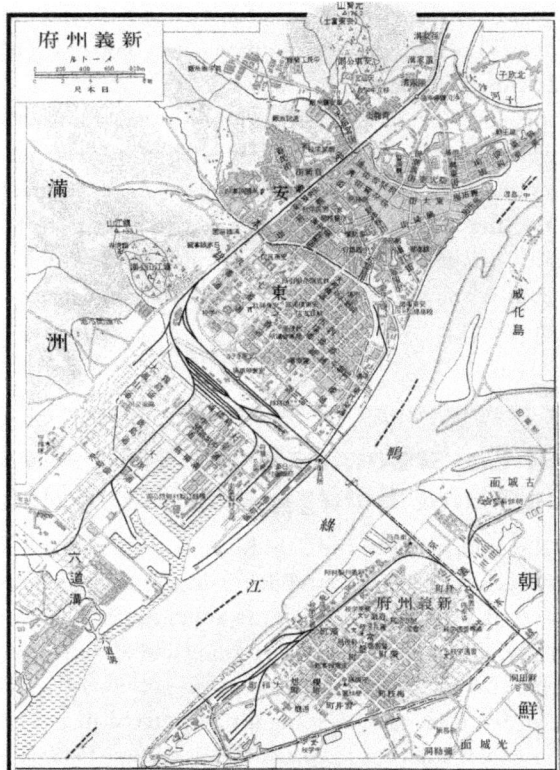

FIGURE 4.1. Japanese map of the twin border cities of Andong (upper left) and Sinŭiju (lower right) intersected by the Yalu River.

Source: Kaizōsha, ed., Nihon chiri taikei 12-kan: Chōsen hen (Tokyo: Kaizōsha, 1930).

As this description of Liudaogou shows, the liquid geographies of Yalu smuggling extended not just to the main channel of the Yalu but also to the numerous small creeks abutting the river and extending into places like Liudaogou. In the spring through autumn months, such streams allowed nimble smugglers' boats to approach safety while preventing access to larger customs surveillance vessels.[20] For the smuggler seeking to evade customs detection, an intimate knowledge of the Yalu's riparian topography was thus an essential survival tool. Chinese customs officials repeatedly encouraged merchants to take their trade across the bridge as an antismuggling preventative measure, showing the degree to which the river environment was seen as hostile to their control.[21]

A 1921 report by the Andong customs office noted that Liudaogou was "considered a dangerous place for a Customs Officer to try and function, especially at night." As evidence, the same report cited an incident two years prior on October 2, 1919, in which an ethnically Korean tidewaiter (an officer who boarded and inspected incoming ships) named Y. P. Kim had been seized by smugglers in their boat, only managing to escape by jumping into the frigid river and swimming to shore.[22] Considering that the Yalu typically froze over by late November, water temperatures at this autumnal time of year would have been cold indeed. Appeals for help from the Japanese concession police, the same report noted, had largely been in vain.

In addition to the serrated topography of the Yalu shoreline, the river's seasonal variations also fundamentally shaped the flow of smuggled goods between the Andong and Sinŭiju shorelines. The methodically kept diaries of Roy Maxwell Talbot, a US national employed by the Chinese Maritime Customs Service as commissioner of Andong customs, carefully describe the effects of seasonal change on smuggling operations. Talbot embraced the initial arrival of the wintertime icebound season, when floating chunks of ice in the river impeded the regular flow of cross-border traffic. Writing in a frustrated tone after ice failed to materialize one evening in late November, the commissioner explained: "Continuous mild when I want ice in river to stop the smuggling temporarily at least. It is getting on my nerves now."[23] But once ice on the river froze completely, Talbot found himself consumed by the burst of smuggling activity that followed. By the springtime thawing of the ice, Talbot's diary welcomed the end of the anarchic accessibility of the frozen river. "Ice on river becomes unsafe. All smuggling on ice consequentially ceases. Feel that it will never be as bad again as we contain it better by water."[24]

From an administrative standpoint, winter was easily the most difficult season of all for smuggling regulation—a fact borne out in both qualitative and quantitative evidence from the period. A December 18, 1923, article in the *Tonga ilbo* described how both Chinese and Japanese officials were intensifying searches of handheld goods in response to the new "freedom" of movement offered by the river's frozen surface.[25] A report by the Andong customs commissioner a few months later detailed how since the freezing over of the river there "had not been a single night when rice smuggling had not occurred." All throughout that winter, the report detailed, large groups of mostly Korean smugglers hired by Japanese merchants in Andong had been transporting sacks of grain across the river ice to Korea. When confronted by Chinese officials, the bootleggers would retaliate by throwing stones and otherwise resisting arrest.[26] Talbot's own diary recounts an episode one January evening where he and other customs officers encountered hundreds of Korean smugglers standing around fifty to sixty loaded sledges atop the Yalu ice, waiting for an opportue movement for the goods to be quickly rushed ashore and onto safety. "Our small patrol," Talbot writes, "was powerless to cope with them."[27] Talbot also claimed that smugglers were plied with sake to make themselves "warm" and "courageous" during the bitter cold winter nights.[28] Courage was certainly needed, not only for possible confrontations with officials but also for braving a frigid pathway that occasionally cracked open and plunged smugglers to an icy death.[29]

In terms of quantitative evidence for the regulatory challenges of the "icebound season," a statistical analysis of smuggling enforcement data gathered and compiled from reports produced by the Andong customs office over a nearly two-decade period (1912–1930) shows that the three-month period from January to March had noticeably lower citations than the remainder of the year (see figure 4.2).[30] Such data could indicate a wintertime decline in the amount of smuggling. However, when paired with qualitative evidence like those sources discussed previously, the statistics suggest that the fewer citations were due to the overall decreased efficacy of the wintertime customs rather than smugglers' unwillingness to brave the cold.

By piloting boats in the spring through autumn months or riding sledges across the frozen wintertime Yalu, smugglers became intimately acquainted with the river's seasonal transformations. But who were these smugglers that did battle

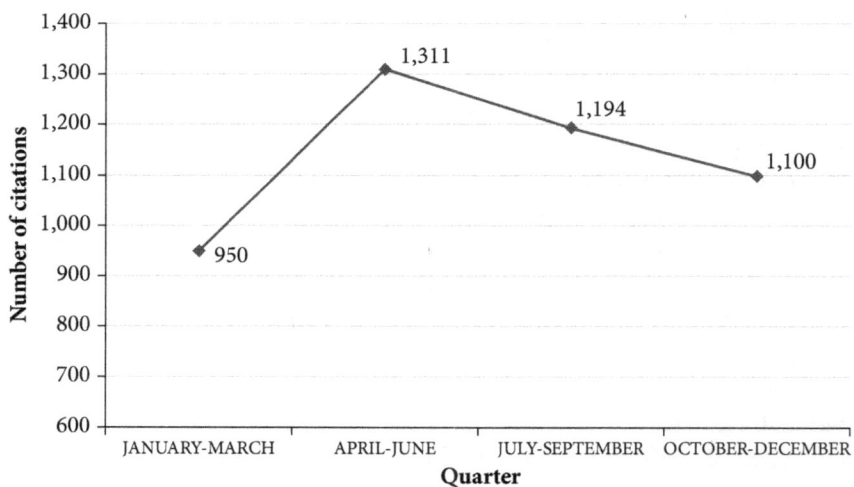

FIGURE 4.2. Line chart showing data for smuggling citations by Chinese customs officials in Andong. The data is organized into four three-month quarters, roughly corresponding with annual seasons, and draws on data reported between 1912 and 1930 (except for 1929, for which data is inconsistent).

Source: Zhongguo bianjiang shi di yanjiu zhongxin, Dongbei bianjiang dang'an xuanji, (Guilin: Guangxi shifan daxue chubanshe, 2007), v. 60:235–281, 436–508; 61:136–219, 376–424; 62:1–76, 181–266, 372–440; 63:1–58, 189–227, 353–405; 64:1–44, 227–254, 359–391; 66:384–412; 67:261–317; 68:118–177; 69:116–174.

with the river as well as customs officials? As the value of goods traded across the Yalu steadily grew, Koreans gradually became the dominant ethnic group among Manchurian-Korean border smugglers. Whereas ethnic Koreans made up only 4.3 percent of smugglers caught in Andong during the year 1914 (Japanese, by contrast, made up nearly 80 percent), by a decade later (1924) that percentage had grown to approximately 45.2 percent, or nearly half of all smuggling citations. At the end of the 1920s, Koreans made up two-thirds of those cited for smuggling.[31] This phenomenon of growing Korean participation in smuggling encouraged an official image of Koreans as inherently lawless and prone to illicit trade. Chinese customs authorities spoke with alarm of the increasing number of Korean "ruffians" (baotu), many of them employed by Japanese merchants in the Andong concession, who regularly transported grain, salt, and other goods across the river.[32] Cattle were even occasionally smuggled to avoid border controls for veterinary disease.[33] In the racist words of one American commissioner: "By nature a Korean takes to smuggling like a duck to water."[34] Across the river, a similar perception of Sinŭiju developed as a smuggler's haven and an unruly frontier city. 'What thing is most plentiful in Sinŭiju?" a 1923 article in the Korean magazine Kaebyŏk rhetorically asked its readers. "Grain? Cargo? Fish? No. Then maybe sorghum wine? ... No, it is none of those things. It is smugglers."[35]

Blaming smuggling on Koreans' ethnicity was easier than dealing with the systemic factors that fueled Korean participation in this illicit trade. One major issue was economic disenfranchisement. Even relatively elite Koreans in the border city of Sinŭiju complained about their exclusion from the city's most profitable industry, timber processing, which was overwhelmingly in the hands of Japanese settler capitalists.[36] Another factor encouraging Korean participation in Yalu smuggling was widespread rural poverty under colonial rule and the subsequent migration of ethnic Koreans to Andong and other cities in southern Manchuria, where they enjoyed extraterritorial status as subjects of the Japanese Empire. Whereas only 50 Koreans lived in the Andong railway concession in 1908, by 1917 that number had grown to 1,843, expanding further by 1929 to 8,102 of 58,440 settlement residents (approximately 14 percent).[37] These Korean residents frequently acted as brokers between Japanese and Chinese merchants in Andong and Sinŭiju. Participation in the illicit (though hardly underground) economy penetrated all levels of Korean migrant society, with marginalized, lower-class Koreans doing the dangerous day-to-day labor of transporting goods while elites provided capital and negotiated with Japanese and Chinese merchants for further investment.[38]

Of course, widespread Korean involvement in smuggling would have been unimaginable without the protection offered by Japanese police authorities in the railway concession. As a result of the Chinese Maritime Customs Service's inability to carry weapons in the Andong railway concession, gangs of smugglers took to throwing stones, wielding clubs, and otherwise openly resisting arrest when confronted by customs representatives. A report sent by the Andong customs to the governor of Fengtian Province related how even large groups of twenty customs agents had been attacked by well over a hundred stone-throwing Korean grain smugglers. The report's author then accused Japanese concession police of providing "implicit protection" for smugglers' activities by refusing to intervene.[39] In another case, Chinese customs officers approached the Japanese police for help confiscating smuggled goods that had recently arrived from the Korean side of the river. Not only did the police refuse, but one Chinese customs officer allegedly heard the smugglers using the police station telephone to tell the owner of the goods that the goods had landed safely.[40] Whether or not Japanese police actually let smugglers avail themselves of police station telephones, Japanese officials and settlers alike thought they had much to lose and little to gain by aiding Chinese customs enforcement, as the following episode from the winter of 1930–1931 shows.

Sino-Japanese Diplomatic Tensions and a Wintertime Crackdown

By the late 1920s, Sino-Japanese conflicts over the issue of Yalu River smuggling were escalating in a manner that mirrored mounting tensions between the two countries. The successful unification of China under the Nationalist regime of Chiang Kai-Shek in 1927, after over a decade of divisive warlord politics, also brought portentous changes to the Chinese Maritime Customs Service. One key change was the new Nationalist regime's recovery of tariff autonomy. Not only was the Customs Service staffed at its highest levels by foreigners, but the Qing and later Republican governments had been compelled by Western powers to maintain customs duties at an artificially low rate. Seeking a source of revenue to support their long-term state-building goals, the new Nationalist government successfully concluded negotiations to regain control over customs rates in 1928.[41] Just months later, on February 1, 1929, Nationalist leaders dramatically raised customs rates on goods traveling into the country.

While the increase in customs taxes did generate significant revenue for the Nationalist state, it also added dangerous fuel to the already volatile issue of Yalu River smuggling. Faced with the dramatic escalation of cross-border smuggling and a mandate to increase customs revenues for the new Nationalist government,

Customs Service officials unsuccessfully tried to seek help from Japanese authorities. Internal documents from the Japanese Foreign Ministry show the agency's consular representatives in Andong trying to intercede on behalf of the Chinese Customs Service to secure help from Japanese police officials in Sinŭiju and Dalian, only to back away in response to opposition from Japanese merchants in the Andong and Fengtian Chambers of Commerce. In May 1929, for example, the Foreign Ministry convinced the Andong concession police to help "preserve international trust" by devoting more personnel and police boats to smuggling patrol.[42] By late June, concession police had recovered ten thousand pieces of luggage and 3,000 yen in lost customs fees.[43] Yet after Japanese merchants in Andong complained about the threat to their livelihood and even began mobilizing disgruntled Korean smugglers to threaten the Andong consul, the intensity of Japanese officials' desires to aid the Chinese Customs Service quickly cooled.[44] Not only did smuggling regulation threaten an-all-too lucrative source of income for the local Japanese settler economy, but officials also cited a potential security threat from thousands of unemployed Koreans.[45]

Japanese authorities' unwillingness to help Chinese customs officials had violent consequences. In one May 1930 incident, customs officers engaged three sampans filled with approximately 10,000 yen worth of clothing. The Korean smugglers on board first resisted attempts to confiscate the materials. Accounts differ of what occurred afterward, with Chinese officials claiming that the fleeing smugglers all leapt into the river and escaped, while the Japanese Foreign Ministry claimed that one of the smugglers was beaten on the forehead severely before falling in the river and drowning.[46] The next day, a large group of enraged Koreans brought the body of the alleged victim to a Customs Service station. Laying their comrade's body down in front of the station doors, they then began breaking windows, smashing doors, and otherwise wrecking the station while the frightened customs officials on duty fled for safety. Accounts also diverge here in regard to the police response: the Chinese account claimed that the Japanese police did "nothing" to stop the violence, while the Japanese Foreign Ministry report claimed otherwise.[47]

Such violence, along with the repeated entreaties of the Chinese Maritime Customs Service and the powerful Western interests backing them, compelled Japanese authorities to once again consider adopting a hardline stance toward smuggling enforcement. In January 1931, Kwantung Leased Territory officials issued the sternest set of regulations to date on smuggling. Colonial officials in Korea indicated their support of these measures, with Sinŭiju police authorities promising to add one extra policeman to every customs and police substation along the river in addition to requiring licenses (*menkyo*) for transporting goods across the winter ice.⁴⁸ Across the river Andong police officials met with local merchants and chambers of commerce to warn them about smuggling while also imposing stricter surveillance of the Yalu shoreline.⁴⁹

It is not coincidental that the timing of these new regulations came with the arrival of the wintertime icebound season, a time in the year conventionally considered more difficult for smuggling enforcement. Japanese sources themselves noted the freezing over of the river and the commencement of traffic atop the ice as key factors giving urgency to their actions.⁵⁰

Despite the challenges of ice and cold, by all accounts this newest regulatory push enjoyed promising initial success. On February 12 the North P'yŏngan Province police chief relayed to superiors in Seoul that the amount of goods arriving at Sinŭiju station had decreased by a dramatic 60 percent since the new regulations were issued.⁵¹ Chinese customs records also show a sharp uptick in the number of smuggling citations, the number of citations for January–March being nearly double that of the previous year's figure for the same period.⁵² The same factors that undermined previous regulatory attempts, however, soon challenged this crackdown. Japanese merchants in the Andong concession loudly protested the new measures, claiming that they not only hurt business interests but also damaged Japan's international reputation. Merchants complained about alleged inequity in the application of this regulation, stating that Japanese businesses were uniquely targeted while "corrupt" Chinese officials and merchants were profiting from the less stringent enforcement outside the concession.⁵³

Regulation also failed to address the systemic issues fueling participation in the illicit economy, including a lack of economic opportunities for Koreans living along the Yalu River border. Estimates for the number of Koreans employed full-time in the smuggling trade varied; conservative estimates placed the figure around one thousand, while others claimed double that number in Sinŭiju and the Andong concession.⁵⁴ In response to the January 1931 crackdown, Koreans in Andong and Sinŭiju involved in smuggling, including members of one laborers' association that represented over 250 Korean members, began making requests to local Japanese authorities for help being placed in other local industries. Japanese officials responded by temporarily employing some Korean smugglers in timber-processing plants or as street cleaners, but these opportunities failed to expand to the needed scale as Japanese organizations continued to exhibit a strong preference for cheaper Chinese workers.⁵⁵ It is no surprise then that many Koreans turned to the underground economy, where they encountered a more favorable reception from Japanese settler capital as smugglers.

The fate of this short-lived wintertime crackdown validated Chinese claims of Japanese border officials' complicity in cross-border smuggling. Even as Foreign Ministry diplomats pushed for greater cooperation with Chinese officials,

Japanese border police in colonial Korea and the Andong railway concession quickly backed down in the face of pressure from local Japanese merchants. Their implicit allowance of this commerce would persist even after the Japanese occupation of Manchuria, which would result in fractious intraimperial clashes over how best to manage the liquid geographies of Yalu smuggling.

Smuggling in the Era of the Manchukuo Customs

When Japanese troops occupied the city of Andong on the morning of September 19, 1931, the foreign-managed Customs Service was the only official institution they spared. Its fate, as well as that of other Customs Service offices in Manchuria, were left temporarily unresolved. Hundreds of miles away in the city of Shanghai, Roy Maxwell Talbot, a long-time American employee of the Maritime Customs Service, ruminated in his diary on the possible consequences of the Japanese occupation for his career. Talbot had been notified only days earlier of his new position as deputy commissioner of the Andong customs office, an eagerly anticipated promotion that led him to excitedly write "Deputy Commissioner! ☺" with a caricatured smiling face next to it in his journal entry for that day. After reading news of the Manchurian Incident, however, Talbot more anxiously wrote: "My paper says the Japanese have occupied Moukden [sic] & disarmed the Chinese! What a business! This will probably interfere with my appointment at Antung?"[56]

Not only did the Japanese occupation "interfere" (to put it mildly) with Talbot's appointment as commissioner, but after a drawn-out process of failed negotiations and then outright force, Japanese authorities remade the Andong customs into a bureaucratic arm of the newly established Manchukuo government. As a result of the Customs Service's strong ties to the West, Japanese leaders were initially reluctant to directly seize it and risk further alienating already strained Western support for their actions in Manchuria.[57] But even as Chinese and Western outrage mounted, imperial officials quickly realized the Customs Service's value as a revenue source for their Manchukuo state-building project. For months following the Manchurian Incident the Andong customs office existed in a strange limbo, with Chinese customs officials attempting to prosecute their duties and secure whatever help they could from Japanese police while at the same time preparing for a takeover that was increasingly inevitable.[58] On December 17 Talbot wrote in his journal: "Much talk these days about the Japanese taking over the Customs. Very possible. There is no doubt in my mind that they intend to absorb Manchuria as they did Korea."[59] By March 12 Talbot was issued his first demand to hand over the Customs Service office. Refusing to do so without express orders from his superiors in Shanghai, Talbot was finally removed from his position by force on June 28, and a new Japanese director was installed.[60]

In theory, the Japanese takeover of the Andong customs office simplified the "smuggling question" by making it a matter of pure colonial policy instead of Sino-Japanese diplomacy. Indeed, by early 1932 Japanese police and military officials had already begun to take over enforcement duties on the Yalu River with gusto, leading one newspaper to declare that a bloody new "era of terror" was marking the end of previously open smuggling.[61] Yet such sensational declarations proved premature. Just as there had never been such a thing as a unified colonial policy on Manchuria and Korea before the Manchurian Incident, officials from the newly created Manchukuo state soon clashed with those from the Government-General of Korea and Kwantung Leased Territory over the best direction for smuggling regulation. Manchukuo customs officials continued to grapple with many of the same issues that had plagued their Chinese predecessors, including a growing demand for illicit goods among Japanese merchants, a shifting riparian environment, the extraterritorial status of the Andong concession, and unwilling cooperation from authorities on the Korean side of the river.

The chaos following the Manchurian Incident provided fertile conditions for smuggling. Roy Talbot estimated the total loss of revenue for the Andong customs for the year 1931 to be nearly one million yen, a significant sum during a time when overall legal imports were down due to the ongoing global economic depression.[62] In a March 30, 1932, diary entry Talbot wrote that an estimated 50,000 yen worth of goods made its way across the Yalu ice in a single night.[63] Even after the stabilization of the Manchukuo customs office by late 1932, smuggling continued to grow due to Japanese investment in Manchukuo and the rapid economic growth that followed. Much of this traffic was in goods like shoes, cloth, opium, and precious metals.[64] There was also the oft-smuggled salt, which remained subject to government monopoly in both Korea and Manchuria. According to one police official, by 1934 the loss of income due to salt smuggling along the Yalu River for the Andong customs office was a staggering 1.78 million yen.[65]

As was the case prior to the Manchurian Incident, the majority of Yalu smugglers in the border cities of Andong and Sinŭiju were ethnic Koreans. Former Korean residents of Sinŭiju recalled decades later how smugglers dominated the local economy during the early to mid-1930s. Rather than being condemned by fellow Koreans, these smugglers were reportedly viewed positively for their contributions to the economic recovery of depression-era Sinŭiju.[66] An example of this can be found in the life and career of Sinŭiju resident and Korean "smuggling boss" Han Munhwan. Born in 1896, Han was listed as a "grain merchant" in a

1928 newspaper article about Sinŭiju commercial activity.[67] His name and the address of his Sinŭiju storefront also appeared prominently in an advertisement printed in a 1931 local Korean-language gazetteer, suggesting a degree of respectability and active participation within Sinŭiju's small but vibrant Korean bourgeois society.[68] Just a year later, however, Han was arrested by colonial police for gold smuggling, eventually serving three months in prison for his crimes.[69] That same year, an article published in the Dalian-based Japanese magazine *Shin tenchi* listed Han and his associates in the "Samsŏngho" trading company as some of the most notorious "smuggling bosses" along the Manchurian-Korean border.[70]

Han's tempestuous relationship with Japanese imperial authority is revealing of how Korean participation in smuggling was in part a response to rampant economic and political marginalization in Korean border communities. Han's 1932 arrest was not his first brush with the law. In 1921 Han had been arrested and spent a year in prison for his alleged involvement with the Korean independence movement along the border.[71] Han was thus one of many notable Koreans along the border who threw their support behind the anti-Japanese resistance movement in the wake of the March First protests. Whether or not Han's 1930s-era smuggling was also linked to the resistance movement (as is unclear from surviving sources), it is clear that Han had long functioned at the margins of colonial law. Nonetheless, Han's activities as a smuggler, or even the time spent in prison, do not seem to have diminished his prestige among fellow Koreans in Sinŭiju. Throughout the 1930s, Korean-language newspapers like the *Tonga ilbo* reported favorably on Han's donation of large sums to different civic causes in Sinŭiju as well as his prominent participation in different civic organizations. This suggests smuggling bosses were hardly pariahs in their own border community, but rather important patrons and, as occasion required, employers.[72] Figures like Han provided important sources of authority outside of the confines of the colonial state in the ordering of the Yalu's liquid geographies of illicit commerce.

Korean smugglers who worked for smuggling bosses like Han Munhwan made the journey across the Yalu River individually or in large "gangs" (*gyangu*) of as many as a hundred or more members, a distinction often made in gendered terms. In a round-table discussion dedicated to the smuggling issue, Andong Chamber of Commerce director Iino Shōtarō differentiated between "masculine smuggling" and "feminine smuggling" along the border. The former, Iino explained, consisted of mostly male gangs of smugglers who would violently engage customs officials whenever approached. "Feminine smuggling," by contrast, consisted of individual acts of customs subversion by mostly female smugglers that were allegedly regarded as less threatening by officials and often went unpunished.[73] In a 1934 article on smuggling, Sinŭiju police chief Nakamura Mika expressed sympathy for the older female smugglers who braved the frigid winter cold to carry small loads of salt across the Yalu nightly during the icebound season. "When one thinks of their suffering, is it not natural and human enough that the hand of regulation is reluctant to prosecute them?"[74] Yet the reality of customs' officials unrelenting gaze belied such claims of genteel pity. Korean-language newspapers carried multiple articles describing male officials' violent abuse of female border-crossers. In one case customs officials in Ŭiju brutally beat the stomach of a pregnant woman accused of hiding smuggled goods.[75]

The persecuted female Korean smuggler, driven by desperate poverty to gamble her life on the border, became a stock figure in 1930s Korean fiction. A 1933 story in the literary magazine *Samch'ŏlli* (Three-thousand Li) narrated a fictional first-person account of a poor woman in Sinŭiju forced to smuggle alcohol and silk goods by her abusive husband. The story climaxes when a customs official nearly discovers the illicit goods the woman has hidden away under her clothing, only to stop when the protagonist complains of suffering from a "gynecological disease" (*buinbyŏng*).[76] Another 1934 short story published in the women's journal *Sin kajŏng* (New Family) told the story of a single mother who takes up salt smuggling to feed her young son and daughter after her husband, a cloth smuggler, dies trying to evade customs officials (see figure 4.3).[77] The most well-known story in this genre, however, is feminist writer Kang Kyŏngae's 1934 short story "Salt" (*Sogŭm*), also published in *Sin kajŏng*. "Salt" tells the story of a poor Korean migrant to Manchuria who begins smuggling salt across the border after losing her husband to Communist guerrillas and two children to disease. While technically set along the Tumen River boundary, the narrative presented, including a description (censored at the time) of the protagonists' resistance to arrest, would have been familiar to many who lived along the neighboring Yalu as well.[78]

In contrast to Korean-language media portrayals of Korean women as victims of the customs regime, some Japanese-language publications sensationally portrayed these same women as skillful and calculating criminals. The author of a 1936 article for the Japanese settler magazine *Mansen* (Manchuria and Korea) described women who regularly stuffed large silver coins in their vaginas and then attempted to walk nonchalantly across the Yalu River Railway Bridge. The known "customs record," the article proclaimed in lurid tone, was an attempted seventy-seven coins smuggled in this manner, though the "average" was between thirty-five and fifty. Of course, the article reassured its Japanese readers, Japanese women had never been discovered engaging in such degrading acts (though Japanese women were also not likely subjected to the same invasive inspections as their Korean counterparts).[79]

FIGURE 4.3. Illustration of female Korean smugglers nervously making the border crossing.

Source: Ch'oe Chŏnggŏn, "Milsu sangsŭpja," Sin kajŏng, August 1934, 16. Image courtesy of Hyundammungo Foundation.

Continuity and Change in the Seasonal Environments of Smuggling

Running through all these accounts were the seasonal landscapes of the Sino-Korean border. With its undefined borderline and variable topography, the Yalu retained a powerful influence on smugglers' operations even after the 1931 Manchurian Incident. Reports about the challenges posed by the wintertime Yalu and the gangs of smugglers crossing its frozen surface became a stock feature of news reporting in colonial Korea. A 1933 *Tonga ilbo* article related how smugglers waited for the Yalu River to freeze just as eagerly "as the Christians wait for the coming of their Redeemer."[80] In a November 29, 1935, piece, the same newspaper described Sinŭiju officials' nervousness in the face of the upcoming winter. Surging silver prices in Japan led an estimated 9,000–10,000 people to smuggle silver currency between Andong and Sinŭiju that year (a figure that, if true, would have been equivalent to roughly 17 percent of Sinŭiju's total population at the time[81]), and that number was only expected to increase during the "icebound season."[82]

Writings by colonial Korea and Manchukuo customs officials displayed an acute awareness of the heightened dangers of the frozen Yalu. Published in multiple editions throughout the 1930s, the Sinŭiju custom office's booklet *An Introduction to Sinŭiju Harbor (Shingishū minato ippan)* described the icebound season as one in which smuggling was "especially" active, with smugglers moving "freely" between opposite sides of the riverbank. Specific solutions outlined in the booklet included the installation of more telephone lines and the construction of special surveillance huts atop the Yalu ice (see figure 4.4).[83]

Like the policemen discussed in chapter 3, Japanese customs officials implemented a variety of measures to manage the icebound season. The Andong customs office doubled the number of nighttime staff patrolling critical crossing points during the winter.[84] It also took steps to rapidly increase its overall

FIGURE 4.4. Border officials pose in front of a surveillance hut built on top of the Yalu River ice.

Source: "Apkang ŭi milsuch'ul kamsi," Maeil sinbo, *February 5, 1933.*

manpower. The seizure of the office in 1932 precipitated the mass expulsion of Western and Chinese customs workers hostile to the Japanese takeover. While some Japanese and local Chinese employees of the Maritime Customs Service willingly stayed with the new regime, other replacements for lost personnel were hired from Japan.[85] Still faced with a perceived manpower shortage, especially in the face of expanding smuggling operations, the Manchukuo Customs implemented annual exams to hire more officials, adding more than 280 in 1932, as well as 260 in 1933 and 130 in 1934, a significant percentage of whom were stationed in Andong. Additional customs agents were brought over from Japan. In 1933 the Andong customs office also opened new branch offices at strategic points along the upper Yalu, specifically in Linjiang, Ji'an, and Changkuanhekou.[86] The results of this expansion were significant. While the Andong branch of the Maritime Customs Service employed 134 workers at the beginning of 1932—a number that dropped to 36 immediately following the Japanese takeover of the office later that year—by 1942 this number had reached 537. Slightly over half of these employees were Japanese, and the remainder were ethnically Korean or Chinese.[87]

As was the case for the policing of anti-Japanese guerrillas, wintertime smuggling enforcement also entailed the mobilization of animal labor. In November 1934 the *Tonga ilbo* reported that eight "heartless" German Shepherd dogs had been imported for use by the Andong customs office from the Manchukuo Army, a first in the agency's history. Published immediately before the onset of winter, the article predicted a "bloody confrontation" between these dogs and smugglers on the frozen Yalu.[88] This article attracted the attention of colonial censors, who no doubt objected not only to the article's sympathetic portrayal of smugglers who "put their lives on the line" to "feed their families," but also to its negative depiction of guard dogs as demonic specters of the harsh Yalu winter rather than suffering and sympathetic imperial servants.[89] Fears about customs dogs' ferocity were not unwarranted. These dogs fulfilled their responsibilities with deadly efficacy, as was likely the case in January 1936 when a frozen corpse covered in dog-bite wounds was found atop the Yalu ice.[90] But they were also not immune to the allure of bribery. One participant in a 1943 roundtable on Yalu River smuggling, for example, related how smugglers occasionally tried to feed police dogs and then use them for their own purposes (such dogs were no more venal than their human overseers, including seven Japanese and Korean policemen arrested in 1934 in Andong for taking bribes from cloth smugglers).[91]

Of course, the policing of Manchukuo-era Yalu smuggling went beyond the icebound season. As a March 1934 article in the *Tonga ilbo* reported, while the Yalu's ice had retreated that spring, the problem of smuggling had not. Customs officials on both sides of the Yalu were "gravely considering" methods of suppressing this illicit trade, the article related, including the purchase of four high-speed boats for use in Sinŭiju and the erection of searchlights on the Manchurian side of the river.[92] Even with these technologies, however, the constantly shifting geography of the riparian border made prosecution difficult. Because most smuggling took place at night, it was frequently impossible for officials to determine where exactly a smuggling crime had been committed. Using small wooden boats to transport their wares across the river, smugglers exploited the ambiguity of the Korean-Manchurian border on the Yalu to their profit and advantage.[93]

Smuggling was even harder to control along the upper reaches of the Yalu, where the river was much narrower and thus easier to cross at any time of the year. While the bulk of border trade (licit and illicit) occurred between the twin cities of Andong and Sinŭiju, the amount of smuggled goods making their way across the narrow reaches of the upper Yalu was enough to attract the ire of Manchukuo customs officials. Among the officials dispatched to newly built branches of the Manchukuo customs stations along the upper Yalu was the Korean Ŏm Sŭnghwan. Ŏm later recounted his experience working at the Changbai branch office of the Andong customs in an account serialized in the South Korean newspaper *Chungang ilbo*. As one of ten Koreans employed by the Andong office, Ŏm explained that he was chosen to lead smuggling enforcement at the new Changbai substation because "I knew Chinese." While Ŏm's Chinese fluency was considered a valuable asset for work in the region, Changbai was in fact one of the more culturally Korean areas of the Yalu's Manchurian bank, with some 70 percent of the population ethnically Korean. This ethnic affinity encouraged cultural integration between Changbai and the Korean side of the river, as well as economic integration through smuggling. The flourishing of smuggling in the region was also encouraged geographically by the narrow and easily traversable width of the border river. As Ŏm later recounted, after arriving at the Changbai branch office he and his three subordinates found it "impossible" to control smuggling due to the narrowness of the Yalu near its headwaters.[94]

Along the upper Yalu River border where customs employees like Ŏm were few and far between, colonial border police enforced trade regulations through their intrusive full-body searches of border crossers. In addition to searching for smuggled goods, police inspected border crossers regularly for weapons, illicit propaganda, or other indications of anti-Japanese rebel activity. In 1936 Korean journalist Yang Ilch'ŏn described the impact of such body searches on the daily lives of border residents as part of a multi-part travelogue of his journeys along the Yalu border published in the *Tonga ilbo*: "The border! A very short distance of water is like the difference between heaven and earth in people's lives. Goods that cross the river, even just one needle, are subject to customs tax, and people who cross the rivers are subjected to an aggressive body search."[95]

Smuggling, Manchukuo-Colonial Korea Border Tensions, and River Violence

Even while rampant smuggling vexed police and customs officials along the upper Yalu River, the bulk of illicit border trade remained concentrated along the Andong-Sinŭiju corridor, where tensions were heating up between Manchukuo and Korean customs officials over the ill-defined Yalu border. Much to the chagrin of their counterparts in the colonial Korean bureaucracy, Manchukuo customs officials began responding to the border's murky ambiguity by ignoring it altogether. During the Maritime Customs Service era, the sovereignty of the liquid channel between Andong and Sinŭiju had often been in question. While Chinese officials claimed that the border ran through the middle of the river at its deepest point (a point that was impossible to define in practice), Japanese officials in Andong often claimed that the boundaries of the railway concession extended beyond the shoreline to the middle of the river abutting the settlement. Such a claim, as was pointed out by exasperated Maritime Customs Service officials, created an impenetrable "pipe line" of Japanese riparian sovereignty between China and Korea.[96] Yet while Maritime Customs Service employees could only weakly challenge this monopoly, Manchukuo customs officials asserted their presence on the river much more forcefully due to the backing of the Kwantung Army.

Unable to fully police smuggling in the Andong railway concession (which remained independent of Manchukuo until December 1937), Manchukuo officials began aggressively pursuing smugglers on the waterfront. This led to more violent confrontations with smugglers. It also amplified friction between the Andong customs and colonial officials in Sinŭiju. In a January 1935 article on smuggling, Sinŭiju police chief Nakamura Mika identified the Manchukuo customs officers' frequent "invasion" of colonial Korea's territorial waters on the Yalu as a growing threat to regional security.[97] The previous chapter noted colonial Korean police exasperation with Manchukuo authorities' disinterest in policing the border against "bandits." Smuggling enforcement presented an opposite situation, where Manchukuo authorities' aggressiveness earned the ire of Korean officials who stood to gain more from the generally northward-bound illicit trade.

Tensions between Manchukuo and colonial Korea climaxed in the late spring and summer of 1936 over a string of deadly skirmishes between smugglers and

Manchukuo customs officials on the Korean side of the Yalu. On May 23 Manchukuo customs officers approached a group of forty-five Korean smugglers crossing the river by boat. A scuffle quickly ensued, which resulted in the smugglers' vessel flipping over and throwing its occupants into the river. Nine of the smugglers on board drowned as a result. Reporting on this incident days later, the *Tonga ilbo* printed the full names of each of the alleged victims while accusing Manchukuo officials of "murder."[98] Then on August 4, as discussed in the introduction to this chapter, a similarly deadly event occurred as twenty-five Korean smugglers drowned following a battle with Manchukuo customs officials. This incident incited a similarly vociferous response from the vernacular press in colonial Korea, though Manchurian papers were understandably more measured in their own coverage of such events.[99]

Rather than earning the rebuke of colonial censors, strongly worded accusations of Manchukuo "atrocities" in Korean newspapers were tolerated, and even encouraged, by colonial officials. Claims about Manchukuo authorities' "tyranny" were repeated in the *Maeil sinbo* (Daily News), an official mouthpiece of the Government-General of Korea. The *Maeil sinbo* nonetheless deflected the blame from the Manchukuo Customs in general to the specific actions of a few rogue customs agents, calling for their swift punishment after prompt negotiations between officials on both sides of the river.[100]

The mounting tensions over Yalu River smuggling created an open rift in the policies and rhetoric of Manchurian-Korean integration then being promoted by top Japanese officials. Beginning in the mid-1930s, Governor-General Minami Jirō (a former commander of the Kwantung Army) saw Manchuria's rapid industrialization under the aegis of the Japanese military as a chance to advance the industrial development and militarization of the Korean Peninsula. According to this strategic vision, Manchuria and Korea would together act as a "supply base" for further Japanese expansion on the continent. With such top-level pressure to improve Manchurian-Korean relations, it was not long before officials in Andong and Sinŭiju would attempt to put aside their differences. An October 22 meeting between Japanese authorities in the Andong concession and those from the Manchukuo customs office agreed to implement drastic measures such as a complete nighttime ban on boat traffic.[101] In November, Sinŭiju officials also announced their intention to more aggressively pursue the smuggling issue. Abandoning the "passive" approach traditionally adopted by Sinŭiju authorities, by late 1936 customs and police officials were raiding the merchant houses of notorious smugglers and seizing the cargo of boats deemed to be smugglers' vessels. Popular media reported how such measures were "striking fear" in the hearts of the thousands of smugglers who called Sinŭiju home.[102]

The timing of these measures—immediately before the onset of the wintertime icebound season—was also indicative of how climate, as much as intraimperial infighting, helped shape the Yalu River's illicit economies. By 1937 colonial officials achieved some success in their efforts to reduce the number of smuggling incidents on the Yalu, though in the face of wartime economic disruptions and encroaching winter ice these results ultimately proved elusive. As regulation intensified, officials on both sides of the border also cooperated in directing smugglers' labor toward civil engineering projects and other "legitimate occupations." The respite brought by these measures was brief, however. Following the outbreak of the Second Sino-Japanese War in 1937, the cessation of construction projects in the face of the approaching icebound season and rising commodity prices in Manchukuo reinvigorated cross-border smuggling. Despite increased cooperation between cross-border officials, the smuggling issue remained unresolved.[103]

Much like "bandit" and guerrilla activity, smuggling assumed a distinctive seasonal bent as merchants took advantage of the frozen wintertime border to evade officials' disciplinary gaze. Once the ice retreated, smugglers (overwhelmingly Korean by the late 1920s) quickly switched to transporting goods over the river by boat or, less frequently, by rail and foot across the Yalu River Railway Bridge. But as this chapter has demonstrated, navigating the seasonal riverscape of the Yalu was just one part of a smuggler's job. In all instances, the ability to navigate between different zones of sovereignty was also an essential factor behind smugglers' success. Colonial officials in Korea often refused to prosecute goods heading toward southern Manchuria, the destination of most contraband on the Yalu, while Chinese customs officials were unable to operate freely in the Japanese railway concession. Both factors were a source of constant frustration for the Chinese customs office in Andong, and such disputes continued long after the 1931 Manchurian Incident and the Japanese takeover of the Andong office in 1932.

Rather than discouraging smuggling, the creation of Manchukuo led to an unprecedented outburst of smuggling activity. After seizing control of the Andong customs office, Manchukuo authorities attempted to buttress the new state's finances by aggressively policing smuggling. However, such efforts were frustrated by the rapid expansion of smuggling of gold, silver, salt, cloth, and other goods. Like their earlier counterparts in the Chinese Maritime Customs Service, the Manchukuo customs also encountered a freezing and shifting river that readily defied attempts at border demarcation and set a volatile stage for smugglers' exploits and debates with officials in colonial Korea and the Andong concession about river sovereignty.

The Yalu's illicit economy remained relatively unwieldy until Japanese authorities began implementing various measures after 1937 to more thoroughly assimilate the Yalu border. These measures included the abolition of Japanese extraterritoriality in Manchukuo and the corresponding dissolution of the Andong railway settlement in December 1937. They also included the industrial development of the Yalu corridor and construction of the massive Sup'ung Dam between 1937 and 1945, discussed in the following chapter. Together, these changes radically reshaped the liquid geographies of Yalu smuggling and life along the river in general. But even with these changes, the prevalence of smuggling between Andong and Sinŭiju continued to defy official expectation and define imperial border-making efforts.

5

DAM CONSTRUCTION AND "MANCHURIAN-KOREAN UNITY"

Prior to the 1940s, the freezing of the Yalu was a regular occurrence. The question was never if the river would freeze over, but when. During the winter of 1941–1942, however, the icebound season for a significant portion of the lower Yalu River was a full month and a half shorter than the previous yearly average.[1] In subsequent winters, the lower Yalu would not freeze over at all.[2]

The source of this profound transformation in the Yalu's seasonal cycles was the Sup'ung Dam, second largest in the world at the time of its completion in 1944. Japanese engineers intended for this to be the first of seven projected dams along the Yalu, which together would harness the river's flow to provide hydroelectricity for imperial industrial projects in Manchukuo and Korea. Begun in 1937, construction of the dam occurred as Japan waged all-out war in China and later Southeast Asia and the Pacific. Earlier scholarship by Hirose Teizō and Aaron Stephen Moore has demonstrated the massive scale of this undertaking and how it legitimated colonial exploitation through a technocratic discourse of "Scientific Japan."[3] The Sup'ung Dam ultimately required 850,000 tons of concrete and millions of hours of manpower to complete.[4] It also displaced thousands of local Koreans and Chinese and contributed to the disappearance of timber rafts from the lower Yalu, as well as winter ice. In the eyes of border policeman and writer Noritake Kazuo, the Yalu was no longer the free-flowing river of the past, but an electricity-generating "lake."[5]

This chapter specifically focuses on how Sup'ung Dam construction represented the intensification, and ultimate culmination, of long-standing imperial efforts to channel the Yalu River border's liquid geographies. Under the banner of "Manchurian-Korean unity" (*Mansen ichinyo*), officials in Manchukuo and colonial Korea worked collaboratively to transform the Yalu into an "economic river" (*keizai kasen*) that served an empire expanding rapidly into China, Southeast Asia, and the Pacific.[6] This did not entail the erasure of the formal political boundary between Korea and Manchukuo, as some scholars have supposed.[7] Rather, the border was used as a resource for imperial expansion as Japan's military adventurism pushed the empire's frontiers far beyond Northeast Asia. Wartime infrastructural and border policing projects sought to harmonize relations between Korea and Manchukuo and ensure that the human and nonhuman mobilities of the river border flowed in productive and profitable ways. Just as the Sup'ung Dam channeled the Yalu River's roaring current into currents of exploitable hydroelectric power, new harbors, bridges, railways, and other industrial infrastructure—alongside anti-Japanese "bandit" suppression campaigns and crackdowns on Yalu River trade—attempted to channel the dynamic cross-border movements of peoples, goods, water, and ice for the empire's benefit.

Completion of the Sup'ung Dam and successes on other border-making fronts caused Japanese propagandists to exult about their "conquest of nature" and the obliteration of remaining barriers the Yalu posed to imperial expansion. Yet the seasonally changing river, and the mobile actors who traversed its surface, continued to behave in ways that belied Japanese narratives of conquest. The process of reengineering the Yalu border to fit the ideological and material aims of "Manchurian-Korean unity" was undercut by a combination of local human and nonhuman resistance and the internal contradictions of Japanese policy. Infrastructural projects like the Sup'ung Dam met significant challenges from the Yalu's summertime floods. When it came to border surveillance, Chinese and Korean guerrilla fighters continued to launch raids on Japanese border posts until their violent suppression by Japanese police and military forces, while smugglers continuously subverted the border regime by evading customs fees. Administrative tensions between Korea and Manchukuo also manifested over debates about local fishing rights and competing industrial projects. Japan's insistence on maintaining the Manchukuo-Korean political boundary helped contribute to the longevity of these divisions as local bureaucrats defended the interests of stakeholders on respective sides of the border. Amid these challenges and imperial overreach in the Asia-Pacific, the project of "conquering" the Yalu proved ultimately unsustainable, even as the Sup'ung Dam irrevocably altered the river's environment.

Creating "Manchurian-Korean Unity" through Yalu Development

As documented in chapters 3 and 4, the Japanese invasion of Manchuria in 1931 did little to dissipate the long-standing tensions that had developed along the Yalu River border. Like the thick ice that clung to the river into the early spring, it would take more than a flash of heat from the Kwantung Army's guns to melt the frosty distrust that had characterized cross-Yalu relations. Border police in Korea worried about the sudden escalation of anti-Japanese guerrilla raids, while customs officers felt threatened by the increasingly assertive intrusion of Manchukuo customs boats into their territorial waters.[8] Colonial officials across the Korean Peninsula also worried about the sudden attention and resources from the Tokyo government being devoted to the new client state. As Louise Young has convincingly argued, Manchukuo became the "jewel in the crown" of the Japanese Empire after 1931.[9] In the jealous eyes of some Japanese settlers and officials in Korea, Manchukuo's new position as prized "centerpiece" of the Japanese imperium necessarily diminished Korea's former status as the largest and most important colony.[10] Even as migrants flocked to the region for new economic opportunities (both real and imagined) and the allure of new markets caused businessmen in Korea to more eagerly embrace the new Japanese presence, it was not until 1936 that the real groundwork for regional political and economic integration was laid out, with the fluid and seasonally changing Yalu River at center.[11]

The impetus for greater Korean-Manchurian cohesion came from both larger imperial pressures and the personal initiative of the new governor-general of Korea, Minami Jirō. With tensions between Japan and China mounting, senior figures in the Japanese Army felt the need to mold Korea and Manchuria into a unified "military supply base."[12] Among those was former Kwantung Army commander Minami, whose appointment to the position of governor-general of Korea in August 1936 was immediately perceived by the colonial Korean press as an "opportunity" to "deepen relations" between Korea and Manchukuo.[13] In keeping with these expectations, Minami exploited his deep personal connections to Manchukuo's Kwantung Army leaders to bring colonial Korean policy more in line with the client state's plans for industrialization. On October 29, 1936, Minami met with his successor as Kwantung Army commander-in-chief, Ueda Kenkichi, at the Japanese consulate in Tumen along the northeast Sino-Korean border. Also accompanying them to discuss matters of joint security and Manchurian-Korean border policing were the chief of the Kwantung Army military police and the head of the Government-General of Korea (GGK) Police Bureau. Scholars have argued that the phrase "Manchurian-Korean unity" and its political agenda first arose at this meeting, subsequently known as the Tumen Conference.[14]

Among the items discussed at the 1936 Tumen Conference and subsequent meetings was the need for Manchukuo and colonial Korean officials to work together to develop the Yalu River by better harnessing its liquid flows of people, goods, and water.[15] This collaborative effort would include new, jointly built infrastructure such as bridges as well as hydroelectric dams. Bridges would create more corridors for containing flows of commodities and border-crossers across the Yalu, while dams would channel the Yalu's watery current to provide electricity for industrial projects in Korea and Manchukuo. Korean-Manchurian collaboration would also involve intensified policing of the river border to achieve political and economic stability in what had long been a volatile frontier. In their own separate meeting at the Tumen Conference, Kwantung Army and GGK police officials agreed to cooperate further on issues of border policing against "bandits" and smugglers. It would take further wrangling at the local level to realize these ambitions, but the Tumen meeting provided a significant verbal commitment to ending the tensions that had developed around border enforcement.

It was not long before the rhetoric of "Manchurian-Korean Unity" and the resulting Tumen Conference led to more concrete agreements on collaborative reengineering of the Yalu River border. On December 10, 1936, less than two months after the Tumen meeting, officials from Manchukuo and colonial Korea met in the Manchukuo capital of Shinkyō (Changchun) to ink the "Memorandum Concerning Bridges on the Yalu and Tumen Rivers." As detailed in chapter 2, bridge construction had long been considered integral to the goal of solidifying imperial control in the region. With the original 1911 railroad bridge serving as a critical conduit of trade and surveillance since its completion decades earlier, Japanese officials now sensed the opportunity to build multiple new bridges across the border while ostensibly avoiding the diplomatic rancor that characterized the earlier project. The December 1936 memorandum specifically called for the construction of fourteen bridges across the Yalu and neighboring Tumen River, with eight to be built by the Manchukuo regime and six by the Government-General of Korea.[16]

A month after the completion of the bridge agreement, a meeting between the administrative director-general of Korea and the head of the Manchukuo Transportation Bureau yielded the "Memorandum on the Formation of a Joint Manchurian-Korean Technical Committee on the Yalu River."[17] This new joint committee sought to address what had long been a thorny issue in cross-border relations: namely the colonial Korean government's monopolistic management of the Yalu River trade route, which included the maintenance of buoys and other aids for river navigation as well as periodic hydrographic surveys of the river's mouth. Like other aspects of Yalu border-making, river route maintenance was a seasonal act. The freezing of the Yalu necessitated the removal of river buoys in the winter, while summer flooding could alter the river's course and thus require that navigational markers be relocated. A plan for joint Manchurian-Korean management of the river was first drafted in 1932 by the South Manchuria Railway Company.[18] This plan initially received support from the Japanese Imperial Navy but was later rejected by Governor-General of Korea Ugaki Kazushige. The colonial Korean government had ignored earlier Chinese petitions for joint river management prior to 1931, and it had little intention of relinquishing its monopoly in this new era of border relations.[19] It was only after protracted negotiation, and assurances by Manchukuo officials that they would not challenge the Korean government's claim to Hwanch'op'yŏng and other river islands, that agreements were made that put in place the chain of events leading to the creation of the Joint Committee.[20]

While Japanese officials in Manchukuo and colonial Korea had to overcome mutual distrust to achieve agreements on Yalu waterway management, they readily united around the need to monopolize cross-border trade and commodity flows by muscling out foreign competition. One of the most significant foreign competitors for Japanese merchants in Andong was a British merchant named George Shaw. Shaw was a multinational figure who capitalized on his unique cultural identity and Western extraterritorial privilege in ways that cut against the Japanese imperial project. Born to an Irish father and Japanese mother in the southern Chinese treaty port of Fuzhou, Shaw moved to Andong following its opening as a treaty port and found success as a ship owner and proxy for the UK-based Swire Trading Company.[21] Not only did Shaw irk Japanese rivals by successfully driving business away from Japanese-owned trading companies in Andong and Sinŭiju, but he also provoked Japanese authorities by allegedly harboring Korean anti-Japanese guerrillas in his Andong office.[22] Furthermore, Shaw repeatedly refused to comply with Japanese regulations that stipulated the hiring of Japanese boat pilots to take ships around Korean river islands when traveling upstream to Andong, preferring to use his own hired Chinese pilots instead.[23] After repeatedly failing to outcompete him, Japanese authorities in Manchukuo eventually bought out much of Shaw's shipping interests and turned them over to the quasi-governmental Daan (Great Peace) Steamship Company in 1935, though Japanese officials would not succeed in completely driving him out of the region until 1938.[24] Such measures illustrated the dramatic lengths to which Japanese authorities tried to manipulate the Yalu's trade flows for their own benefit.

Plans to monopolize flows of riparian commerce were followed by even more radical ambitions to dam the river, thereby converting its powerful, flowing current into currents of hydroelectricity. The dream of harnessing the river's energy had been held by imperial planners and promoters in the region long before the era of "Manchurian-Korean unity." Engineers from the South Manchuria Railway Company (SMRC) conducted multiple surveys of the Yalu between 1922–1928, collecting data on the river's current and possible sites for future dam projects while avoiding attacks from Korean guerrillas. In 1923 SMRC officials also secured a concession from Manchurian warlord Zhang Zuolin for a proposed Sino-Japanese hydroelectric company that would structurally resemble the Yalu River Timber Company created a decade and a half earlier.[25] Not to be outdone by their Manchurian counterparts, officials from Korea conducted their own hydroelectric surveys of the Yalu. The Government-General of Korea's Communications Bureau (Teishinkyoku) first measured the streamflow of the Yalu as part of its larger Second Hydropower Study (1921–1929) of rivers throughout the Korean Peninsula, followed by even more detailed surveys of the river in 1936.[26]

The importance of harnessing the Yalu's volatile current to broader goals of borderland pacification was clear for early dam proponents. In a 1923 report, Japanese technician Kurihara Chūzō expounded the benefits of a proposed Yalu dam for regional stability and "border security" through increased industrialization.[27] But it was precisely factors like continued political instability and cross-border tensions that postponed the realization of these plans until August 1937, when a memorandum on the hydroelectric development of the Yalu River was drawn up between the Manchukuo and Japanese governments. After debate among technicians in Manchukuo and colonial Korea, the decision was made to build the first of seven proposed dams along the river at Sup'ung-dong, a site located some forty miles upstream from Sinŭiju.[28] Construction would be directed by separate Manchukuo and Japanese corporations collectively referred to as the Yalu River Hydropower Company (Ōryokkō Suiryoku Hatsuden Kabushiki Kaisha), though in reality both entities shared the same management and personnel. The founding capital for the Yalu River Hydropower Company was set at one hundred million yen. The Manchukuo government supplied half of this amount, while the other half was raised from a group of private and quasi-governmental organs in colonial Korea that included the Bank of Korea and Noguchi Jun's Chōsen Nitrogenous Fertilizer Company, which planned to use the electricity to power new chemical fertilizer plants.[29]

The Sup'ung Dam was conceived by imperial technocrats as centerpiece of a new Yalu River "industrial belt" that would include not only the Sup'ung Dam but also six additional dams, bridges, grand harbor projects at the mouth of the river, and mineral exploitation of the upper Yalu.[30] Such industrialization would be the harbinger of a new regional order based on cross-border cooperation in the spirit of "Manchurian-Korean unity." Japanese bureaucrats in Korea and Manchukuo were hardly alone in thinking grandiosely about dams during this period. As Christopher Sneddon argues, large dams became the ultimate symbols of technical "modernization" in the twentieth century, embraced by powerful countries across the globe.[31] Promoters of the US Grand Coulee Dam heralded it as the harbinger of a "new kind of civilization,"[32] while the Soviet ideologue Leon Trotsky called for dams to "give lights to cities, to drive factories, and to enrich ploughland."[33] The Sup'ung Dam project thus did not emerge in isolation, but was a local manifestation of a worldwide trend toward highly intensive forms of hydraulic engineering. Japanese engineers themselves learned from this global dam-building expertise, touring major dam sites in the United States during the 1930s and eventually ordering the Sup'ung Dam's turbines from engineering firms in the United States and Germany.[34]

The Sup'ung Dam project drew on transnational expertise and material, but rather than inspire peaceful global coexistence, the Sup'ung Dam was instead mobilized to further Japanese imperial conquest. Once completed, hydroelectricity generated by channeling the Yalu's powerful liquid current would go on to power the industrial transformation of Korea and Manchukuo into ostensibly united "military supply bases" for bloody campaigns in China, and after 1941, the greater Asia-Pacific.[35]

Challenges to "Manchurian-Korean Unity" and Yalu River Development

The fluid human and nonhuman mobilities, or liquid geographies, of the Yalu border region had long been a vital, but also perennially troublesome, element of Japanese expansion into Korea and Manchuria. This dynamic continued throughout the process of Yalu industrialization and the creation of a border regime of "Manchurian-Korean unity." Persistent raids by anti-Japanese guerrillas, lingering rivalries between local populations and governments on both sides of the river, and dramatic summertime floods all revealed ways in which the fluid, and seasonally variant, movements of human and nonhuman actors spilled outside the channels set by Japanese border officials.

Skirmishes with anti-Japanese guerrillas continued even as imperial planners made grand plans to develop the frontier river. The Northeastern United Anti-Japanese Army (Dongbei kang Ri lianjun), formed under the aegis of the Chinese Communist Party as an alliance of previous guerrilla groups, was one major group that defied Japanese border development.³⁶ The same year that construction of the Sup'ung Dam began, a raid by two hundred guerrilla fighters under *lianjun* commander Kim Il-sung shook the confidence of border police officials in Korea. The June 3, 1937, attack on the upper Yalu town of Poch'ŏnbo succeeded in destroying local government offices as well as setting fire to a Japanese police box, the local elementary school, and post office. Altogether, Kim's forces occupied the town for a full day before retreating into Manchuria.³⁷ Preparation for the attack began days earlier as Kim's forces established contact with anti-Japanese activists on the Korean side of the river and later constructed a raft bridge across the flowing summertime Yalu. As was later related in Kim's autobiography, "a strange tension" gripped his "entire body" as he and his forces made their way across the river, which he was surprised to find less heavily patrolled than he had expected.³⁸ The temporary success of Kim's guerrillas at Poch'ŏnbo drew comparisons by colonial police to earlier wintertime attacks like the Tonghŭng Incident of 1935 (discussed in chapter 3), and as a result, renewed efforts were made to strengthen the security apparatus around the Yalu.³⁹ Memory of the successful Poch'ŏnbo raid would also form an eventual cornerstone of Kim's cult of personality as ruler of North Korea.

"Bandit suppression" accelerated amid the pressing need to secure the Sup'ung Dam and other new industrial projects under the new regime of "Manchurian-Korean unity." After high-level police and military officials from colonial Korea and Manchukuo met during the October 1936 Tumen Conference, both sides agreed to provide greater support and increase mutual communication during bandit suppression campaigns timed primarily for the fall and winter.⁴⁰

Seasonal patterns of border security continued to define Japanese counterinsurgency efforts. In a 1940 report to Communist officials, Chinese guerrilla leader Wang Zhengmin described how Japanese police and military utilized the summer months to conduct reconnaissance missions and distribute soldiers throughout the geographically remote forest and mountain regions preferred by guerrilla forces.⁴¹ The most intensive anti-guerrilla suppression campaigns then took place during the late fall and winter, when climatic and material conditions posed greatest difficulties for guerrilla fighters and their paths were exposed by the freshly fallen snow.⁴² These border suppression campaigns yielded some significant results, including the capture and execution of "bandit" leader Wang Fengge in March 1937.⁴³ Yet the newly formed Northeast Anti-Japanese United Army continued to actively resist Japanese military and industrial campaigns in the region. A 1939 report published by the Manchukuo province of Tonghua, which included the upper Yalu counties of Changbai and Linjiang, detailed how nearly a thousand "Communist bandits" still operated within the province's boundaries. The majority of these "bandits," the same report explained, were ethnic Koreans who participated in anti-Japanese guerrilla activities during the 1920s. These groups now comprised a multiethnic body led by figures such as the Koreans Kim Il-sung and Ch'oe Hyŏn, and Chinese guerrilla leader Yang Jingyu.[44]

Amid "bandit" suppression and other forms of seasonal border-making, early construction of the Sup'ung Dam took place under intense surveillance and a prominent police presence. Japanese engineer Satō Toshihiko later recalled being accompanied by five machine-gun-wielding border policemen on an initial Yalu dam site survey conducted by propeller boat.[45] Once work began, border police were mobilized not only to continually patrol the massive construction site against possible attack or infiltration but also to monitor the movements of the more than seventy thousand Korean and Chinese villagers displaced by the dam's construction.[46] The same security measures were undertaken for other Yalu industrial projects. The Dongbiandao Development Company (Tōhendo Kabushiki Kaisha), a quasi-governmental Manchukuo corporation founded in 1938 to exploit mineral resources along the upper Yalu River basin, hired a private police force from Japanese border police and soldiers experienced in "bandit suppression," establishing a direct personnel link between border pacification efforts and regional industrialization.[47]

Despite cooperative efforts to subjugate unruly guerrillas and tame the river, massive infrastructure projects like the Sup'ung Dam exposed persistent intraimperial tensions along the Yalu's banks. No matter how diligently imperial boosters proclaimed the need for "Manchurian-Korean unity," the border's continued existence, buttressed by imperial Japan's insistence on Manchukuo sovereignty, served as a flash point for long-held regional rivalries.

Competing local interests on the border were especially clear when it came to the twin ice-free harbor projects of Dadong and Tasa-do. For decades promoters of regional development on both sides of the border had bemoaned the Yalu's insufficiencies as a channel for waterborne trade. These included the river's shallow depth and its dramatic seasonal variability, especially flooding in the summer and the layer of thick ice that covered the river for almost a third of the year.[48] Larger marine ships bound for the railway boomtowns of Andong and Sinŭiju had to stop and unload their wares at ports located far away at the river's mouth. Thus, in the eyes of local officials, the region's further development would require the construction of new harbors at these spots at the river's mouth that did not freeze over in winter. Among the locations considered for new harbor construction were two small Korean islands near the mouth of the river collectively referred to as Tasa-do. Tasa-do's value as an ice-free port that could be readily linked by railway to Sinŭiju was first recognized by Japanese officials in 1904 during the Russo-Japanese War.⁴⁹ Despite repeated surveys and private attempts to develop the harbor, however, it was not until 1935 that construction of the full-fledged railway link began under the quasi-governmental Tasa-do Railway Company.⁵⁰ Construction of the harbor itself proceeded in three stages, with the first beginning in 1927 and later phases commencing in 1936 and 1938. Each stage of construction brought greater ambition and heftier budgets, with projected expenditures growing from half a million yen in 1927 to thirteen million yen by 1938.⁵¹

While Tasa-do was originally conceived as the primary port of call for future Yalu development,⁵² by 1937 officials and entrepreneurs in the city of Andong were pushing for their own ice-free harbor on the Chinese side of the river's mouth. Plans for the "Dadong" (Great East) harbor project called for a massive industrial port city that would house over four hundred thousand people and feature dozens of factories powered by cheap Yalu electricity.⁵³ Once construction began in 1939, the project's proponents were all too eager to denigrate the value of the Tasa-do harbor while highlighting Dadong's advantages. A January 1940 series of articles in one Manchurian newspaper criticized Tasa-do's lack of facilities for industrial development while maintaining that "development of Dongbiandao should of course take place through Dadong."⁵⁴ Meanwhile, a June 1940 article in a Korea-based newspaper pointed out multiple flaws in the Dadong plan while stating that Yalu development "must still rely on Tasa-do."⁵⁵ Despite multiple proclamations by top-level Japanese authorities that both harbors were necessary for the Yalu's development, regional loyalties demonstrated the persistence of border divisions in the era of "Manchuria-Korea unity."⁵⁶

Cross-border rivalries were also evident in debates over Yalu fishing rights and access to the springtime icefish harvest. As discussed in chapter 1, these feuds first emerged in the Protectorate period (1905–1910), when Japanese officials aggressively expelled Chinese fishermen from the Yalu's fishing grounds. A 1935 South Manchuria Railway Company study complained that little had changed since then, as officials in colonial Korea continued to pursue "monopolistic" fishing policies.⁵⁷ Even into the late 1930s and the era of "Manchurian-Korean unity" local officials in North P'yŏngan Province and Andong Province repeatedly failed to reach a compromise on the issue. Adding urgency to these debates were dramatic declines in springtime icefish harvests due to overfishing and pollution caused by runoff from the Sup'ung Dam construction site and other new industrial sites. In June 1938, major newspapers in Korea reported that whereas the annual icefish catch typically amounted to 25,000–30,000 *kan* (or roughly 93,000–112,000 kilograms), as of late May 1938 fishermen had only harvested 4,000 *kan*, a fraction of the yearly average. As fish populations plummeted, competition intensified for this underwater resource.⁵⁸ Just when both parties finally seemed to be reaching a consensus in September 1940, however, talks collapsed again due to what one Korean newspaper called the "fickle attitudes" of Manchukuo officials and the concerted pleas of Korean and Japanese fishermen "willing to die" before they yielded their three-decade-long control of the lower Yalu's icefish fishery.⁵⁹

Maps were also mobilized by the participants of this fiery debate. When North P'yŏngan and Andong officials reconvened to discuss the fisheries issue in spring 1941, the Andong delegation tried to refute colonial Korea's claims to almost all of the river's fishing rights by explaining how even official Japanese Army maps drew the border between Manchukuo and Korea in the middle of the river.⁶⁰ As such arguments demonstrated, as long as the border's existence was reified on official maps it would remain a point of division and contention between Korea and Manchukuo (See figure 5.1). By April 8, 1941, both sides eventually came to an agreement that allowed for a limited number of licensed Chinese fishermen to harvest icefish in the lower Yalu—a first since 1909.⁶¹

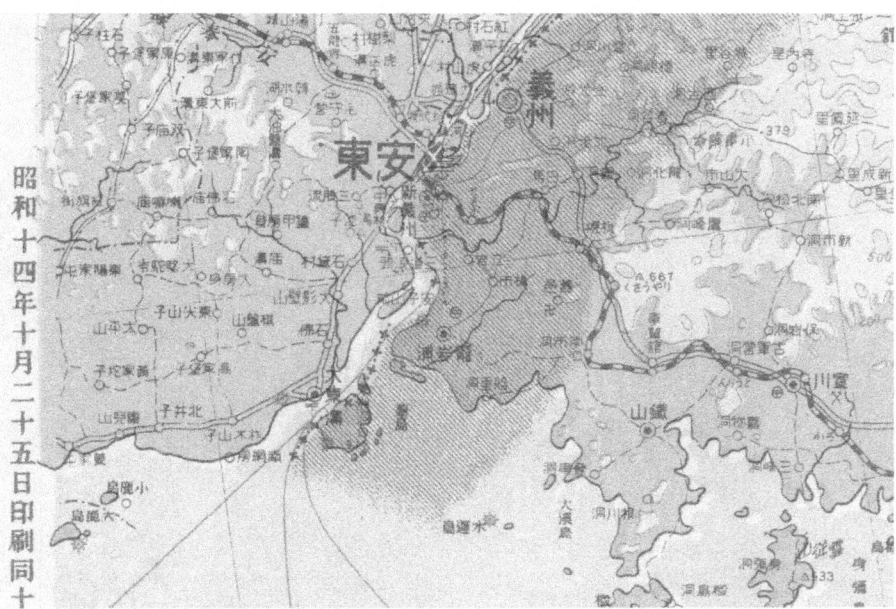

FIGURE 5.1. Detail from 1939 map of Manchukuo produced by the Japanese Army. The map shows much of the lower Yalu River as being on the Manchukuo side of the borderline (drawn with crosses).

Source: *Dai Nippon Teikoku Rikuchi Sokuryōbu*, Manshūkoku yochizu: hyakumanbun no ichi, *1939, available at https://searchworks.stanford.edu/view/9684408.*

Summer Floods and the Seasonality of Dam Construction

While rivalries centered around cartographically reinforced boundaries between Korea and Manchuria challenged efforts to build "Manchurian-Korean unity," the Yalu River itself remained a formidable obstacle to border industrialization. This became evident in the construction of the Sup'ung Dam, which Japanese engineers increasingly framed as an attempt to "conquer nature" (*daishizen o seifuku shi*) and subjugate the river.[62] "Conquering" the river through dam construction involved mobilizing hundreds of thousands of Chinese, Korean, and Japanese workers, some of whom were prisoners and forced laborers, from all across Japan's empire.[63] It also meant displacing approximately 70,000 Korean and Chinese farmers from the dam site, who were given only minimal reimbursement for their lost land before being sent to locations as far away as northern Manchuria.[64]

Even as the considerable labor resources and disciplinary tools of the Japanese Empire were marshaled for the Sup'ung project, the river had its own way of seemingly fighting back. Annual summertime floods posed the most intractable problem for dam construction. In 1938 torrential floods of 20,000 cubic meters per second destroyed ongoing work, while floods continued to delay dam construction the following summers (see figure 5.2).[65] Altogether, such damage pushed back the dam's final completion by two years.[66]

FIGURE 5.2. A June 1940 flood destroyed a construction bridge in front of the Sup'ung Dam.

Source: Chōsen Ōryokkō Suiryoku Hatsudensha, Suihō kensetsu kinen shashinchō *(Sakju: Chōsen Ōryokkō Suiryoku Hatsuden Kabushiki Kaisha, 1943).*

The power of the Yalu's torrential floods humbled the engineers who supervised dam construction. In a memoir, Japanese engineer Satō Toshihiko recalled meeting a senior colleague who had worked on the 1911 Yalu River Railway Bridge. When the latter remarked how "crazy" it was to try to dam the powerful Yalu River, Satō countered by explaining how construction plans for the dam had already made careful allowances for the river' natural force. Most of the pouring of concrete for the structure would take place during the winter when the river's current was at its weakest, Satō explained. In the summer, construction would mostly cease as powerful floods would be allowed to wash over the site. Although this plan managed to convince the skeptical bridge builder, in practice accommodating the Yalu's seasonal variability was more of a challenge.[67] Later in his memoir Satō recounted how a 20-meter tall and 1.5-meter thick concrete block was suddenly washed away one day without a trace during a summer flood. "This made me realize the incredible power of water," Satō remarked.[68]

The intensity of the Yalu's summer floods was tied to decades of human interference in the forested ecosystems of the upper Yalu watershed. The link between deforestation, soil erosion, and flooding was well-understood among foresters and state officials throughout East Asia. In his study of Japanese colonial forestry in Korea, David Fedman describes how colonial foresters often repeated the four-character phrase *chisan chisui* (tame the mountains, tame the waters) in their injunctions to colonized Koreans to plant trees.[69] At the same time, revered "founder of modern China" and first president of the Republic of China Sun Yatsen similarly urged his government to adopt afforestation methods to combat rampant flooding.[70] Despite such rhetoric, the sheer size of the Yalu's forests, protected for centuries by Qing isolationist policy and their remoteness, led many to ignore the flooding problem while assuming that the region's timber resources were uniquely "limitless."[71] Logging of the rich stands of timber along the upper Yalu River Basin accelerated following Japanese expansion into the region and the 1908 creation of the Sino-Japanese Yalu River Timber Company. By the 1930s, dozens of timber processing facilities were operating in the twin border cities of Sinǔiju and Andong.[72] Timber-felling grew more rapid following the outbreak of the Second Sino-Japanese War in 1937, as the Japanese state mobilized forestry resources throughout the empire to fuel the war effort. By 1942 total forest cover in northern Korea had fallen to just 68 percent of its 1927 level, while forest cover in Manchuria also declined precipitously.[73]

In addition to the mass extraction of timber sponsored by the colonial state, the activity of swidden farmers, known in Korea as "fire-field farmers" (K: hwajŏnmin), also hastened Yalu forest degradation and flooding. Like slash-and-burn agriculturalists in other parts of the world, these farmers subsisted on marginal mountainous lands by burning down forests (often state-owned) and harvesting crops in the resulting open land. In the eyes of Japanese officials, slash-and-burn agriculturalists not only subverted the imperial state's command over forest resources but also posed a larger security threat along the Manchurian-Korean border.[74] Among fire-field farmers, many of them former tenant farmers driven by poverty to this hardscrabble existence, illicit practices like salt and tobacco smuggling, as well as opium cultivation, were a way of life and necessary means of survival.[75] The various measures undertaken by Japanese officials to sedentarize these slash-and-burn agriculturalists included resettlement programs as well as strict punishments for those who violated the state's forestry laws. Despite these measures, the numbers of hwajŏnmin continued to climb. As of 1936 over 300,000 families were engaged in such marginal farming, a 300 percent increase since 1916.[76]

As the Yalu's forests were slowly depleted, observers near and far ruminated on the link between timber-felling and the region's floods. In his 1943 book about Manchurian forests, forestry science expert Murayama Jōzō bemoaned the "naked red earth" along the upper Yalu caused by timber overharvesting that began in the late Qing period and continued under the Yalu River Timber Company.[77] When dramatic floods hit the region earlier in 1935, Korean intellectual Yun Ch'iho commented in his diary, "The conscienceless and heartless cutting down of the forests on the mountains from which the Yalu receives its mighty volume of water must be largely responsible for this fearful flood."[78] As such observations indicate, engineers trying to dam the Yalu amid powerful summer floods were realizing the results of decades of intensive timber-cutting. The same problems also affected other industrial projects along the river. In August 1940, for example, rising river levels caused an estimated 750,000 yen of damage to factories being constructed near the Dadong harbor site.[79]

In addition to summertime floods, other recurring disasters at the Sup'ung Dam construction site included fires, landslides, and deadly falls. In December 1939, for instance, landslides took the lives of seven laborers and seriously injured five others.[80] Such "accidents" were exacerbated by unsafe work conditions, which included twelve-hour work shifts under the unrelenting surveillance of Japanese police and overseers. Estimates of the total number of worker deaths during construction, many of them caused by accidents as well as the communicable diseases that spread rapidly in the cramped workers' quarters, range from a few hundred to several thousand.[81]

The inhumane conditions for workers at Yalu industrial sites laboring through the region's cycles of hot and cold, flowing water and ice are captured in the recollections of Zhou Hongzuo, a laborer at the Dadong harbor project interviewed decades later by a local historian in Northeast China.[82] As Zhou recounts, laborers at the Dadong site subsisted on a meager diet of cornbread and pickled radish while working under pickax-armed foremen who would violently strike any workers seen slacking off on the job. The same kinds of communicable diseases that ravaged workers at the Sup'ung Dam site also afflicted Dadong workers, though Japanese overseers took few measures other than to isolate the sickest in "quarantine rooms" (*gelifang*). As Zhou recalled, "once someone was sent to the quarantine room, we knew they were done for." Laborers also bore the brunt of the Yalu's climatic extremes. Workers trying to escape the hot summer sun would wrap the underside of empty cement bags around their arms, a desperate tactic that resulted in "their arms being covered with scars." The intense heat alternated with heavy summer rains, which added to the workers' hardships by flooding the construction site. Once winter approached, workers would then tie empty cement bags around their bare feet to alleviate the pain of working the frozen earth. The bodies of workers who died the same season were thrown into the river to flow into the ocean.[83]

The suffering of ordinary laborers was downplayed, however, in Japanese reports that stressed Japanese engineers' own exertion and ingenuity in the face of seemingly insurmountable challenges from the river environment. *Overview of the Construction of the Sup'ung Dam* (*Suihō hatsudenjo kōji taikan*), published in 1942, contained transcripts of interviews with several leading Japanese engineers on the project. These engineers and project overseers were quite eager to detail the natural challenges to dam construction and the ways in which they were skillfully overcome. Far less often mentioned was the back-breaking labor needed to move the tons of dirt and concrete that ended up blocking the river's flow.[84] In their focus on Japanese triumphalism, reports like the *Overview of the Construction of the Sup'ung Dam* also only briefly acknowledged the role of the many Koreans and Chinese involved with the dam project, whether as skilled engineers, contractors, clerks, or as day laborers. The *Overview* gives a multipage table of contractors involved in the dam's construction but lists only twenty-five identifiably Korean and Chinese names. It also neglects to include any names of the thousands of day laborers who toiled on the project, the vast majority of whom were non-Japanese.[85]

The Yalu Conquered(?)

The Sup'ung Dam's promoters saw its completion as a definitive symbol of their "conquest of nature" and successful integration of the Sino-Korean border. Imperial engineers and officials greeted the first successful transmission of electricity from recently imported German turbines at the Sup'ung Dam with considerable fanfare. At a special "transmission of electricity ceremony" in August 1941, president of the Yalu River Hydropower Company Noguchi Jun declared that the dam showed the "greatness of our country" and the "fulfillment of Japanese-Manchukuo unity," while Governor-General Minami proclaimed "the conquest of nature by human might."[86]

"Conquering" the Yalu entailed not only the channeling of the river's flow into electric currents but also the shortening and, eventually, erasure of the wintertime icebound season. For years, the ice had been one of the most distinctive features of the Yalu's seasonal topography. But beginning in early 1941, just as the dam's initial phase of construction was nearing completion, observers noticed that part of a two-kilometer stretch of the river below the dam had failed to freeze over despite temperatures plunging to thirty degrees below Celsius. The explanation for this strange phenomenon proposed by one contemporary newspaper was rising water temperatures caused by the movement of the river's water through the dam's water gates and turbines.[87] While this might have played a factor, water stored at the bottom of the massive Sup'ung reservoir was also insulated against changes in surface temperature. Once released downstream, it caused the lower stretches of the river to become comparatively colder in the summer and warmer in the winter. The following winter (1941–1942), the same phenomenon occurred on a wider scale as the frozen-over period for the entire stretch of river from the Sup'ung Dam to the Yalu's mouth was shortened by over a month.[88] In subsequent winters, the river below the dam would not freeze over at all.[89]

By lessening the dramatic effects of the icebound season, dam construction made the river's seasonal cycle more congenial to the aims of the colonial state. The frozen paths across the border that had bedeviled customs officials and police officials for decades no longer existed along the lower Yalu. Police deployment statistics showed a possible effect of the declining seasonal threat as officials no longer bolstered police numbers during the winter after 1940.[90] It seemed to many that Japanese technology had finally conquered this colonial frontier. The disappearance of the winter ice did cause some to reflect with wistful nostalgia on the passing of an earlier era. In his 1943 book *Ōryokkō* (The Yalu River), Japanese writer and former border police officer Noritake Kazuo remarked how dam construction had robbed the Yalu of its free-flowing essence by turning it into an electricity-producing "lake."[91] But other observers were more optimistic. For instance, the authors of the 1942 *Antō sangyō keizai gaikan* (Summary of Andong's Economy and Industry) argued that the shortened icebound season and division of the river into "lakes" as a result of dam construction would significantly aid river transport and regional development.[92]

In addition to the disappearance of the lower Yalu's ice, Japanese officials' optimism in the wake of dam construction was inspired by an increasingly stable security situation around the Manchurian-Korean border. Successive joint counterinsurgency campaigns by Japanese and Manchukuo soldiers and police officers, which included brutal "scorched-earth" tactics aimed at alienating popular support for guerrillas, seemed to have dealt the final blow to the fierce insurgency that had challenged Japanese hegemony for decades. "Bandit suppression" had been a goal of Manchukuo security forces ever since the creation of the client state. It was not until after the Japanese invasion of mainland China reached a stalemate in 1938, however, that military forces in Manchuria devoted their full attention to the remaining guerrilla resistance. Beginning in October 1939, a massive combined Japanese and Manchukuo Army force of 75,000 troops launched simultaneous counterinsurgency campaigns in the Manchukuo provinces of Jilin, Jiandao, and Tonghua.[93] On February 23, 1940, influential Communist guerrilla leader Yang Jingyu, commander of the First Route Army of the Northeast Anti-Japanese United Army, was killed in a gunfight with Manchukuo policemen.[94] Kim Il-sung and Ch'oe Hyŏn managed to escape such a fate only by fleeing to the Soviet Union later that year.[95] Just as the ice of the lower Yalu was fading into memory, wintertime border raids appear to have ended as well. By 1944 Government-General of Korea propagandists confidently stated that the history of "banditry" in the region had been relegated to the watery depths of the new Sup'ung Reservoir.[96]

In the wake of dam completion and guerrilla pacification came grand schemes to develop the Sup'ung Reservoir as the "world's number-one fish hatchery."[97] Pollution from dam construction had an initially detrimental effect on the river's fish populations. Suggestions to install a fish ladder on the Sup'ung Dam to help fish travel over the massive concrete barrier were also refused by dam engineers, who believed that the costs of ladder installation and maintenance outweighed any potential economic benefit.[98] Instead, officials on both sides of the border began promoting the idea of farming fish in the Sup'ung Reservoir, which they predicted would increase the value of the Yalu's annual yield from 60,000–70,000 yen to 3–4 million yen.[99] In July 1941 fisheries officials in colonial Korea and Manchukuo announced plans to build hatcheries on the reservoir that would raise salmon, pond loach, eels, and various types of carp, with a total projected budget of one million yen.[100] Wartime scarcity meant that these plans were later scaled back.[101] Yet despite such limitations, by October 1943 fishery technicians had already moved thirty million sweetfish eggs from an aquacultural facility in the nearby Ch'ŏngch'ŏn River to the Sup'ung Reservoir. The results were "encouraging," officials reported, and provided the basis for additional aquacultural experiments the following year.[102]

Completion of the Sup'ung Dam also ignited ambitions to turn the reservoir into a tourist hotspot. In her study of tourism in the Japanese colonial empire, Kate McDonald argues that Japanese officials actively promoted travel as a means of "legitim[izing] imperial claims to colonized land."[103] Before 1940, tourist guidebooks produced by the South Manchuria Railway Company or the Government-General of Korea's Railway Bureau typically only mentioned the Yalu River border region as part of a brief stop in Andong or Sinŭiju on the railway route from Korea to Manchuria.[104] While such guides often highlighted the railway bridge or historic Russo-Japanese War sites in Andong's immediate vicinity, travel further up the frontier Yalu would have been dangerous and less likely for the well-heeled Japanese tourists reading these publications. But as "bandit suppression" and Yalu industrialization picked up speed, local boosters promoted a new image for the formerly contested border region. An article in the Sinŭiju Chamber of Commerce's monthly newsletter titled "The Value of the Sup'ung Dam for Tourism" argued that the dam and reservoir offered opportunities for new types of recreational sport fishing and boating. The Sup'ung Dam was additionally only a two-and-half-hour drive from Sinŭiju, putting it in closer proximity to major rail lines than more remotely located large dams in the countryside of the Japanese archipelago.[105] Such writings show how the Yalu was being reimagined and transformed from a remote and dangerous colonial periphery to a sedate stop on a tourist itinerary.

A Contested and Incomplete Conquest

Completion of the Sup'ung Dam brought with it imperial Japanese optimism that unruly elements of the Yalu's liquid geographies had finally been tamed and contained, especially as the subjugation of anti-Japanese guerrillas also spelled the end of previous seasonal cycles of border violence. Yet while officials and engineers proudly declared the dam a hallmark of "Scientific Japan," not all local stakeholders saw the accompanying transformation of the Yalu River in rosy terms.[106] Among the disenchanted were the poorly remunerated laborers whose "sacrifice" was hardly acknowledged by dam proponents. There were also the poor Korean and Chinese farmers forcibly displaced to make way for the massive new Sup'ung reservoir. Compelled to sell their homes at the artificially low prices set by Japanese officials before being relocated to new settlements hundreds of miles away, these forced migrants and their mournful plight caught the imagination of local writers. In a series of articles for the Korean-language *Mansŏn ilbo*, journalist Kang Ikhyŏn followed these farmers (while under heavy police surveillance) as they prepared to abandon their homes. While Kang himself was generally supportive of Japanese plans for the region, he ruminated on the fate of these migrants in the face of colonial policy and their nostalgic attachment to a landscape that would soon disappear: "For those villagers forced to leave behind their beloved hometowns, land, familiar mountains and rivers, and their friends and family only to enter relocation groups and start their lives anew, can you really expect them to understand the policy of 'constructing a New Asia'? For them it is simply the greatest disaster of their lives."[107]

Even privileged Japanese timber merchants in the Yalu border cities of Sinŭiju and Andong saw the dam's completion as an all-out attack on their way of life, as the region's traditionally most profitable industry was predicated on using the river's unimpeded flow to transport timber. Since the dam's construction was first announced in 1937, timber merchants in these cities aggressively lobbied dam engineers for measures that would allow timber rafts to continue to float downstream. As discussed in previous chapters, timber rafts—commemorated in popular songs such as the "Ōryokkō bushi" (Yalu River melody)—were a veritable economic lifeline for the downstream "timber cities" of Andong and Sinŭiju, with their annual presence on the springtime Yalu numbering well into the thousands. Dam engineers' inability to accommodate the movement of timber rafts and imperial planners' unwillingness to forsake larger plans to industrialize the region signaled that the electricity-producing "economic river" had replaced the "timber river" of old.[108] As a result, the heart of the Yalu's lumber processing industry was compelled to move from Andong and Sinŭiju to the upper Yalu cities of Manp'ojin and Ji'an.

Dam construction also severed a river route that had long been a source of profit for local boatmen. In order to stem protests from river boat captains, the Yalu River Hydropower Company simply purchased most river transportation companies and brought them under its monopoly (much as the Daan Steamship Company had done earlier with shipping interests near Andong).[109] Yet the sundering of the river by the newly completed dam still dealt a crushing blow to boat captains' livelihoods. Decades later, one Chinese boatman recalled that while the Sup'ung Dam "contributed to the industrial development of the northeast," it had "completely severed river transit, and brought significant inconvenience to the river transportation business."[110]

Efforts to monopolize river transit extended to the suppression of smuggling. After flourishing for years in the uneven spaces of riparian sovereignty along the Andong-Sinŭiju corridor, smugglers' activities receded for a brief period after 1937. Increased cooperation between customs and police authorities in Andong and Sinŭiju was one major factor that helped contain smuggling, especially when cross-border officials collaborated on such measures as banning nighttime river traffic.[111] Another decisive factor was the December 1937 abolition of Japanese extraterritoriality in Manchukuo. The extraterritorial status of the Japanese railway settlement in Andong had long provided a safe haven for smugglers and their sponsors. By the mid-1930s, however, calls mounted to abolish extraterritoriality and bring railway settlements under the legal jurisdiction of the Manchukuo regime. The legal privileges enjoyed by concession residents exposed the hypocrisy behind the Manchukuo nation-building project, but more importantly Japanese authorities also saw residents' exemption from Manchukuo taxes as a major fiscal liability amid the Kwantung Army's capital-intensive commitment to Manchukuo's heavy industrialization.[112] The disappearance of the Andong settlement, along with newly lowered customs rates, seemed to end the spectacle of large smuggling "gangs" making their way across the Yalu between Andong and Sinŭiju. Whereas Andong customs officials prosecuted a total of 2,982 smuggling incidents in 1936 and 1,518 in 1937, by 1938 the number dropped to a mere 169.[113]

The late 1930s decline in smuggling proved short-lived, however, as the movements of smugglers and illicit goods once again spilled outside the channels for river trade set by border officials. The Japanese military's increased demand for materials to fuel its ongoing war in China led the colonial Korean and Manchukuo governments to implement increasingly strict economic controls. These included the rationing and setting of officially mandated prices on basic commodities to curb inflation following the outbreak of the Asia-Pacific War in December 1941.[114] But even with the creation of special "economic police" (*keizai keisatsu*) to enforce these regulations, growing demand for increasingly scarce basic commodities and a desire to circumvent wartime rationing encouraged smuggling and other forms of illicit trade to flourish. From a low of only 69 persons cited for smuggling in Andong in 1938, the number jumped to 310 in 1939 and 603 by 1942.[115]

Part of this flourishing illicit trade was a thriving traffic in opium. As discussed in chapter 3, opium was a significant cash crop for border residents, including impoverished Korean "fire-field" farmers. Indeed, as one period article claimed, opium was second only to rice in terms of importance and value to migrant Korean communities in Manchuria.[116] Manchukuo authorities initially allowed cultivators to grow opium poppies in the border counties of Linjiang and Changbai to supply the Manchukuo state's lucrative official opium monopoly. Some of this opium was even allegedly smuggled across the Yalu in timber rafts drilled with holes to hide smugglers' goods.[117] Opium was also widely grown on the Korean side of the Yalu, as the GGK permitted legal opium cultivation in the border provinces of South and North Hamgyŏng to supply its own opium monopoly.[118] But by 1936 Manchukuo authorities, increasingly concerned that the sale of border opium was being used to fund anti-Japanese guerrilla groups, issued an ultimatum banning all opium cultivation in the region.[119] As a result, smuggled Korean-grown opium, already known on the Manchurian side of the river for being "high-quality," gained even more market share.[120] One of the multiple routes by which Korean opium made its way into southern Manchuria was by the Yalu River itself, as opium traveled downstream from cultivation areas in South Hamgyŏng to major consumption centers like the lower Yalu border city of Andong. A 1941 article published in a Japanese military police (*kenpei*) periodical described how Manchukuo authorities were aware of the smuggling issue in the mid-1930s but were too busy with guerrilla suppression to devote much attention to it. But as insurgent strength diminished by the end of the decade, Manchukuo officials began addressing the issue with greater urgency. The article's author speculated that completion of the Sup'ung Dam would alter the river-borne opium trade, though reports of continued smuggling suggests that the dam was a rather inadequate obstacle to opium marketeering.[121]

Smuggling in opium and other illicit goods continued even as the shortening, and eventual disappearance, of the lower Yalu's icebound season affected the traditional dynamics of wintertime smuggling. After the delayed onset of the icebound season in 1941–1942 due to dam construction, there was a reported "sudden spike" in the number of smuggling incidents in the Andong-Sinŭiju region once the river froze. Police estimated that an average of fifty incidents occurred daily as smugglers took advantage of the river ice and a dramatic rise of wartime commodity prices in Manchukuo.[122] The following winters there was no ice for smugglers to traverse. As a result, many took their illicit trade instead to railway cars traveling across the Yalu River Railway Bridge. Smugglers had to be more subtle and less brazen than in previous years, but a rise in black markets to counteract wartime commodity controls provided sufficient economic incentive for smuggling to continue.[123] Troubles with smuggling beguiled Japanese officials along the Andong-Sinŭiju corridor even as river engineering and border regulation efforts elsewhere met with increased success. One history of the Manchukuo police force noted that since 1940, Andong had become the de facto capital of black-market activities in Manchukuo.[124]

Amid these ongoing border issues, special meetings between Japanese representatives in Andong and Sinŭiju sought to address the lingering tensions behind "Manchurian-Korean unity." On November 14, 1941, and again on March 22, 1942, the Andong and Sinŭiju Chambers of Commerce held discussion forums featuring local officials and businessmen from both border cities. While the stated goal of the gatherings was to help integrate the bifurcated cross-border economy and bring it more "in line" with national policy, the discussion quickly turned to a laundry list of outstanding grievances against the wartime border regime.

As stated by one attendee of these meetings, "Manchurian-Korean unity is far easier said than done."[125] Many complained about escalating price differences between Andong and Sinŭiju, a major factor behind the smuggling resurgence. As Andong Chamber of Commerce president Senoguchi Fujitarō explained, while earlier "free-trade" policies had kept commodity prices on both sides of the border more or less equal, after the implementation of price controls in Korea the cost of goods in Sinŭiju was more similar to the southern Korean port city of Pusan than Andong. Meanwhile, in Andong prices reflected the planning of officials in the far-off Manchukuo capital of Shinkyō rather than local circumstances.[126] The implications of government-set prices were dramatic for those living along the Yalu River border. Whereas fifteen kilograms of rice cost 4.30 yen in Sinŭiju, for example, the same amount cost 5.96 yen in Andong, a difference of approximately 38.6 percent.[127] Little wonder that an illicit trade in rice and other goods thrived along the river. As a November 1940 article in the *Mansŏn ilbo* declared, "One just has to cross the Yalu and they can earn nine yen of profit on one *sŏk* of rice."[128] The temptation was also great for railway workers and officials along the border to engage in corrupt speculation. On December 14, 1942, a twenty-year old Japanese employee of a customs office in Manp'ojin was arrested along with another young Japanese railroad assistant conductor for impersonating customs agents, capturing contraband from smugglers, and then selling these goods on the black market for exorbitant prices.[129]

Another source of frustration for attendees at the November 1941 Andong and Sinŭiju economic discussion forum was the failed promise of hydroelectric development and other Yalu industrialization projects to improve life along the border. Not only had the dam severed Andong and Sinŭiju's access to waterborne timber rafts, the traditional economic lifeblood of the two cities, but the promise of cheap and plentiful hydroelectricity for industrial development had also run aground on wartime realities. As detailed by Aaron S. Moore, the Yalu River Hydropower Company and the Government-General of Korea received permission from the Manchukuo government in 1941 to raise the electricity rate from the originally agreed eight rin per kilowatt-hour to one sen one rin per kilowatt-hour.[130] The cost hike, which came after construction expenses expanded due to summertime floods and the higher cost of wartime materials, caused industrial promoters in Andong and Sinŭiju to worry that the increased price for electricity would pose an undue "shock" for factories in the region.[131]

In addition to the higher cost of electricity, wartime material shortages were hampering grand schemes to turn the Yalu River into a unified Manchurian-Korean "industrial belt." This was evident in the case of the ongoing harbor construction projects at the river's mouth. At the 1941 Andong and Sinŭiju economic discussion forum, a government civil engineer based in Sinŭiju noted that the recently completed cargo unloading docks at the Tasa-do harbor were only 30 percent of their original projected size, while a representative of a shipping company called the current facilities at Tasa-do "extremely insufficient."[132] The pace of construction at the Dadong harbor project was also slowing due to wartime material shortages. As one 1944 publication by the Manchukuo government's Bureau of Transportation euphemistically noted, it was "difficult to be optimistic" about the project's timely completion.[133] These infrastructural projects required massive inflows of resources such as concrete, steel, and fuel from other parts of Japan's wartime empire. But as the needs of wartime mobilization diverted these flows of goods elsewhere, the ambitions of Japanese colonizers to further transform and channel the liquid geographies of the Yalu border began to collapse.

A Collapsing Imperial Border Regime

Japan's declining fortunes in its prolonged war with the United States and other Allied powers dealt the final blow to the hubris-filled imperial project of "conquering nature" and fulfilling "Manchurian-Korean unity" at the Yalu. Successive Japanese defeats in the battles of Midway (1942) and Guadalcanal (1942–1943) translated into increasingly desperate attempts to provision Japan's overextended wartime empire—an empire that, in the euphoric rush of initial post–Pearl Harbor victories, had ballooned dramatically.[134] As critical materials were diverted to the battlefront, Japanese engineers and officials along the Manchurian-Korean border attempted to adapt by modifying existing plans for river engineering projects, a decision that came with its own deadly consequences.

Following completion of the Sup'ung Dam, engineers from the Yalu River Hydroelectric Company turned their attention to two new dam projects at Unbong and Ŭiju, both of which were ultimately left unfinished due to Japan's imperial collapse. The Unbong Dam, which began construction in July 1942, was located near the upper Yalu River border cities of Manp'ojin and Ji'an. These formerly remote cities on opposite sides of the border were linked by a new railway route completed in 1939, and with the completion of the Unbong Dam Japanese engineers hoped that cheap electricity could further drive the region's industrial transformation.[135] Yet from the start, construction was hampered not only by material shortages but also by Japanese engineers' own pride and miscalculation. In his memoir, Japanese engineer Satō Toshihiko recalled how he and his colleagues felt overconfident coming off the successful Sup'ung project, and as a result, decided to use a simple suspension bridge for work on the dam's body rather than a sturdier structure like the one used at Sup'ung. This plan failed to anticipate strong winds in the narrow river valley where the project was taking place, and the bridge had to be replaced.[136] While completion of the dam was originally set for 1948, it was only about 30 percent complete at the time of Japan's defeat in 1945.[137]

The Ŭiju Dam project, begun at the same time along the lower portion of the river, also saw delays and material shortages, with deadly consequences for on-site workers. As detailed in Satō's memoir, the upper portion of the airtight caissons used in the dam's foundation work were built of wood due to the difficulties of procuring steel. The lack of a back-up electrical generator to power the caissons' air-pressure regulating compressor also meant that when an unexpected power outage occurred at the dam site, water quickly flooded into the chamber, drowning all of the workers laboring inside.[138] Such nightmarish working conditions ended only with Japan's defeat, which left the Ŭiju Dam just 20 percent complete.[139]

The realities of impending imperial collapse caused Japanese officials to even begin dismantling some of the regulatory infrastructure of the Korea-Manchukuo border. The celebration greeting the first transmission of electricity from the Sup'ung Dam in August 1941 inspired booster hyperbole about the "eradication" of the Sino-Korean border.[140] These statements echoed claims from three decades earlier about the border's disappearance with the completion of the Yalu River Railway Bridge. But the idea of actually eliminating the police and customs inspections that reified the border's existence was not under discussion—until the exigencies of war caused Japanese leaders to decide otherwise. First, in 1943 Manchukuo customs officials granted customs tax exemptions for goods destined for use on the Unbong and Ŭiju dam construction sites. Official explanations for the new exemptions cited the importance of both border engineering projects to Korea and Manchukuo.[141] Finally, in July 1944 officials from the Government-General of Korea, Manchukuo, and the South Manchuria Railway Company abolished customs taxes altogether on goods traveling across the Manchurian-Korean border. Officials stressed that this was only a temporary measure to expedite cross-border transport that would be removed within one year following Japanese victory in the Asian-Pacific war. Imperial officials' reluctance to cede the border's utility for channeling flows of goods and peoples is evident in the fact that it took until 1944 for such a law to be passed. And while custom taxes were abolished, border inspections continued as part of an ultimately unsuccessful effort to limit the outflow of hard currency from Manchukuo.[142]

As symbolized by the appearance of American B-29 bombers in the skies above the Yalu River in February 1945, the hoped-for wartime victory that would cement Japanese power in the region and across the Asia-Pacific never came. As difficult as it was to defend the Yalu border on the ground, the aerial Manchurian-Korean boundary was even more difficult to secure. The river itself was never bombed during World War II, but by 1945 American pilots en route from bombing raids in the Manchurian interior crossed the boundary line with impunity as the limited aircraft resources of the Japanese military were diverted elsewhere.[143] Japanese military officials also looked with increased concern to the Soviet-Manchukuo border as Soviet leaders mulled declaring war on Japan, a decision finally made on August 9, 1945. The subsequent Soviet occupation of Manchuria and northern Korea, combined with the Japanese surrender to the Allied forces on August 15, spelled the abrupt end of the Japanese Empire.

As the rapid collapse of the Japanese imperial project demonstrates, the "conquest" of the Yalu River's "nature" and reengineering of its border to serve wartime aims proved an unsustainable ambition. On the one hand, industrial projects like the Sup'ung Dam did transform the Yalu environment, overcoming floods, ice, and other challenges to make the river more amenable to imperial control. Promotion of "Manchurian-Korean unity" also encouraged successful cross-border cooperation on issues like river management and anti-guerrilla counterinsurgency campaigns. The violent guerrilla resistance that had challenged Japanese rule in the region for decades was destroyed by 1941, and for a fleeting time the border region no longer seemed to pose any overt challenge to Japanese rule.

But even prior to the ultimate dissolution of the Japanese Empire in 1945, the lingering tensions underlying the rhetoric of "Manchurian-Korean unity" were clear. Illicit trade continued to thrive, and regional rivalries between local governments along the border persisted. Finally, the subjugation of the Yalu River itself required a level of material commitment that was difficult to sustain during wartime. The flooding of the Ŭiju Dam caisson and other incidents like it revealed the "power of water" (*mizu no chikara*): a foundational and oft-subversive element of the region's liquid geographies that would continue to confront post-1945 regimes that emerged in the wake of Japan's surrender.

CONCLUSION

Border police pursuing contraband-carrying smugglers across a frozen river. Illicit border crossers drowning in a murky river after their boat capsizes. Floods threatening border policing infrastructure. These could well be stories from the early twentieth-century Yalu River. But they are in fact from twenty-first-century news reports about the St. Lawrence River bordering the United States and Canada and the Rio Grande River bordering the United States and Mexico.[1]

I mention these stories from the northern and southern peripheries of the United States, where I currently reside, as a way of highlighting how this book addresses key themes common to the bordering experience across time and space. The fraught intersections of mobile border crossers, seasonally changing riparian environments, and state-led attempts to channel these liquid geographies can be found in many different contexts beyond the early twentieth-century Yalu. According to a recent United Nations report, there are 286 river basins worldwide that cross multiple national boundaries.[2] Besides rivers, forests, mountains, deserts, and other types of environments act in concert with human actors to challenge the rationalizing impulses of state control and boundary-drawing.

The colonial Yalu River boundary offers a compelling case study for understanding the challenge border environments present to modern states due to its dynamic flows of water and ice as well as people and goods. Far from being a sealed-off edge of empire, the Yalu River was a strategically vital conduit for flows of people and goods integral to Japanese expansion. By encouraging trade and the movement of multiethnic imperial subjects across the river, colonial officials attempted to project power north into Manchuria as well as cement control over

Korea. But flows of people and commodities could, and did, spill outside of the regulatory channels enforced by colonial police and customs officials. The Yalu's seasonal patterns of water and ice further shaped the mobility of border crossers, including colonial officials, to provide opportunities and obstacles for the expansion of imperial power. The dynamics of seasonal border-making were not constant. Rather, they changed over time, especially as imperial engineers reengineered the river environment to channel human and nonhuman flows for self-serving ends. When, on the eve of Japan's imperial collapse, ice no longer formed on the lower Yalu River due to the Sup'ung Dam's completion, it presaged an era in which the loss of ice due to climate change and other effects of industrialization would have dramatic consequences not just for boundary-making, but for human society and politics in general.

In our contemporary era, neoliberal political regimes are ever-reliant on cross-border commerce and migration to sustain economic and political expansion. They also construct walls and fences and checkpoints to keep "undesirable elements" out. Yet just as imperial Japan's efforts to maintain its selectively permeable membrane at the Yalu collided with the physical realities of life along this seasonally changing riparian border, contemporary states are finding their efforts to channel the mobilities of human actors complicated by the flowing rivers, mountains, deserts, and other dynamic environments where political borderlines are drawn. As numerous commentators have pointed out in the case of the US-Mexico border, proposals to strengthen river borders by building fences or other physical fortifications betray a lack of common-sense knowledge about how rivers flood, shift course, and otherwise function as dynamic environments.[3] Climate change also poses new challenges to border policing in the form of increased flooding along river borders, rising sea levels along ambiguous marine boundaries, or as a factor behind economic displacement driving cross-border migration. The link between expanding fossil-fuel use and global climate change blurs the already fuzzy distinctions between human agency and nonhuman power in the creation and contesting of state boundaries.[4]

Drawing insights from ecology, environmental historians and scholars in the environmental humanities have long pushed us to see history not as the creation of discrete human actors but as the product of complex relationships between humans and the nonhuman environment. As spaces "where land and water meet," to quote Nancy Langston, rivers and riparian zones have proven to be particularly rich sites for this kind of inquiry.[5] Whether by examining the "Yellow River–Hebei complex" in premodern China, "riparian relations" in modern Japan, or the "organic machine" of North America's Columbia River, to name a few examples, historians of river environments have tried to bridge persistent artificial distinctions between human-made systems and the nonhuman world.[6]

By focusing on what I call the Yalu's liquid geographies, this book has applied similar insights to the history of political boundaries and border-making. Only recently have scholars begun to interrogate the anthropocentrism of conventional border studies and think through borders as more-than-human spaces. Borders are haphazardly imposed on all types of physical landscapes, but much as river studies have yielded tremendous analytical fruit in the field of environmental history, rivers can be key sites for considering how human and nonhuman flows intersect to define political boundaries.[7] This book has narrated the history of the Yalu River border through the interconnected and seasonally changing movements of water and ice, as well as human actors, yielding a fuller picture of how this strategically significant boundary was constituted and experienced.

While revealing key insights into the nature of borders, the story of the colonial Yalu also provides meaningful interventions in the historiography of East Asia. It joins recent studies of Manchuria in foregrounding how the mountains, forests, and rivers of this transnational frontier were central to the development of Northeast Asia as a whole. It also pushes historians of Korea to look beyond the colony's urban spaces and toward the peninsula's northern periphery for understanding the violent workings of colonial power. And when it comes to histories of the Japanese Empire, this examination of the Manchurian-Korean boundary provides new insight into the internal tensions of Japan's imperial expansion into Northeast Asia. Following the Japanese invasion of Manchuria in 1931 and the creation of the puppet state of Manchukuo a year later, the Yalu River was putatively transformed from an international border into an intraimperial boundary. But even amid official proclamations of "Manchurian-Korean unity" the border between Manchukuo and Korea remained a site of tension and conflict. Disputes over smuggling regulation, fishing rights, border policing, and other cross-border issues showed that cooperation between colonial regimes in Korea and Manchukuo was not a given, but rather a protracted and contentious process that frequently ran aground on local rivalries and bureaucratic divisions along their shared border that lasted all the way until imperial collapse in 1945.

Epilogue: The Yalu's Postcolonial Liquid Geographies

In 1949 Korean author Kim Mansŏn published a semi-autobiographical short story about the experience of crossing the Yalu border immediately after Japan's surrender. "Yalu River" depicts a Korean migrant to Manchuria, Wŏnsik, and his efforts to cross the Yalu and return home to Korea amid the tumult of imperial collapse. Wŏnsik's travails represented the very real plight of the many thousands of Korean migrants who were relocated to Manchuria to work as agricultural laborers and factory workers during World War II, only to try to journey back to Korea once Japan surrendered and its colonial empire fell apart. Traveling with Wŏnsik's family on a crowded train from northern Manchuria are hundreds of fellow Korean refugees. After the train is forced to stop in the border city of Andong, Wŏnsik joins the other refugees in nervously heading for a nearby ferry crossing. "If only I can cross the river and set foot in Sinŭiju, then all of my worries will disappear," Wŏnsik thinks to himself. It is not until he finally reaches the Korean side of the river that "his heart was put at ease."[8] For both the fictional Wŏnsik and his real-life compatriots, the act of Yalu border crossing, fraught as it was, symbolized the shaking off of colonial displacement and the earnest hope of building new, better postcolonial futures in their ancestral homelands. The liquidity of the border to these refugee flows would soon be affected, however, by events outside their control.

The politics and porosity of the postcolonial Yalu shifted with larger conflicts in the region. With the Japanese defeat and imperial retreat in 1945 came two new occupying powers on the Korean Peninsula—both firmly committed to an ideology of anticolonialism, but often neocolonial in their own foreign policy. As part of a "trusteeship" agreement negotiated in the waning days of World War II, the Soviet Union occupied the northern half of Korea from the southern banks of the Yalu to the 38th Parallel, while the United States occupied the peninsula's southern half. The Soviet occupation of northern Korea lasted until 1948, during which occupation authorities oversaw the installation of anti-Japanese guerrilla Kim Il-sung as supreme leader and the remaking of the country into a bastion of socialist "revolution."[9] Meanwhile, on the Chinese side of the Yalu, Manchuria became a battleground between competing Chinese Communist and Nationalist armies in the Chinese Civil War (1945–1949) following a year-long occupation by the Soviet Union.

Whereas the constant cross-border flow of peoples and goods formed an important part of Japanese imperial policy, Soviet and Chinese forces adopted comparatively stricter restrictions on civilian river traffic. As one former Japanese settler repatriated from the region recollected, the arrival of Soviet troops saw the end of the distinctive "propeller boats" that had previously plied the river's course.[10] While propeller boats and other river vessels had been integral to Japan's project of welding together Korea and Manchuria, the postcolonial era viewed this bustling river-borne commerce as a potential security threat.

Amid the raging Chinese Civil War, officials in Soviet-occupied North Korea sought to channel the Yalu's human flows in ways that aided Chinese Communist allies while hindering Chinese Nationalist troops. In June 1946 Soviet occupying forces allowed Communist soldiers fleeing Nationalist offensives in the border cities of Andong and Tonghua to cross the river and take refuge in northern Korea.[11] At the same time officials in occupied North Korea opened the border to Chinese Communists, they vigorously policed "illegal" border crossings by Nationalist forces. As was the case before 1945, these efforts to channel the Yalu's liquid geographies were inherently seasonal in nature. During the winter of 1946–1947, for example, North Korean officials engaged in seasonal border-making counted more than two dozen border raids by Chinese Nationalists, including a group of soldiers who allegedly kidnapped a young Korean student on the surface of the frozen upper Yalu.[12]

Chinese Nationalists, who briefly controlled parts of the Yalu River basin from 1946 to 1947, attempted to fortify their own faltering influence in the region by reasserting claims to the disputed Hwangch'op'yŏng river islands. Nationalist forces accused officials in North Korea of using the islands to harbor Chinese Communist rebels.[13] Such protests did little to solidify Chinese claims to the islands, however, which remained under the control of Soviet-occupied North Korea until 1948 and the newly created Democratic People's Republic of Korea afterward. It also did little to reverse the eventuality of Nationalist defeat in the Chinese Civil War. By June 1947 Communist forces succeeded in driving Nationalist troops out of the border city of Andong, and by 1949 the northern bank of the Yalu became part of the newly created People's Republic of China (PRC).

The tumultuous conflicts that racked the postcolonial Yalu saw little break with the outbreak of the Korean War (1950–1953), which thrust the river directly to the center of Cold War geopolitics. The Korean War initially began as a civil war initiated by the new North Korean regime to reunify the peninsula. But events beyond Korea resulted in it becoming a proxy conflict for the global Cold War. Seeing its commitment to "containing" international Communism threatened, the United States intervened in Korea under the banner of a United Nations–authorized "police action." After achieving quick victory over North Korean forces in an ambitious amphibious attack on the Korean city of Inch'ŏn, the UN commander Douglas MacArthur pushed for an ill-fated "march to the Yalu" that he imagined would eradicate the Communist presence on the entire peninsula.[14] In a euphoric and hubris-filled string of post-Inch'ŏn victories, UN forces reached the border in a matter of weeks. South Korean troops accompanying UN forces even sent a canteen full of "Yalu water" to South Korean president Syngman Rhee. This event continues to be commemorated in South Korea, with a canteen bearing the words "Yalu water" (Amnokkang su) proudly displaced in the War Memorial of Korea museum in Seoul.[15] But what MacArthur,

Rhee, and ordinary soldiers failed to anticipate was the psychology of Chinese officials across the Yalu's waters.

The UN march to the Yalu's southern bank alarmed Mao Zedong and other leaders of the newly formed PRC. Determined to both aid their Communist ally North Korea and protect their own vulnerable periphery, Chinese leaders began deploying thousands of "volunteer" troops across the Yalu in October 1950. After weeks of surreptitiously sending scouts and supplies to the Korean War frontline, PRC leader Mao Zedong openly proclaimed the mobilization of a "People's Volunteer Army" to support North Korea. From this point until the conflict's end in 1953, the Chinese effort to turn the tide of the Korean War started first at the Yalu River. As the most popular Chinese propaganda song of the Korean War proclaimed, "Valiantly, militantly, [we] cross the Yalu River! To protect peace and defend the motherland."[16]

Just five years after the end of World War II, the Yalu River's seasonal dynamics and Japanese-built infrastructure were shaping battles between new regional hegemons. US troops arriving near the Yalu border were rapidly overcome not only by attacking Chinese troops but also by an early, harsh winter. In the words of a *New York Times* reporter, the frigid cold "caused more trouble to our troops than did enemy action."[17] Meanwhile Chinese troops attempting to maintain critical bridge routes across the Yalu were challenged by unrelenting US air raids. American bombers destroyed the original Yalu River Railway Bridge completed by the Japanese in 1911. Built to Japanese fanfare decades earlier as a symbol of the "obliteration" of the Yalu's natural barriers, the 1911 bridge itself was now obliterated. American bombers also severely damaged, but failed to destroy, a neighboring bridge completed in 1942.[18] That bridge, built by the Japanese during the height of the Asia-Pacific War, featured an "air-raid resistant" double-diagonal truss bridge design that proved remarkably durable under repeated American attacks. American military officials in occupied Japan even tried to recruit one of the bridge's designers, former Government-General of Korea engineer Oda Yanosuke, to help destroy it. Rather than accepting the offer, Oda refused, citing his own distaste for war born of his World War II experience. According to Oda's memoir, this led one American officer to ruefully joke that Oda would soon be receiving a prize from the Soviet Union for his indestructible bridge design.[19]

The imminent onset of the Yalu winter could have obviated the need for such bridges, but the effects of the Japanese-built Sup'ung Dam meant that the Yalu's ice no longer provided a reliable cross-border pathway. While much of the upper Yalu remained frozen in the winter and thus conveniently accessible to Chinese supply lines, Chinese engineers were compelled to maintain temporary bridges across the still-flowing parts of the lower river even in the depths of winter. One of the most iconic images of China's involvement in the Korean War shows a line of troops using a makeshift bridge to cross the lower Yalu near Andong in the midst of a snow-covered landscape. Since 1951 this photograph (figure 6.1) has become the definitive image of the Chinese Yalu crossing, having been frequently reproduced in textbooks, news articles, documentaries, and other media about the Korean War.[20] But what most viewers miss about this image is the environmental transformation displayed under the soldiers' feet.

If the photo had been taken only a decade earlier, a thick layer of ice would have covered the Yalu and there would have been no need for a temporary bridge like the one seen in the photograph. The lack of ice, despite the obvious freezing temperatures, was the direct result of the Japanese-built Sup'ung Dam further upriver. The winter of 1950–1951 in northern Korea was famously cold—a fact attested by the common depictions of snow and ice in Korean War media and in the title of the popular American Korean War history, *The Coldest Winter*.[21] Large portions of the lower Yalu River that had not frozen over in the years after the Sup'ung Dam's completion iced over once again. Yet there remained places where, even in February, Chinese soldiers could not rely on the help of the river ice to cross over. To the Chinese soldiers who walked solemnly across this pontoon bridge in February 1951, there was no guarantee that their "valiant,"

FIGURE 6.1. Chinese troops near Andong cross the Yalu River into Korea.

Source: "Zhongguo renmin zhiyuanjun zhange," Jiefangjun huabao, April 1951.

"militant" march across the Yalu would not be interrupted by UN fire. If such an attack had occurred, they would have almost certainly plunged into the frigid, flowing waters of the Yalu below.

Decades after the Korean War, the Yalu remains a heavily militarized and seasonally variable boundary between China and North Korea. Disastrous floods exacerbated by rampant deforestation struck the region in August 2010, resulting in thousands of evacuations.[22] Meanwhile, the unsanctioned movement of peoples and goods continues to thrive in this seasonally changing frontier space. Recent attempts to close the border against the fearful plague of COVID-19 collided with the liquid mobilities of borderland communities. Border trade severely decreased amid the "excessive" and often violent vigilance of border police. Nonetheless, smuggling operations persisted with the tacit cooperation of local residents and other border authorities.[23] Stories also abound of defectors and smugglers making the wintertime crossing from North Korea into China across the frozen upper Yalu.[24] To this day, the Yalu border's destiny continues to be shaped by the movements of people, water, and ice.

Notes

ABBREVIATIONS

The following abbreviations are used in the notes:

CTS   *Chōsen tōchi shiryō 9: Enkyō*
DBDX   *Dongbei bianjiang dang'an xuanji*
JACAR Japan Center for Asian Historical Records
SHAC   Second Historical Archives of China
TM   *T'onggambu munsŏ*

FOREWORD

1. Élisabeth Vallet, "The World Is Witnessing a Rapid Proliferation of Border Walls," *Migration Policy Institute*, March 2, 2022, https://www.migrationpolicy.org/article/rapid-proliferation-number-border-walls.

2. Josh Smith and Sudev Kiyada, "North Korea Spent the Pandemic Building a Huge Border Wall," *Reuters*, May 27, 2023, https://www.reuters.com/graphics/NORTHKOREA-BORDER/byvrlwjreve/.

3. Seuikee Jang, "Lax Patrols Lead to Spike in Smuggling Across China–North Korea Border," *Daily NK*, April 3, 2023, https://www.dailynk.com/english/lax-patrols-lead-spike-smuggling-across-china-north-korea-border/.

INTRODUCTION

1. Ishimaru Gin'ichi, *Kokkyō shashin daikan* (Shingishū [Sinŭiju]: Ōkō Nippōsha, 1929). Another recounting of the Yalu timber rafters' perilous journeys can be found in David Fedman, *Seeds of Control: Japan's Empire of Forestry in Colonial Korea* (Seattle: University of Washington Press, 2020), 125–126.

2. "Pyŏktong taean e panman'gun," *Tonga ilbo*, May 31, 1935.

3. Hildi Kang, *Under the Black Umbrella: Voices from Colonial Korea, 1910–1945* (Ithaca, NY: Cornell University Press, 2001), 81.

4. The idea of "knowing" a river through labor is borrowed from Richard White's now-canonical environmental history of the Columbia River. See Richard White, *The Organic Machine: The Remaking of the Columbia River* (New York: Hill & Wang, 1995).

5. "Amnokkang," Kukka chisik p'otŏl: Pukhan chiyŏk chŏngbo net, http://www.cybernk.net/infoText/InfoNatureCultureDetail.aspx?mc=BN0104&id=BN010200000628&rightType=%20&direct=1&direct=1 (accessed August 31, 2023). For a detailed early twentieth-century source on Yalu geography, see Hermann Lautensach, *Korea: A Geography Based on the Author's Travels and Literature*, trans. Katherine and Eckart Dege (Berlin: Springer Verlag, 1988), 244–253.

6. The stele's rediscovery in the late nineteenth century, just as Japanese imperialists were starting to encroach on the Korean Peninsula, caused a sensation among nationalist Koreans looking for ancient heroes to inspire resistance to new foreign threats. For more, see Andre Schmid, *Korea between Empires, 1895–1919* (New York: Columbia University Press, 2002), 1–22.

7. A historical description of the Koguryŏ kingdom from the Tang dynasty-era text *Tongdian*, compiled in 801 CE, records the following: "Mazishui [an alternate historical name for the Yalu] is also known as the Yalu. . . . it is known as this because the water is the color of a duck's head." For a recent summary of debates around the etymology of the term "Yalu," see Yi Sŭngsu, "Amnokkang myŏngch'ing ko," *Han'guk minjok munhwa* 81 (March 2022): 29–52.

8. Koryŏ cultural perceptions of the northern border are explored in Remco Breuker, "Within or Without? Ambiguity of Borders and Koryŏ Koreans' Travels during the Liao, Jin, Song and Yuan," *East Asian History* 38 (February 2014): 47–62. On general Koryŏ relations with these northern dynasties, see Peter Yun, "Rethinking the Tribute System: Korean States and Northeast Asian Interstate Relations, 600–1600" (PhD diss., University of California, Los Angeles, 1998), 43–129.

9. Seonmin Kim, *Ginseng and Borderland: Territorial Boundaries and Political Relations between Qing China and Chosŏn Korea, 1636–1912* (Berkeley: University of California Press, 2017), 29–30.

10. Kim, *Ginseng and Borderland*, 29–30.

11. Nianshen Song, *Making Borders in Modern East Asia: The Tumen River Demarcation, 1881–1919* (Cambridge, UK: Cambridge University Press, 2018), 61. On the ideological importance of Manchuria for the Qing state, see also Mark C. Elliot, "The Limits of Tartary: Manchuria in Imperial and National Geographies," *Journal of Asian Studies* 59, no. 3 (2000): 603–646.

12. For more on Qing policies toward Manchuria and the consequences of *fengjin* and its uneven enforcement, see David A. Bello, *Across Forest, Steppe, and Mountain: Environment, Identity, and Empire in Qing China's Borderlands* (Cambridge, UK: Cambridge University Press, 2015); and Jonathan Schlesinger, *A World Trimmed with Fur: Wild Things, Pristine Places, and the Natural Fringes of Qing Rule* (Redwood City, CA: Stanford University Press, 2017).

13. Qing efforts to protect its ginseng monopoly and enforce the Sino-Korean border are extensively detailed in Kim, *Ginseng and Borderland*.

14. Kang Sŏkhwa, "Chosŏn hugi P'yŏngan-do chiyŏk Amnokkang byŏn ŭi pangŏ ch'egye," *Han'guk munhwa* 34 (December 2004): 191.

15. In 1796, for example, one major flood wiped out over a thousand homes and killed several hundred people near Ŭiju. *Chŏngjo sillok* 45:20 (August 20, 1796), http://sillok.history.go.kr/id/kva_12008020_002.

16. Kim, *Ginseng and Borderland*, 89. For more on how climate shaped Chosŏn frontier administration, see Wenjiao Cai, "Coping with the Cold: Nature and State on Chosŏn Korea's Northern Frontier" (PhD diss., Harvard University, 2022).

17. The original text of this report, known as the *Kangbuk ilgi* (Diary of [travels] north of the [Yalu] River), can be found through the Korea University Center for Overseas Resources on Korean Studies database, http://kostma.korea.ac.kr/dir/list?uci=RIKS+CRMA+KSM-WM.1872.0000-20090720.RICH_0047. The report and its significance are analyzed in detail in Kwangmin Kim, "Korean Migration in Nineteenth-Century Manchuria: A Global Theme in Modern Asian History," in Wen-Hsin Yeh, ed., *Mobile Subjects: Boundaries and Identities in the Modern Korean Diaspora* (Berkeley, CA: Institute of East Asian Studies, 2013), 17–37.

18. Song, *Making Borders in Modern East Asia*, 120–126.

19. *Pipyŏnsa tŭngnok* 247 (Ch'ŏlchong 11 nyŏn 1 wŏl), accessed through the National Institute of Korean History Korean History Database (Kuksa P'yŏnch'an Wiwŏnhoe Han'guksa Deit'ŏbeisŭ), http://db.history.go.kr/id/bb_247_001_01_0110.

20. *Kangbuk ilgi*.

21. Kim, *Ginseng and Borderland*, 137.

22. Kirk Larsen, *Traditions, Treaties, and Trade: Qing Imperialism and Chosŏn Korea, 1850–1910* (Cambridge, MA: Harvard University Asia Center, 2008), 90. The original classical Chinese text of this agreement, along with English translation, can be found in Imperial Maritime Customs, *Treaties, Conventions, etc., between China and Foreign States*, vol. 2 (Shanghai: Statistical Department of the Inspectorate General of Customs, 1908), 1528–1537.

23. On Russian imperialism in late Qing Manchuria, see Victor Zatsepine, *Beyond the Amur: Frontier Encounters between China and Russia, 1850–1930* (Vancouver: University of British Columbia Press, 2017).

24. Masuda Tadao, *Manshū kokkyō mondai* (Tokyo: Chūō Kōronsha, 1941), 12.

25. For a nuanced and informative take on early Japanese "borders," see Bruce L. Batten, *To the Ends of Japan: Premodern Frontiers, Boundaries, and Interactions* (Honolulu: University of Hawai'i Press, 2003).

26. "Amnokkang ch'ŏlgyo ŭi ilil kyotong nyang," *Tonga ilbo*, March 5, 1935.

27. A cogent critique of the Enlightenment-era "Man vs. Nature" binary is presented in Anna Tsing's influential study, *The Mushroom at the End of the World: On the Possibility of Life in Capitalist Ruins* (Princeton, NJ: Princeton University Press, 2015), vii–viii. For a recent essay that cites Tsing and other thinkers in advocating for the applicability of the "more-than-human" to environmental history, see Emily O'Gorman and Andrea Gaynor, "More-Than-Human Histories," *Environmental History* 25 no. 4 (October 2020): 711–735.

28. Richard White, *The Organic Machine*; Sarah Pritchard, *Confluence: The Nature of Technology and the Remaking of the Rhone* (Cambridge, MA: Harvard University Press, 2011). For East Asia–focused river histories that similarly challenge simple human-nature binaries, see Micah S. Muscolino, *The Ecology of War in China: Henan Province, the Yellow River, and Beyond, 1938–1950* (Cambridge, UK: Cambridge University Press, 2015); David A. Pietz, *The Yellow River: The Problem of Water in Modern China* (Cambridge, MA: Harvard University Press, 2015); Ruth Mostern, *The Yellow River: A Natural and Unnatural History* (New Haven, CT: Yale University Press, 2021); and Roderick I. Wilson, *Turbulent Streams: An Environmental History of Japan's Rivers, 1600–1930* (Leiden: Brill, 2021).

29. Dilip da Cunha, *The Invention of Rivers: Alexander's Eye and Ganga's Descent* (Philadelphia: University of Pennsylvania Press, 2019).

30. Many scholars in environmental history and the environmental humanities use the term "agent" to describe these nonhuman entities as well. As Linda Nash notes, this desire to ascribe "agency" to nonhuman entities is borne out of the intellectual tradition of social history, where endowing a historical subject with "agency" recovered its rightful place in the shaping of historical narratives. See Linda Nash, "The Agency of Nature or the Nature of Agency?" *Environmental History* 10, no. 1 (January 2005). At the same time, periodic challenges to the description of nonhuman "agency" are raised by those who associate the term with philosophical intentionality or choice, which may be present among certain nonhuman actors like animals but is lacking among nonsentient entities such as rivers or mountains. While I agree with the desire to make room for nonhuman forces in historical narratives, I believe that the philosophical connotations of "agency" make the term "nonhuman actors" I employ more fitting for this context and no less powerful rhetorically.

31. Sandro Mezzadra and Brett Nielson, *Border as Method, or the Multiplication of Labor* (Durham, NC: Duke University Press, 2013), 3. For classic border and border-making histories, see Peter Sahlins, *Boundaries: The Making of France and Spain in the*

Pyrenees (Berkeley: University of California Press, 1989); and Thongchai Winichakul, *Siam Mapped: A History of the Geo-Body of a Nation* (Honolulu: University of Hawai'i Press, 1994).

32. Mezzadra and Nielson, *Border as Method*, 7. On borders as "motors" of circulation, see Thomas Nail, *Theory of the Border* (Oxford, UK: Oxford University Press, 2016), 7–8.

33. See, for example, Lissa K. Wadewitz, *The Nature of Borders: Salmon, Boundaries, and Bandits on the Salish Sea* (Seattle: University of Washington Press, 2012); C. J. Alvarez, *Border Land, Border Water: A History of Construction on the US-Mexico Divide* (Austin: University of Texas Press, 2019); Frederico Freitas, *Nationalizing Nature: Iguazu Falls and National Parks at the Brazil-Argentina Border* (Cambridge, UK: Cambridge University Press, 2021).

34. Xavier Oliveras-Gonzalez, "Beyond Natural Borders and Social Bordering: The Political Agency of the Lower Rio Brave/Grande," *Geopolitics*, https://doi.org/10.1080/14650045.2021.2016706.

35. For more on the environments of border-making along the US-Mexico border, see Alvarez, *Border Land, Border Water*. On the Mekong, see David Biggs, *Quagmire: Nation-Building and Nature in the Mekong Delta* (Seattle: University of Washington Press, 2010). For a recent more-than-human account of the Korean DMZ border, see Elena Kim, *Making Peace with Nature: Ecological Encounters along the Korean DMZ*. (Durham, NC: Duke University Press, 2022).

36. The Climate History Network maintains an extensive online database of works on climate history: http://www.climatehistory.net/bibliography.

37. Thomas M. Wickman, *Snowshoe Country: An Environmental and Cultural History of Winter in the Early American Northeast* (Cambridge, UK: Cambridge University Press, 2018). For an East Asia–focused study on winter that embraces a similar seasonal perspective, see Norman Smith, "'Hibernate No More!': Winter, Health, and the Great Outdoors," in Norman Smith, ed., *Empire and Environment in the Making of Manchuria* (Vancouver: University of British Columbia Press, 2017), 130–151.

38. Recent works on the transnational history of modern Manchuria include Victor Zatsepine, *Beyond the Amur*; Emer Sinéad O'Dwyer, *Significant Soil: Settler Colonialism and Japan's Urban Empire in Manchuria* (Cambridge, MA: Harvard University Asia Center, 2015); Sören Urbansky, *Beyond the Steppe Frontier: A History of the Sino-Russian Border* (Princeton, NJ: Princeton University Press, 2021); Koji Hirata, "Made in Manchuria: The Transnational Origins of Socialist Industrialization in Maoist China," *American Historical Review* 126, no. 3 (September 2021): 1072–1101; Victor Seow, *Carbon Technocracy: Energy Regimes in Modern East Asia* (Chicago: University of Chicago Press, 2021); and Ruth Rogaski, *Knowing Manchuria: Environments, the Senses, and Natural Knowledge on an Asian Borderland* (Chicago: University of Chicago Press, 2022). The term "cradle of conflict" comes from Sinologist Owen Lattimore's influential early study of Manchuria. See Owen Lattimore, *Manchuria: Cradle of Conflict* (New York: Macmillan, 1932).

39. See, for example, Smith, *Empire and Environment in the Making of Manchuria*; Seow, *Carbon Technocracy*; and Rogaski, *Knowing Manchuria*. The environmental focus has been pronounced in early modern histories of the region. See Bello, *Across Forest, Steppe, and Mountain*; Schlesinger, *A World Trimmed with Fur*; and Rogaski, *Knowing Manchuria*, chaps. 1–3.

40. Andre Schmid, *Korea between Empires*, 199–223; Esselstrom, *Crossing Empire's Edge: Foreign Ministry Police and Japanese Expansionism in Northeast Asia* (Honolulu: University of Hawai'i Press, 2009), chaps. 2–4; Kim, *Ginseng and Borderland*; Song, *Making Borders in Modern East Asia*; Alyssa M. Park, *Sovereignty Experiments: Korean*

Migrants and the Building of Borders in Northeast Asia, 1860–1945 (Ithaca, NY: Cornell University Press, 2019).

41. On this "urban bias," see Fedman, *Seeds of Control*, 9. For another recent effort to correct this bias, see Holly Stephens, "Agriculture and Development in an Age of Empire: Institutions, Associations, and Market Networks in Korea, 1876–1945" (PhD diss., University of Pennsylvania, 2017).

42. Gi-Wook Shin and Michael Robinson, eds., *Colonial Modernity in Korea* (Cambridge, MA: Harvard University Asia Center, 1999).

43. David Ambaras, *Japan's Imperial Underworlds: Intimate Encounters at the Borders of Empire* (Cambridge, UK: Cambridge University Press, 2018), 28. On imperial borders and borderlands, see also Sakura Christmas, "The Cartographic Steppe: Spaces of Development in Northeast Asia, 1895–1945" (PhD diss., Harvard University, 2015); Paul D. Barclay, *Outcasts of Empire: Japan's Rule on Taiwan "Savage Border," 1874–1945* (Berkeley: University of California Press, 2017); Kate McDonald, *Placing Empire: Travel and the Social Imagination in Japan* (Berkeley: University of California Press, 2017), 83–102; Hiroko Matsuda, *Liminality of the Japanese Empire: Border Crossings from Okinawa to Colonial Taiwan* (Honolulu: University of Hawai'i Press, 2018); Seiji Shirane, *Imperial Gateway: Colonial Taiwan and Japan's Expansion in South China and Southeast Asia, 1895–1945* (Ithaca, NY: Cornell University Press, 2022); Paul Kreitman, *Japan's Ocean Borderland: Nature and Sovereignty* (Cambridge, UK: Cambridge University Press, 2023) and Takahiro Yamamoto, *Demarcating Japan: Imperialism, Islanders, and Mobility, 1855–1884* (Cambridge, MA: Harvard University Press Asia Center, 2023).

44. An informative discussion of how Japanese imperial borders played a dual role of inclusion and exclusion, as reflected through travelers' narratives, can be found in McDonald, *Placing Empire*, 83–102. The concept of imperial gateways is expounded in Shirane, *Imperial Gateway*, 1–14.

45. Connections between Korean and Manchurian colonizing projects previously analyzed by scholars include Korean migrants—see Song, *Making Borders in East Asia*; and Hyun Ok Park, *Two Dreams in One Bed: Empire, Social Life, and the Origins of the North Korean Revolution in Manchuria* (Durham, NC: Duke University Press, 2005)—surveillance of the Korean resistance movement (Esselstrom, *Crossing Empire's Edge*), and dam construction—Aaron Stephen Moore, "'The Yalu River Era of Developing Asia': Japanese Expertise, Colonial Power, and the Construction of Sup'ung Dam," *Journal of Asian Studies*, 72, no. 1 (2013): 115–139. Most English-language scholarship on Japanese colonialism in Northeast Asia focuses specifically on either Korea or Manchuria rather than both regions, but even in such Korea- or Manchuria-focused studies some attention is usually given to the links between these colonizing projects. See, for example, Yoshihisa Tak Matsusaka, *The Making of Japanese Manchuria, 1904–1932* (Cambridge, MA: Harvard University Asia Center, 2001), 198–204; Jun Uchida, *Brokers of Empire: Japanese Settler Colonialism in Korea, 1876–1945* (Cambridge, MA: Harvard University Asia Center, 2011), chap. 7; and Fedman, *Seeds of Control*, 132–138.

1. REEDS, FISH, TIMBER, AND DEFINING THE YALU BORDER

1. Ōsaki Mineto, *Ōryokkō: Man-Kan kokkyō jijō* (Tokyo: Maruzen, 1910), 1–2, inset.

2. See Seonmin Kim, *Ginseng and Borderland: Territorial Boundaries and Political Relations between Qing China and Chosŏn Korea, 1636–1912* (Berkeley: University of California Press, 2017), 140–151; Nianshen Song, *Making Borders in Modern East Asia: The Tumen River Demarcation, 1881–1919* (Cambridge, UK: Cambridge University Press, 2018); Alyssa M. Park, *Sovereignty Experiments: Korean Migrants and the Building of Borders in Northeast Asia, 1860–1945* (Ithaca, NY: Cornell University Press,

2019). The lack of interest in the Yalu is not just a feature of the English-language historiography. As noted by Zhang Zhongyue, scholars outside the United States have tended to devote more significant attention to the politics of the Tumen River boundary between China and Korea than the Yalu. Zhang Zhongyue, *Qing dai yi lai Yalu Jiang liuyu yimin yanjiu* (Jinan: Shandong renmin chubanshe, 2017), 1.

3. Song, *Making Borders in Modern East Asia*, 267.

4. Gao Jian-hua et al., "Sediment Transport in Yalu River Estuary," *Chinese Geographical Science* 13, no. 2 (2003): 157–163.

5. Yu Yunfeng, *Andong xian zhi*, vol. 1. Reprint in *Zhongguo fangzhi congshu: Dongbei difang*: di 18 hao (Taibei: Chengwen Chubanshe, 1974), 60–61.

6. "Kokkyō fukin tōsho sasu ni kansuru chōsa," National Archives of Korea, CJA0002277, 545–546.

7. "Ōryokkō ishū no shozoku ni kansuru keisō ikken: Dai-ikkan," Japan Center for Asian Historical Records [hereafter JACAR], B03041224100, 595–596.

8. "Kokkyō fukin tōsho sasu ni kansuru chōsa," 545.

9. Disputes over ownership of river islands had taken place in earlier periods, however. For a study of early seventeenth-century Ming-Chosŏn conflicts over Yalu River islands, see Jing Liu and Yan Piao, "Expansion, Contestation, and Boundary Making: Chosŏn Korea and Ming China's Border Relations over the Yalu River Region," *International Journal of Korean History* 25, no. 2 (August 2020): 105–142.

10. Kim Chŏng-ju, ed., *Chōsen tōchi shiryō* [hereafter abbreviated as *CTS*], vol 9: *Enkyō kankei* (Tōkyō: Kankoku Shiryō Kenkyūjo, 1970–1972), 69.

11. See, for example, *Chŏngjo sillok*, March 6, 1786 (CJ 21.03.06).

12. "Kokkyō fukin tōsho sasu ni kansuru chōsa: Kōsōhei," 548–549. For more on the broader dynamics of Qing-Chosŏn border interactions during this period, see Kim, *Ginseng and Borderland*.

13. For studies on the Han colonization of Manchuria, see James Reardon-Anderson, *Reluctant Pioneers: China's Northward Expansion, 1644–1937* (Stanford, CA: Stanford University Press, 2005).

14. "Kokkyō fukin tōsho sasu ni kansuru chōsa: Kōsōhei," 552.

15. Antō Shōkō Kōkai, *Antōshō no iseki* (Antō: Antō Shōkō Kōkai, 1942), 1, 8.

16. Antō Shōkō Kōkai, *Antōshō no iseki*, 14–15.

17. "Kōsōhei gaikyō," unpublished manuscript, University of California, Berkeley, library.

18. "Kokkyō fukin tōsho sasu ni kansuru chōsa," 546.

19. "Kōsōhei gaikyō."

20. *CTS*, 67.

21. "Kokkyō fukin tōsho sasu ni kansuru chōsa," 552.

22. For more on the politics of collaboration in protectorate-era Korea, see Yumi Moon, *Populist Collaborators: The Ilchinhoe and the Japanese Colonization of Korea, 1896–1910* (Ithaca, NY: Cornell University Press, 2013).

23. "Kokkyō fukin tōsho sasu ni kansuru chōsa," 553.

24. "Yalu Jiang xiayou zhang tan Huangcaoping wei cao bei Jinteng qiang yun," Archives of the Institute of Modern History, Academia Sinica, Waijiaobu: Chaoxiandang, 02-19-006-01-027.

25. Kuksa P'yŏnch'an Wiwŏnhoe, *T'onggambu munsŏ*, vol. 1, pt. 6, no. 12, "Kankoku shisei kaizen ni kansuru kyōgikai dai jūni kaigi roku." This and all other references to the *T'onggambu munsŏ*, hereafter abbreviated as *TM*, are from the National Institute of Korean History online database: http://db.history.go.kr/. Titles of individual entries are romanizations of the Korean titles assigned by the compilers, except in cases where a Japanese title is present, in which case a romanization of the Japanese is used.

26. *CTS*, 29.
27. For a detailed discussion of implications of Narita's 1906 survey of the lower Yalu, see O Pyŏng-han, "1906-nyŏn Ilbongun Andonghyŏn kunjŏngsŏ ŭi hagu chosa sŏnggyŏk kwa ŭiŭi," *Hanguk kŭnhyŏndaesa yŏn'gu* 80 (March 2017): 69–95.
28. *CTS*, 71–72.
29. *TM* 3:2:185, "Hwangchŏp'yŏng chugwŏn munje e kwanhan kŏn."
30. "Kankoku shisei kaizen ni kansuru kyōgikai."
31. *TM* 3:2:183, "Yongamp'o taean Hwangchŏp'yŏng wi yech'wigwŏn e kwanhan kŏn."
32. *CTS*, 90.
33. *CTS*, 90.
34. *TM* 4:5:7, "Hwangchŏp'yŏng kaltae yech'wigwŏn maesu kŏn."
35. *CTS*, 90.
36. *CTS*, 90.
37. Eiko Maruko Siniawer, *Ruffians, Yakuza, Nationalists: The Violent Politics of Modern Japan, 1860–1960* (Ithaca, NY: Cornell University Press, 2011), 1. For her discussion of *tairiku rōnin*, see pages 52–57.
38. *CTS*, 90.
39. *CTS*, 91.
40. *CTS*, 91–92.
41. "Kokkyō fukin tōsho sasu ni kansuru chōsa," 557.
42. "Qing cui Ri shi pai Han yuan yu difangguan huitong lü kan Huangcaoping wei tang jiexian," Archives of the Institute of Modern History, Academia Sinica, Waijiaobu: Chaoxiandang, 02-19-007-01-007.
43. *TM* 10:4:13, "Kōsōhei-tō mondai ni kansuru ken."
44. Yi Chusŏn, "Ōryōkkō chūshū o meguru Kan-Shin keisō to teikoku Nihon: Kōsōhei no jirei o chūshin ni," *Nihon rekishi* 763 (December 2011): 62; *TM* 4:7:174, "Hwangch'opyŏng ro suhwaek kongdong kwalli ha e hanbun yŏngyu cheŭi kŏn."
45. Yi, "Ōryōkkō chūshū o meguru kanshin keisō," 64
46. "Fengtian xing Sheng gongshu wei Andong tianshuigou wei tang bei Ri-ren zhanju chi Dongbiandao du chi ban shi," Liaoning Provincial Archives, JC010-01-032347.
47. "Qing cui Ri shi pai Han yuan yu difangguan huitong lü kan Huangcaoping wei tang jiexian."
48. "Hwangchŏp'yŏng kaltae yech'wigwŏn maesu kŏn."
49. For more on the Ilchinhoe's anti-tax campaigns, see Moon, *Populist Collaborators*, 194–240.
50. Yi, "Ōryōkkō chūshū o meguru Kan-Shin keisō," 64. Moon notes that Ilchinhoe interest in the island's reeds, including allegedly seizing reeds from Korean harvesters, began even earlier in 1905. See Moon, *Populist Collaborators*, 208.
51. *CTS*, 136–137.
52. *CTS*, 136–137.
53. *CTS*, 163.
54. *CTS*, 165–167.
55. Yi, "Ōryōkkō chūshū o meguru Kan-Shin keisō," 65–67.
56. *CTS*, 173–179; Chŏng Angi, "20 segi ch'oyŏp Hwangch'op'yŏng ŭi yŏngt'o punjaengsa yŏn'gu," *Yŏngt'o haeyang yŏn'gu* 13 (June 2017): 92.
57. *TM* 5:12:23, "Hwangch'opyŏng sojae nojŏn kyŏngyŏnggwan munje haegyŏl e kwanhan kŏn."
58. "Kokkyō fukin tōsho sasu ni kansuru chōsa," 560.
59. "Ōryokkō Ni-Shi kakkai mondai ikken fu tosenjō mondai, tōsho mondai, JACAR, B03041228700.

60. For an excellent summary of the Hwangch'op'yŏng dispute's Cold War-era resolution, see Chŏng Angi, "20 segi ch'oyŏp Hwangch'op'yŏng ŭi yŏngt'o punjaengsa yŏn'gu."

61. Chŏng Mungi, *Amnokkang ŏbo*, 1940, manuscript, Yonsei University Library.

62. For two essays on the expansion of Japan's marine fisheries, see William Tsutsui, "The Pelagic Empire: Reconsidering Japanese Expansion," and Micah Muscolino, "Fisheries Build Up on the Nation: Marine Environmental Encounters between Japan and China," in Ian Jared Miller et al., ed., *Japan at Nature's Edge: The Environmental Context of a Global Power* (Honolulu: University of Hawai'i Press, 2013), 21–38 and 56–72.

63. Chōsen Sōtokufu Suisan Shikenjō, *Ōryokkō no sakana* (Fuzan [Pusan]: Chōsen Sōtokufu Suisan Shikenjō, 1940), 2–3.

64. Minami Manshū Tetsudō Kabushiki Kaisha Chōsaka, *Manshū no suisangyō* (Dairen [Dalian]: Minami Manshū Tetsudō Kabushiki Kaisha, 1931), 57; "Chŏsonjŏk myŏngmul in baekŏ ŏro kaesi," *Maeil sinbo*, April 13, 1933.

65. Chang Suho, *Chosŏn sidae mal Ilbon ŭi ŏŏp ch'imt'alsa: kaehang esŏ 1910-yŏn kkaji Ilbon ŭi ŏŏp ch'imt'al e kwanhan yŏn'gu* (Seoul: Susan Kyŏngje Yŏn'guwŏn, 2011), 101–110.

66. "Ōryokkō gyogyō kankei zassan," JACAR, B11091940400.

67. Ōryokkō gyogyō kankei zassan," JACAR, B11091940400.

68. *TM* 10:19:35,"Kantei haken ni kansuru ken."

69. *TM* 10:19:34, "P'yŏngan nambuk-to yŏnan ŭi mirŏsŏn sanghwang pogo ich'ŏp."

70. "Yalu Jiang Huaren yuye shili zhi shuwen," *Huashang lianhe bao* 6 (1909): 3; "Yalu Jiang yuye zhi shiquan Fengtian," *Shen bao*, May 9, 1909.

71. Zhongyang yanjiuyuan jindaishi yanjiusuo, *Qing ji Zhong Ri Han guanxi shiliao* 10 (Taipei: Zhongyang yanjiuyuan jindaishi yanjiusuo, 1972), 6976.

72. "P'yŏngan-pukto, mirŏja ch'wich'e ŏmjung," *Maeil sinbo*, May 7, 1916.

73. *Yalu Jiang hua jie an cankao wenjian*, manuscript, Seoul National University Library.

74. Kanno Naoki, "Ōryokkō Saiboku Kōshi to Nihon no Manshū shinshutsu—shinrin shigen o meguru taigai kankei no hensen," *Kokushigaku* 172 (August 2000): 47.

75. S. C. M. Paine, "The Chinese Eastern Railway from the First Sino-Japanese War until the Russo-Japanese War," in Bruce A. Elleman and Stephen Kotkin, eds., *Manchurian Railways and the Opening of China: An International History* (Armonk, NY: M. E. Sharpe, 2010), 17.

76. Vladimir M. Vonliarliarskii, "Why Russia Went to War with Japan: The Story of the Yalu Concession," *Fortnightly Review*, May 1910, 821.

77. Vonliarliarskii, "Why Russia Went to War with Japan," 825–826.

78. Japanese lumbermen first arrived in the region following the Sino-Japanese War, and the first Japanese surveys of Korea's forests also took place during this same conflict. See David Fedman, *Seeds of Control: Japan's Empire of Forestry in Colonial Korea* (Seattle: University of Washington Press, 2020), 38.

79. Ōryokkō Saiboku Kōshi, ed., *Ōryokkō ringyōshi* (Antō [Dandong]: Ōryokkō Saiboku Kōshi, 1919), 46.

80. David Fedman, "The Saw and the Seed: Japanese Forestry in Colonial Korea, 1895–1945" (PhD diss., Stanford University, 2015), 190.

81. Naoki, "Ōryokkō Saiboku Kōshi to Nihon no Manshū shinshutsu," 57.

82. Fedman, "The Saw and the Seed," 182. For a detailed overview of the work of the Forest Management Bureau, see Fedman, *Seeds of Control*, 119–147.

83. Nishida Mataji and Nakamuta Gōrō, *Ōryokkō ryūiki shinrin sagyō chōsa fukumeisho* (Tokyo: Nōshōmushō Sanrinkyoku, 1905), 25.

84. Statistical Department of the Inspectorate General of Customs, *Decennial Reports on the Trade, Industries etc. of the Ports Open to Foreign Commerce and on the Condition and Development of the Treaty Port Provinces: 1902–1911, Volume 1: Northern and Yangtze Ports* (Shanghai: Statistical Department of the Inspectorate General of Customs, 1913), 103.

85. Antō Kōseikyoku, *Keizai kasen 'Ōryokkō' no bekken* (Antō [Andong]: Manshūkoku Kokumuin Kōtsūbu Antō Kōseikyoku, 1935), 8; Ishimaru Ginichi, *Kokkyō shashin daikan* (Shingishū [Sinŭiju]: Ōkō Nippōsha, 1929).

86. Nishida and Nakamuta, *Ōryokkō ryūiku shinrin sagyō chōsa fukumeisho* 24; "Ōryokkō Saiboku Kōshi gyōmu kansa hōkokusho," JACAR, B09040887600, 11.

87. Yumi Moon, "From Periphery to a Transnational Frontier: Popular Movements in the Northwestern Provinces, 1896–1904," in Sun Joo Kim, ed., *The Northern Region of Korea: History, Identity, and Culture* (Seattle: University of Washington Press, 2010), 204–205.

88. "Mokuhi jiken songai baishō," JACAR, C03020446700.

89. "Mokuhi jiken songai baishō."

90. Government-General of Chosen, *The Third Annual Report on Reforms and Progress in Korea (1909–1910)* (Seoul: Chōsen Sōtokufu, 1910), 12.

91. Guojia tushuguan gujiguan, ed., *Guojia tushuguan guancang Qingdai minguo diaocha baogao congkan* 30 (Beijing: Beijing Yanshan chubanshe, 2007), 460; Naoki, "Ōryokkō Saiboku Kōshi to Nihon no Manshū shinshutsu," 58.

92. *TM* 10:1:77, "Mokuha Ō Heitai no ken."

93. *TM* 10:20:45, "Ikadanorifu sōnan dai-kyuu kai hōkoku."

94. Antō-ken Shōkō Kaigisho, *Ōryokkō no mokuzai to Manshū ni okeru mokuzai jijō* (Antō [Dandong]: Antō-ken Shōkō Kaigisho, 1931), 30–31; Paek Ŭlsŏn, "Kankoku kokuyūrin ni okeru basshutsu, ikurin jigyō no tenkai katei ni kansuru shiteki kenkyū," *Hokkaidō Daigaku Nōgakubu enshūrin kenkyū hōkoku* 47, no. 1 (1990): 14. As David Fedman notes, the Forest Management Bureau would eventually train more Koreans in Japanese-style timber rafting techniques. Fedman, *Seeds of Control*, 125.

95. "Ōryokkō eirinsho kankei zassan Dai-ichi ken bunkatsu 3," JACAR, B0401 1183700.

96. *TM* 10:1:80, "Shinkoku mokuhi bōryoku tenmatsu."

97. "Yalu Jiang Ri ren she jing qing yan jie Ri shi zhuan ling chetui bing jiang Wang Bingtai shihui," Archives of the Institute of Modern History, Academia Sinica, Waijiaobu, 02-30-002-01-009.

98. "Memorandum on: The Yalu River Timber Concession," Box 115, "China: Yalu River Timber Concession, Memo On, 1921," Stanley Kuhl Hornbeck papers, 1900–1966, Hoover Institution Archives.

99. *TM* 10:20:48, "Amnokkang sangnyu esŏ ŭi Ch'ŏngin p'okhaeng e taehan chosa pogo kŏn"; *TM* 10:1:80, "Shinkoku mokuhi bōryoku tenmatsu."

100. *TM* 10:20:45, "Ikadanorifu sōnan dai-kyuu kai hōkoku."

101. *TM* 6:1:471, "Shinkoku hatō mokuha nado bōryoku jiken no genin ni tsuite."

102. "Yalu Jiang Riren she jing qing yan jie Ri shi zhuan ling chetui bing jiang Wang Bingtai shihui."

103. *TM* 10:20:45, "Ikadanorifu sōnan dai-kyuu kai hōkoku."

104. "Amnokkang hongsu sokpo," *Hwangsŏng sinmun*, July 31, 1909.

105. *TM* 10:1:80, "Shinkoku mokuhi bōryoku tenmatsu."

106. "Yalu Jiang linye weilai zhi fengchao," *Shen bao*, June 20, 1909.

107. "Disturbance on the Yalu," *Japan Times*, August 24, 1909; "Mokpa p'oktong," *Hwangsŏng sinmun*, August 24, 1909.

108. "The Questions between China And Japan," *Times* (London), August 3, 1909.

109. "Yalu Jiang Riben yinglinchang laoqu piao mu chun yong qiangying shouduan yi chou shanhou fangfa," Archives of the Institute of Modern History, Academia Sinica, Waijiaobu, 02-30-002-01-009.

110. *TM* 10:1:60, "Ōryokkō hyōryūboku seiri ni kanshi Tohendō dōtai to shōgi no ken."

111. "Mokuha yizen fuon," *Asahi shinbun*, September 1, 1909; "Timber-Feller's Disturbance," *Japan Times*, August 26, 1909.

112. Phrase borrowed from James Scott, *Weapons of the Weak: Everyday Forms of Peasant Resistance* (New Haven, CT: Yale University Press, 1985).

113. Naoki, "Ōryokkō Saiboku Kōshi to Nihon no Manshū shinshutsu," 58–59.

114. *TM* 10:1:60, "Ōryokkō hyōryūboku seiri ni kanshi Tohendō dōtai to shōgi no ken"; *The Third Annual Report on Reforms and Progress in Korea (1909–1910)*, 12.

2. BRIDGING THE YALU

1. General Staff, War Office, *The Russo-Japanese War: Reports from Officers Attached to the Japanese Forces in the Field*, vol. 1 (Tokyo: Ganesha Publishing, 2000), 53.

2. Railway Bureau Government-General of Chosen, *Report on the Construction of the Yalu River Bridge* (Ryūzan [Yongsan]: Chōsen Sōtokufu Tetsudōkyoku, 1914), 1.

3. "Shuchō: Man-Sen no renraku naru," *Chōsen*, December 1911, 12.

4. "Lun Zhongguo wei Chaoxian shi bu ke bu yu Riben yi zhan," *Shen bao*, July 21, 1894.

5. *Qing Guangxu chao Zhong Ri jiaoshe shiliao* (Beijing: Gugong bowuyuan, 1932), vol. 21, 37.

6. *Qing Guangxu chao Zhong Ri jiaoshe shiliao*, vol. 22, 6.

7. *Qing Guangxu chao Zhong Ri jiaoshe shiliao*, vol. 20, 15.

8. *Qing Guangxu chao Zhong Ri jiaoshe shiliao*, vol. 21, 37.

9. Kawada Etsu, ed., *Kindai Nihon sensōshi: Nisshin, Nichi-Ro sensō* (Tokyo: Dōdai Keizai Konwakai, 1995), 213.

10. Stewart Lone, *Japan's First Modern War: Army and Society in the Conflict with China, 1894–1895* (New York: St. Martin's Press, 1994), 38.

11. Yabuki Shūichi, "Ōryokkō kakyō oyobi wataribune shōhō," Japan Center for Asian Historical Records [hereafter JACAR], C0606203920, 233.

12. Yabuki, "Ōryokkō kakyō oyobi wataribune shōhō," 218.

13. Yabuki, "Ōryokkō kakyō oyobi wataribune shōhō," 216.

14. Kawada, *Kindai Nihon sensōshi*, 213–214.

15. Shimizu Yoshihiro, *Shintai gunjin yōbun* (Osaka: Hamamoto Meishōdō, 1895), 194–195; Hattori Seiichi, *Tsūzoku seishin senki* (Tokyo: Tōkyō Tosho Shuppan, 1897), 97–99; "Brave Japanese Soldiers," *Aspen* (Colorado) *Daily Times*, January 31, 1895.

16. Hattori, *Tsūzoku seishin senki*, 97–99.

17. Yabuki, "Ōryokkō kakyō oyobi wataribune shōhō," 228.

18. Lone, *Japan's First Modern War*, 75–77.

19. "Ryūhō ni taisuru Ōryokkō kakyō sagyō," *Asahi shinbun*, February 13–15, 1895.

20. "Ryūhō ni taisuru Ōryokkō kakyō sagyō."

21. "Ryūhō ni taisuru Ōryokkō kakyō sagyō."

22. Richard Harving Davis et al., *The Russo-Japanese War: A Photographic and Descriptive Review of the Great Conflict in the Far East* (New York: P. F. Collier & Son, 1904), 2.

23. John W. Steinberg, "Operational Overview," in John W. Steinberg et al., *The Russo-Japanese War in Global Perspective: World War Zero* (Leiden: Brill, 2005), 110–112.

24. Kawada, *Kindai Nihon sensōshi*, 486.
25. "Ōryokkō kakyō no shukō," *Tōkyō Asahi shinbun*, May 7, 1904.
26. General Staff, War Office, *The Russo-Japanese War*, 53.
27. General Staff, War Office, *The Russo-Japanese War*, 53.
28. General Staff, War Office, *The Russo-Japanese War*, 53.
29. General Staff, War Office, *The Russo-Japanese War*, 54.
30. General Staff, War Office, *The Russo-Japanese War*, 54.
31. Mishima Sōsen, *Nichi-Ro gekisen Ōryokkō* (Tokyo: Kinkōdō Shoseki, 1904), 101.
32. General Staff, War Office, *The Russo-Japanese War*, 39.
33. Etsu, *Kindai Nihon sensōshi*, 486.
34. Tamon Jirō, *Tamon Jirō Nichi-Ro sensō nikki* (Tokyo: Fuyō Shobō, 1980), 36.
35. Mizokami Sadao, *Nichi-Ro sensō jūgunki: gun'i no jinchū nikki* (Kyoto: Shibunkaku Shuppan, 2004), 41.
36. Steinberg, "Operational Overview," 110.
37. Steinberg, "Operational Overview," 112.
38. "Abyŏng p'oksang," *Hwangsŏng sinmun*, May 11, 1904.
39. Jack London, "The Yellow Peril," https://www.marxists.org/archive/london/revolution/ch12.htm (accessed September 2, 2023).
40. Chōsen Sōtokufu Tetsudōkyoku, *Ōryokkō kyōryō kōji gaikyō* (Keijō [Seoul]: Chōsen Sōtokufu Tetsudōkyoku, 1911), 3.
41. For a detailed study of the diplomatic processes leading up to the conclusion of the protectorate treaty and the later 1910 annexation of Korea, see Peter Duus, *The Abacus and the Sword: The Japanese Penetration of Korea, 1895–1910* (Berkeley: University of California Press, 1998).
42. Chōsen Sōtokufu Tetsudōkyoku, *Ōryokkō kyōryō kōji hōkoku* (Keijō [Seoul]: Chōsen Sōtokufu, 1912), 1.
43. "Jian zhu Yalu Jiang tieqiao zhi guanxi," *Wanguo shangye yuebao* 14 (1909): 57.
44. For a few examples of preexisting scholarly literature on Japanese colonial railways, see Yoshihisa Tak Matsusaka, *The Making of Japanese Manchuria, 1904–1932* (Cambridge, MA: Harvard University Asia Center, 2001); and Chŏng Chaejŏng, *Ilche ch'imnyak kwa Han'guk ch'ŏlto: 1892–1945* (Seoul: Seoul Taehakkyo Ch'ulp'anbu, 1999).
45. Duus, *The Abacus and the Sword*.
46. *Shingishū shi* (Osaka: Shōbunkan Insatsujo, 1911), 8.
47. Emer O'Dwyer, *Significant Soil: Settler Colonialism and Japan's Urban Empire in Manchuria* (Cambridge, MA: Harvard University Asia Center, 2015), 74.
48. "Nihon teikoku no kokubō hōshin," JACAR, C14061024600.
49. Nagano Fukai, "Ōryokkō kyōryō, Chōsen hoteru oyobi Keijō eki no kenzō ni tsuite," *Chōsen*, October 1, 1923, 223.
50. Wada Takashi, *Shingishū shi* (Shingishū [Sinŭiju]: Shimada Sōbunkan, 1911), 9–10.
51. For a discussion of Sinŭiju's history as well as prominence in the regional timber trade, see David Fedman, *Seeds of Control: Japan's Empire of Forestry in Colonial Korea* (Seattle: University of Washington Press, 2020), 128–131.
52. Yu Yunfeng, *Andong xian zhi*, vol. 1. Reprint in *Zhongguo fangzhi congshu. Dongbei difang*: di 18 hao (Taibei: Chengwen Chubanshe, 1974), 69–70.
53. Antō-ken Shōgyō Kaigisho, *Antō shi* (Antō [Andong]: Antō-ken Shōgyō Kaigisho, 1920), 2.
54. "Lü zhu Andong Ri-ren zhi zeng jia," *Shen bao*, December 7, 1906.
55. Railway Bureau, *Report on the Construction of the Yalu River Bridge*, 3.
56. Railway Bureau, *Report on the Construction of the Yalu River Bridge*, 5–6.

57. Railway Bureau, *Report on the Construction of the Yalu River Bridge*, 7–8.
58. Railway Bureau, *Report on the Construction of the Yalu River Bridge*, 7.
59. Asano Shunkō et al., *Hazamagumi hyakunenshi*, vol. 1 (Tokyo: Kabushiki Kaisha Hazamagumi, 1989), 172.
60. Railway Bureau, *Report on the Construction of the Yalu River Bridge*, 4.
61. Railway Bureau, *Report on the Construction of the Yalu River Bridge*, 16. This report also refers to the bridge's trusses as "girders," though the two terms have different meanings in contemporary engineering parlance.
62. "Ōryokkō tetsudō kakyōsetsu keikaku ni kansuru ken," JACAR, C03027073100, 526.
63. For a full English-language version of the 1903 treaty, see John Van Antwerp MacMurray, ed., *Treaties and Agreements with and Concerning China, 1894–1919* (New York: Oxford University Press, 1921), 423–432.
64. First articulated in US Secretary of State John Hay's 1899 "Open Door Note," the "Open Door Policy" referred to the proposal to keep China open on an equal basis to foreign trade rather than dividing the country into separate spheres of foreign interest. On the Open Door Policy and its consequences for US-China relations, see Gordon H. Chang, *Fateful Ties: A History of America's Preoccupation with China* (Cambridge, MA: Harvard University Press, 2015), 103–109.
65. This discussion of this controversy is derived from the account provided in John Espy Merrill, "American Official Reactions to the Domestic Policies of Japan in Korea, 1905–1910" (PhD diss., Stanford University, 1954), 247–259.
66. Merrill, "American Official Reactions," 252.
67. Railway Bureau, *Report on the Construction of the Yalu River Bridge*, 4.
68. Merrill, "American Official Reactions," 253.
69. Ōryokkō tekkō sekkei ni kansuru ken," November 20, 1908, in *Kōbun zassan: Meiji 41-nen, dai-23 ken*. National Archives of Japan Digital Archive, https://www.digital.archives.go.jp/DAS/meta/listPhoto?KEYWORD=&LANG=eng&BID=F00000000000000009783&ID=M0000000000000246978&TYPE=&NO=.
70. Railway Bureau, *Report on the Construction of the Yalu River Bridge*, 5.
71. Sigatsu sanjūnichi [April 30, 1909], Koike Shin'ichi shi shiryō, Kanagawa Prefectural Archives.
72. July 27, 1909, Koike Shin'ichi shi shiryō, Kanagawa Prefectural Archives.
73. December 26, 1908, and September 1, 1909, Koike Shin'ichi shi shiryō, Kanagawa Prefectural Archives.
74. These laborers were mobilized by a number of different contractors, the largest of which was Hazama-gumi, a Japanese civil works construction company heavily involved in the earlier construction of railroad routes during the Russo-Japanese War. For a detailed description of the relationship between the Yalu River bridge construction project and Hazama-gumi, see the company's official history: Asano, *Hazamagumi hyakunenshi*, 166–185.
75. Railway Bureau, *Report on the Construction of the Yalu River Bridge*, 21.
76. Railway Bureau, *Report on the Construction of the Yalu River Bridge*, 38.
77. Chōsen Sōtokufu Tetsudōkyoku, *Ōryokkō kyōryō kōji hōkoku*, 61.
78. An early, if not the earliest, example of the usage of this technology to construct a railroad bridge in China is the 1894 completion of the Luan River Railroad Bridge in Hebei. Dou Baogao, "Zhongguo xiujian zuizao de tieluqiao: Luan He Daqiao," *Guangmingwang*, http://history.gmw.cn/2011-11/10/content_2943669.htm (accessed June 22, 2022).
79. Railway Bureau, *Report on the Construction of the Yalu River Bridge*, 38. For a brief description of the construction of the Liao River bridge, see "The Liao River Railway Bridge, Manchuria," *Engineering*, January 21, 1910, 71–73.

80. Railway Bureau, *Report on the Construction of the Yalu River Bridge*, 1.
81. Railway Bureau, *Report on the Construction of the Yalu River Bridge*, 58.
82. Railway Bureau, *Report on the Construction of the Yalu River Bridge*, 60.
83. Mark Driscoll, *Absolute Erotic, Absolute Grotesque: The Living, Dead, and Undead in Japan's Imperialism, 1895–1945* (Durham, NC: Duke University Press, 2010), 54.
84. Railway Bureau, *Report on the Construction of the Yalu River Bridge*, 59.
85. Railway Bureau, *Report on the Construction of the Yalu River Bridge*, 68.
86. Chōsen Sōtokufu Tetsudōkyoku, *Ōryokkō kyōryō kōji hōkoku*, 171.
87. Chōsen Sōtokufu Tetsudōkyoku, *Ōryokkō kyōryō kōji hōkoku*, 170.
88. Jūgatsu nijūrokunichi [October 26, 1909], Nikki: Jū Meiji 42 nen 7 gatsu 11 nichi itaru onaji 43 nen 12 gatsu 31 nichi. Koike Shin'ichi shi shiryō, Kanagawa Prefectural Archives.
89. Railway Bureau, *Report on the Construction of the Yalu River Bridge*, 111. This was the wage given to caisson laborers during the first months of bridge construction, August–December 1909. Afterward they were paid only .450 yen for ten hours of work.
90. Railway Bureau, *Report on the Construction of the Yalu River Bridge*, 59.
91. Railway Bureau, *Report on the Construction of the Yalu River Bridge*, 4.
92. Railway Bureau, *Report on the Construction of the Yalu River Bridge*, 113.
93. Guo Tingyi et al., *Qing ji Zhong Ri Han guanxi shiliao*, vol. 10 (Taibei Shi: Zhongyang yanjiuyuan jindaishi yanjiusuo, 1972), 6997.
94. Chōsen Sōtokufu Tetsudōkyoku, *Chōsen testudōshi* (Keijō [Seoul]: Chōsen Sōtokufu Tetsudōkyoku, 1929), 470.
95. "The Yalu Bridge and China's Protest," *Japan Times*, January 30, 1910.
96. "Ōryōkko kakyō ni kansuru nisshin obegaki," JACAR, B13090915800.
97. Chōsen Sōtokufu Tetsudōkyoku, *Ōryokkō kyōryō kōji hōkoku*, 62.
98. Railway Bureau, *Report on the Construction of the Yalu River Bridge*, 32, 75.
99. Railway Bureau, *Report on the Construction of the Yalu River Bridge*, 104.
100. Railway Bureau, *Report on the Construction of the Yalu River Bridge*, 96–97.
101. Railway Bureau, *Report on the Construction of the Yalu River Bridge*, 113.
102. *Andong Xian zhi*, 60–61.
103. Railway Bureau, *Report on the Construction of the Yalu River Bridge*, 5; Chōsen Sōtokufu Tetsudōkyoku, *Ōryokkō kyōryō kōji hōkoku*, 4.
104. Chōsen Sōtokufu Tetsudōkyoku, *Ōryokkō kyōryō kōji hōkoku*, 293.
105. Chōsen Sōtokufu Tetsudōkyoku, *Ōryokkō kyōryō kōji hōkoku*, 295.
106. Chōsen Sōtokufu Tetsudōkyoku, *Ōryokkō kyōryō kōji hōkoku*, 253.
107. "Amnokkang chŏlgyo ibo nyŏn pisa," *Tonga ilbo*, July 15, 1934.
108. "Amnokkanggyo kaet'ongsik," *Maeil sinbo*, November 1, 1911.
109. "Kaet'ongsik yŏhŭng gwa kisaeng," *Maeil sinbo*, November 1, 1911.
110. Railway Bureau, *Report on the Construction of the Yalu River Bridge*, 1.
111. Jūichigatsu ichinichi [November 1, 1911], Jūyō nikki: Meiji 44 nen. In a later diary entry, Koike Shin'ichi also describes receiving a commemorative gold watch as part of the completion festivities. Jūichigatsu yokka [November 3, 1911].
112. For more on the rhetoric of "boundary breaking" centered on infrastructural projects like the Yalu River Railway Bridge and its promotion in imperial travel literature, see Kate McDonald, *Placing Empire: Travel and the Social Imagination in Imperial Japan* (Berkeley: University of California Press, 2017), 83–102.
113. MacMurray, *Treaties and Agreements with and Concerning China, 1894–1919*, 914–916.
114. Kate L. McDonald, "The Boundaries of the Interesting: Itineraries, Guidebooks, and Travel in Imperial Japan" (PhD diss., University of California, San Diego, 2011), 39–41.

115. Shingishū Zeikan, *Shingishū minato ippan* (Shingishū [Sinŭiju]: Shingishū Zeikan, 1932), 3.
116. O'Dwyer, *Significant Soil*, 75.
117. Kanno Naoki, "Chōsen-Manshū hōmen kara mita Terauchi Masatake zō no ichi danmen: Ōryokkō Saiboku Kōshi nado to no kankei o tsūjite," *Higashi Ajia kindaishi* 16 (March 2013): 97–99.
118. O'Dwyer, *Significant Soil*, 120.
119. Heian Hokudō Keisatsu Buchō, "Keppyōki keibi ni kansuru ken," Heihoku hi 997 gō. National Archives of Korea, CJA0002478.
120. Nakamura Mika, "Shingishū no mitsuyu," *Keimu ihō*, January 1935, 94–95.

3. SEASONS OF YALU RIVER BORDER POLICING

1. Heian Hokudō Keisatsubu, ed., *Kokkyō keibi* (Shingishū [Sinŭiju]: Heian Keishō Henshūbu, 1936), 47; "Keppyōki keibi ni kansuru ken," National Archives of Korea, CJA0002478.
2. Kim Ilsŏng, *Segi wa tŏburŏ*, vol. 6 (Pyongyang: Chosŏn Nodongdang Ch'ulp'ansa, 1995), 5.
3. "Liaoning Sheng zhengfu wei Ji'an xian cheng bao xia fang buzhi qing xing shi," Liaoning Provincial Archives, JC010-01-018956.
4. Kosako Shintarō, *Kokkyō no hana* (Shingishū [Sinŭiju]: Shingishū Insatsu Kabushiki Kaisha, 1936), 1.
5. See Matsuda Toshihiko, *Nihon no Chōsen shokuminchi shihai to keisatsu: 1905-1945-nen* (Tokyo: Azekura Shobō, 2009), 322–341; and Erik Esselstrom, *Crossing Empire's Edge: Foreign Ministry Police and Japanese Expansionism in Northeast Asia* (Honolulu: University of Hawai'i Press, 2009), 65–91.
6. Murakami Masatsugu, *Manshūkoku oyobi shūhen ni okeru shokasen no tōketsu* (Dairen [Dalian]: Minami Manshū Tetsudō Kabushiki Kaisha Chōsakyoku, 1944), 64–67.
7. Heian Hokudō Keisatsubu, *Kokkyō keibi*, 167.
8. Kobayashi Kaneshige, *Kokkyō to sono keibi* (Keijō [Seoul]: Chōsen Sōtokufu Keibi Engōkai, 1936), 19.
9. The response of the colonial Korean government and military police to a "mounted bandit" raid in 1915 on a Yalu River Timber Company office in the Chinese border county of Changbai is analyzed in Kanno Naoki, "Chōsen-Manshū hōmen kara mita Terauchi Masatake zō no ichi danmen: Ōryokkō Saiboku Kōshi nado to no kankei o tsūjite," *Higashi Ajia kindaishi* 16 (March 2013): 97–113.
10. Nianshen Song, *Making Borders in Modern East Asia: Tumen River Demarcation, 1881–1919* (Cambridge, UK: Cambridge University Press, 2018), 226–232.
11. For more on border policing in the 1910s, see Matsuda Toshihiko, "1910 nendai ni okeru Chōsen Sōtokufu no kokkyō keibi seisaku," *Jinbun Gakuhō* 106 (April 2015): 53–79.
12. For a full translated text of the declaration, see Yŏngho Ch'oe, Peter H. Lee, and Wm. Theodore de Bary, eds., *Sources of Korean Tradition, Volume II: From the Sixteenth to the Twentieth Centuries* (New York: Columbia University Press, 2000), 336–339.
13. The most comprehensive examination of the March First Movement in English remains Frank P. Baldwin Jr.'s 1969 dissertation, "The March First Movement: Korean Challenge and Japanese Response" (PhD diss., Columbia University, 1969).
14. Chong-Sik Lee, *The Politics of Korean Nationalism* (Berkeley: University of California Press, 1963), 157–162.
15. Xu Wanmin, *Zhong Han guangxi shi: jindai juan* (Beijing: Shehui kexue wenxian chubanshe, 1996), 200–201; Erik Esselstrom, *Crossing Empire's Edge*, 65. Esselstrom

also discusses Sino-Japanese conflicts over the policing of Korean rebels (with a particular focus on the role of the Japanese Foreign Ministry Police in Kando) in chap. 3 of his book. See Esselstrom, *Crossing Empire's Edge*, 65–91.

16. Matsuda, *Nihon no Chōsen shokuminchi shihai to keisatsu*, 322–341.

17. "Kakai kaihyō ni okeru futei kōdō ni kansuru ken," Japan Center for Asian Historical Records [hereafter JACAR], C06031159300.

18. "Yalu Jiang Ri ting youyi," *Dagong bao*, April 30, 1920.

19. For more about Zhang's complex relationship with the Japanese, see Chi Man Kwong, *War and Geopolitics in Interwar Manchuria: Zhang Zuolin and the Fengtian Clique during the Northern Expedition* (Boston: Leiden, 2017), 77–78.

20. Zhongguo bianjiang shi di yanjiu zhongxin, *Dongbei bianjiang dang'an xuanji* [hereafter *DBDX*] (Guilin: Guangxi shifan daxue chubanshe, 2007), 8:267–270.

21. *DBDX*, 8:289–295.

22. China: The Maritime Customs, *Decennial Reports, 1922–1931* (Shanghai, 1933), 270; Tani Mitsuyo, *Manshū kasenshi* (Shinkyō [Changchun]: Manshū Jijō Annaijo, 1940), 260.

23. In the words of one German geographer who traveled to northern Korea in 1933, the Yalu was "a very busy river, despite its adverse natural conditions and its boundary character." Hermann Lautensach, *Korea: A Geography Based on the Author's Travels and Literature*, trans. Katherine and Eckart Dege (Berlin: Springer Verlag, 1988), 248.

24. "Liaoning Sheng zhengfu wei Andong shangbu gonganju chang chengbao jieshou ji chouban dongji lian fang deng shi," Liaoning Provincial Archives, JC010-01-001142.

25. "Kakai kaihyō ni okeru futei kōdō ni kansuru ken."

26. "Yalu Jiang shang mingwu fei chuan kaishi yunhang," *Shengjing shibao*, April 8, 1938.

27. Kinnosuke Adachi, *Manchuria: A Survey* (New York: R. M. McBride, 1925), 2.

28. While the exact origins of the song are unclear, Yuasa Chikusanjin, a scholar of ballads from the Meiji to the early Showa period, suggests that the tune did in fact originate among the Yalu timber raftsmen depicted in the song's lyric. Yuasa also notes the role of *kisaeng* and other pleasure district workers in popularizing the song, a fact also supported by a 1926 *Tonga ilbo* article that describes the song as one often sung by *kisaeng*. See Yuasa Chikusanjin, *Kōta yawa* (Tokyo: Shinsakusha, 1924), 79–120; "Ponŭn ttaero . . ." *Tonga ilbo*, August 8, 1926.

29. Chōsen Sōtokufu Keimukyoku, *Kōtō keisatsu kankei nenpyō* (Keijō [Seoul]: Chōsen Sōtokufu Keimukyoku, 1930), 145.

30. "Ubu majŏkdan ch'ulhyŏn pŏlbu samyŏng ŭl sasal," *Maeil sinbo*, June 1, 1928.

31. Gondō Kyūshū, "Seibu kokkyō o mawarite," *Keimu ihō*, June 1923, 31.

32. Gondō, "Seibu kokkyō o mawarite." For more on Tada, a larger-than-life figure who was referred to by contemporaries as the "governor-general of the border" (J: *kokkyō sōtoku*), see David Fedman, *Seeds of Control: Japan's Empire of Forestry in Colonial Korea* (Seattle: University of Washington Press, 2020), 131.

33. Tani Mitsuyo, *Manshū kasenshi*, 268.

34. "Kukkyŏng iltae e majŏk toryang," *Tonga ilbo*, May 27, 1928.

35. "3: Chōsen kokkyō bazoku shūgeki jiken," JACAR, B13081174600.

36. "Chaetŭng ch'ongdok ilhaeng sŭpkyŏk sagŏn hubo," *Tonga ilbo*, May 21, 1924.

37. Kim Chŏngju, ed., *Chōsen tōchi shiryō 9: Enkyō kankei* [hereafter *CTS*] (Tōkyō: Kankoku Shiryō Kenkyūjo, 1970–1972), 598–600.

38. *CTS*, 602.

39. *DBDX*, 38:113–118.

40. "Chosŏn tongnip undong ŭi mudanhwa," *Tonga ilbo*, August 18, 1920.

41. Kobayashi, *Kokkyō to sono keibi*, inset.

42. Andō Kesaichi, "Heihoku keisatsu gaikyō," *Keimu ihō*, July 1923, 23.
43. Robert Baird, "A Journey Down the Yalu" (manuscript), Baird Family Papers, National Archives of the Presbyterian Church, USA.
44. Chōsen Sōtokufu Keimukyoku, *Chōsen keisatsu no gaiyō* (Keijō [Seoul]: Chōsen Sōtokufu Keimukyoku, 1925), 118.
45. Susukida Yoshitomo, "Kokkyō ni okeru keisatsukan no seikatsu," *Keimu ihō*, August 1923, 35.
46. Chōsen Sōtokufu Keimukyoku, *Chōsen keisatsu no gaiyō*, 118–119.
47. Lautensach, *Korea: A Geography*, 240.
48. Soldiers from the Nineteenth and Twentieth Divisions of the Japanese Imperial Army, known as "border garrisons" (*kokkyō shubitai*), numbered 2,068 as of 1926. See Kang Ch'angil, "Chōsen shinryaku no butsuriteki kiban to shite no Chōsengun," in Nikkan Rekishi Kyōdō Kenkyūkai, ed., *Nikkan rekishi kyōdō kenkyū hōkokusho: dai 3 bunka hen gekan* (Tokyo: Nikkan Rekishi Kyōdō Kenkyūkai, 2005), 422. For more on the Japanese Army in Korea, see Tobe Ryōichi's contribution to the same volume, "Chōsen chūton Nihongun no jitsuzō: chian, bōei, teikoku," in *Nikkan rekishi kyōdō kenkyū hōkokusho: dai 3 bunka hen gekan*: 387–409.
49. Heian Hokudō Keisatsubu, *Kokkyō keibi*, 214.
50. MS sei, "Hanmoki ni okeru kokkyō hizoku no sōsa ni tsuite," *Keimu ihō*, July 1931, 98.
51. Ch'oe Chŏnghwa, *Sakchu kunji* (Seoul: Sakchu Kunminhoe, 1991), 249.
52. Ch'ae Yŏngguk, *1920-yŏndae huban Manju chiyŏk hangil mujang t'ujaeng* (Ch'ungch'ŏng-namdo Ch'ŏnan-si: Tongnip Kinyŏmgwan Han'guk Tongnip Undongsa Yŏn'guso, 2007), 17.
53. Wiwŏn Kunji P'yŏnch'an Wiwŏnhoe, *Wiwŏn kunji* (Seoul: Wiwŏn Kunji P'yŏnch'an Wiwŏnhoe, 1971), 90–92.
54. Tani, *Manshū kasenshi*, 259.
55. Yi Sŭngch'un, *Ōryokkō jōryū shinrin shakubatsu jigyō annai* (Hu'chang: Ōryokkō Jōryū Shinrin Shakubatsu Jigyō Annai Hakkōsho, 1931), 76.
56. Heian Hokudō Keisatsubu, *Kokkyō keibi*, 87.
57. "Amnokkang yŏnan e hou," *Tonga ilbo*, August 31, 1928.
58. "Sunsa il myŏng iksa," *Tonga ilbo*, September 2, 1921.
59. "Fengtian Sheng gongshu wei Ya Hun liang jiang shui shang jingju cheng qing ba kuan xiu bei shui chong mo ge ju fang bing song ju dan shi," Liaoning Provincial Archives, JC010-01-018581.
60. "Yalu Jiang Ri jing han tang zhi pao huo shen," *Yishi bao*, August 26, 1923.
61. For more on the relationship between migrant communities' opium cultivation and banditry, see Pak Kang, "1920 nyŏndae majŏk kwa Hanin, kŭrigo ap'yŏn," *Han'guk minjok undongsa yŏn'gu* 88 (2016): 41–80.
62. "Ch'ulmol musang han majŏktan yuksip yŏ dongp'o napgŏ," *Tonga ilbo*, August 20, 1928.
63. "Changbaek-hyŏn e majŏk Chosŏnch'on sŭpkyŏk," *Tonga ilbo*, August 23, 1928.
64. Lowest temperatures were -43.6 degrees Celsius recorded for winter, compared to 38 degrees Celsius for summer. Lautensach, *Korea: A Geography*, 91.
65. Kodama Toshimitsu, *Natsukashi no Nihon uta zenshū* (Kagoshima-shi: Chiran Tokkō Irei Kenshōkai, 1972), 338.
66. Heian Hokudō Keisatsubu, *Kokkyō keibi*, 85.
67. Chōsen Sōtokufu Keimukyoku, *Kōtō keisatsu kankei nenpyō*.
68. Kosako Shintarō, *Kokkyō no hana*, 5–18.
69. "Chosŏn tongnip undong ŭi mudanhwa" and "Dong sheng teyue tongxin," *Yishi bao*, May 14, 1921; for a detailed analysis of depictions of "rebellious Koreans" in

Japanese media, including fictional works, see Andre Haag, "Fear and Loathing in Imperial Japan: The Cultures of Korean Peril, 1919-1923" (PhD diss., Stanford University, 2013).
70. Lee, *The Politics of Korean Nationalism*, 157-162. As Lee describes, other armed nationalist groups also fled from Kando to Siberia and northern Manchuria.
71. Heian Hokudō Keisatsubu, *Kokkyō keibi*, 213.
72. "Suksu chung toryŏn sagyŏk," *Tonga ilbo*, August 14, 1924.
73. "Susaektae ch'uldong ŭl chŏtae, *Tonga ilbo*, September 4, 1925.
74. Totsukawa Hanzō, "Shakai bidan: kokkyō keibi no jojōfu," *Kingu*, January 1, 1929, 190-199.
75. Ueda Gunji, *Kokkyō nihyaku ri* (Keijō [Seoul]: Kokkyō Nihyaku Ri Hakkōjo, 1929), 114-115.
76. "Yubunyŏ rŭl nŭngyok, kanggan koso haettago satok," *Tonga ilbo*, August 15, 1924; "Kanggye sagŏn e taehayŏ," *Tonga ilbo*, August 17, 1924.
77. "Mi jian," Archives of the Institute of Modern History, Academia Sinica, 03-33-037-02-036.
78. Xu, *Zhong Han guangxi shi*, 200-201.
79. Erik Esselstrom further delineates the background and consequences of this agreement for relationships between the Government-General of Korea and Japan's Foreign Ministry, the latter operating a large body of consular police in southern Manchuria. See Esselstrom, *Crossing Empire's Edge*, 87-90.
80. For a discussion of the internecine politics of the Korean nationalist movement in southern Manchuria, including the Ch'amŭibu organization that orchestrated the 1924 Saitō Makoto raid, see Sin Chubaek, *Manju chiyŏk Hanin ŭi minjok undongsa, 1920-45: minjokchuŭi undong mit sahoejuŭi undong kyeyŏl ŭi taerip kwa yŏndae rŭl chungsim ŭro* (Seoul: Asea Munhwa, 2002).
81. Kobayashi, *Kokkyō to sono keibi*, inset.
82. "Ōryokkō Ni-Shi kakai mondai ikken," JACAR, B03041228400. Another prominent incident of post-Mitsuya Sino-Japanese tensions came from the Japanese Foreign Ministry's ultimately unsuccessful attempt to open a subconsulate along the Chinese side of the upper Yalu River in Mao'ershan. For more on this episode, see Wang Ju, "1927 nen no iwayuru Rinkō jiken ni kansuru shohoteki bunseki," *Chūgoku kenkyū geppō* 401 (July 1981): 39-58.
83. "Liaoning Sheng zhengfu wei bei zhen ji ge xian choubang xia fang chou bian xiang tuan lian fang banfa shi," Liaoning Provincial Archives, JC010-01-021826.
84. Chōsen Sōtokufu Keimukyoku, *Zaiman Senjin to Shina kanken: tsuketari Manshū ni okeru hainichi undō* (Keijō [Seoul]: Chōsen Sōtokufu Keimukyoku, 1930), 153-155.
85. Kōno Yahei, *Kokkyō keibi kinenshū* (Shingishū [Sinŭiju]: Heian Keishō Henshūbu, 1937), 11.
86. Chōsen Sōtokufu Kansokujo, *Chōsen Sōtokufu Kansokujo kishō gonenhō: Shōwa gannen yori Shōwa 5-nen ni itaru* (Zinsen [Inch'ŏn]: Chōsen Sōtokufu Kansokujo, 1931), 49.
87. Heian Hokudō Keisatsubu, *Kokkyō keibi*, 56-60.
88. Yi Tusan, "Yi si: yedu Yalu Jiang," *Dongfang zhanyou*, May 1939, 10-11.
89. "Yŏhaeng chŭngmyŏng ŭi p'yeji chujang hanora (sang)," *Tonga ilbo*, July 9, 1921.
90. "Amnokkang ŭi ch'wich'e kyŏnghok," *Chosŏn ilbo*, January 19, 1923.
91. Barbara J. Brooks, *Japan's Imperial Diplomacy: Consuls, Treaty Ports, and War in China, 1895-1938* (Honolulu: University of Hawai'i Press, 2000), 143.
92. Heian Hokudō Keisatsubu, *Kokkyō keibi*, 35.
93. Heian Hokudō Keisatsubu, *Kokkyō keibi*, 35.

94. On the politics of Chinese collaboration and nationalism immediately following the Manchurian Incident, see Rana Mitter, *The Manchurian Myth: Nationalism, Resistance, and Collaboration in Modern China* (Berkeley: University of California Press, 2000).

95. For analysis and primary documents on the Chinese Communist Party's role in the Manchurian guerrilla movement, see Dongbei kang Ri lianjun shiliao bianxiezu, *Dongbei kang Ri lianjun shiliao*, vols. 1–2 (Beijing: Zhonggong dangshi shiliao chubanshe, 1987).

96. Chong-Sik Lee, *Revolutionary Struggle in Manchuria: Chinese Communism and Soviet Interest, 1922–1945* (Berkeley: University of California Press, 1983), 214.

97. "Apkang pingsang ŭi tonghaeng kyŏnggye," *Tonga ilbo*, January 9, 1922.

98. Noritake, *Ōryōkkō*, 162.

99. "Amnok kang ch'aebing nyang chŭngga," *Maeil sinbo*, March 6, 1931.

100. Mainichi Shinbunsha, *Nihon shokuminchishi 1: Chōsen* (Tokyo: Mainichi Shinbunsha, 1978), 205.

101. "Keppyōki keibi ni kansuru ken."

102. Nippon Hōsō Kyōkai, "Manshū kara no hikiage taikensha: Takamura Eizō-san." Sensō shōgen aakaibusu. https://www2.nhk.or.jp/archives/movies/?id=D0001130003_000 001 (accessed September 5, 2023).

103. "Keppyōki kokkyō keibi ni kansuru ken," National Archives of Korea, CJA0002489.

104. Ch'oe Kiju, "Kokkyō daiissen kinmu chū no koto," *Heihoku keishō*, August 1, 1933, 111.

105. "Shōwa nana hachi nen chū hizoku Sen nai shinnyū jyōkyō," National Archives of Korea, CJA0002457.

106. After the creation of Manchukuo, "border security" for Manchukuo officials primarily came to refer to the long, contested eastern and northern borders with the Soviet Union. For an extensive study of 1930s Soviet-Manchukuo border conflicts, which culminated in the bloody 1939 Battles of Khalkin Gol, see Alvin D. Coox, *Nomonhan: Japan against Russia, 1939* (Stanford, CA: Stanford University Press, 1985).

107. "Chōsen Sōtokufu bunai rinji shokuin secchisei chū o kaiseisu," National Archives of Japan 1777100, reel number 040800.

108. Chōsen Sōtokufu Keimukyoku, *Chōsen keisatsu no gaiyō*, 117.

109. Chōsen Sōtokufu Keimukyoku, *Chōsen keisatsu no gaiyō* (Keijō [Seoul]: Chōsen Sōtokufu Keimukyoku, 1931–1941).

110. Heian Hokudō Keisatsubu, *Kokkyō keibi*, 25–30.

111. A rumor widespread at the time was that Yi Honggwang himself was a female guerrilla leader. This originated in part, according to the later memoir of one of Yi's Chinese compatriots, went Yi sent a female comrade to interrogate prisoners taken during the raid, who then mistook the interrogator for the Communist leader. Liaoning Sheng dang shi bianweihui, *Dongbei kang Ri douzheng shilunji: di 1 ji* (Shenyang: Liaoning Sheng dang shi bianweihui, 1986), 256.

112. Liaoning Sheng dang shi bianweihui, *Dongbei kang Ri douzheng shilunji: di 1 ji* (Shenyang: Liaoning Sheng dang shi bianweihui, 1986), 256.

113. Heian Hokudō Keisatsubu, *Kokkyō keibi*, 8; "Tonghŭngŭp sŭmnae sigasŏn," *Tonga ilbo*, February 14, 1935.

114. "Ch'onggigo nae ŭi pyŏnggi wa hyŏngŭm obaek wŏn to t'algŏ," *Tonga ilbo*, March 29, 1936.

115. "Kukkyŏng keibi yong piki iwŏl ch'ŏ e toch'ak," *Maeil sinbo*, January 28, 1935.

116. Heian Hokudō Keisatsubu, *Kokkyō keibi*, 48–49.

117. Daqing Yang, *Technology of Empire: Telecommunications and Japanese Expansion in Asia, 1883–1945*, (Cambridge, MA: Harvard University Asia Center, 2011), 46–47.
118. Noritake, *Ōryōkkō*, 236–237.
119. Kim Ilsŏng, *Segi wa tŏburŏ*, vol. 3, chap. 8.6. Ebook, https://dprktoday.com/great/memoirs.
120. Chōsen Sōtokufu Keimukyoku, "Kokkyō Dai ichi, nisen keisatsu haichihyō, Shi Shōwa go-nen ji Shōwajūichi-nen (1930–1936)," National Archives of Korea, CJA0002456; Chōsen Sōtokufu Keimukyoku, "Kokkyō Dai issen, "Dai nisen keisatsukan haichi kankei," Shi Shōwa jūni-nen ji Shōwa jūshichi-nen (1937–1942)," National Archives of Korea, CJA0002457.
121. "Kukkyŏng kyŏngbi ŭi kongnoja chagyŏngdan e chi'sa," *Tonga ilbo*, February 22, 1938.
122. "Kukkyŏng kyŏngbi ŭi kongnoja," *Maeil sinbo*, February 24, 1938.
123. Noritake Kazuo, *Ōryōkkō*, 45; Ushima Yayoshi, "Jikeidan kaku ni shasu," *Heihoku keishō*, August 1, 1933.
124. *Sakchu kunji*, 171
125. Kosako, *Kokkyō no hana*, 18.
126. For more on self-defense corps and the deployment of the *baojia* system in Manchukuo, see Mo Tian, "The Baojia System as Institutional Control in Manchukuo under Japanese Rule (1932–45)," *Journal of the Economic and Social History of the Orient* 59, 4 (2016): 531–554.
127. Tsūka-shō Kōsho, "Kōtoku gonendo fukō kōsaku jisseki hōkokusho" and Antō shō fukō iinkai, "Fukō kōsaku shinpo jōkyō hōkoku," in *Fukō kōsaku jisshi keikaku gaiyō* (Tsūka-shō Kōsho: 1939), manuscript, Takushoku University Library.
128. Heian Hokudō Keisatsubu, *Kokkyō keibi*, 42.
129. Masui Junji, "Inu to nukuyo to," *Heihoku keishō*, August 1, 1933.
130. Heian Hokudō Keisatsubu, *Kokkyō keibi*, 54.
131. Kōno, *Kokkyō keibi kinenshū*, 200–201.
132. "Hokusen Kokkyō keibi,"4; Heian Hokudō Keisatsubu, *Kokkyō keibi*, 53–54.
133. "Hokusen kokkyō keibi," *Asahi gurafu*, July 15, 1936, 4.
134. Aaron Skabelund, *Empire of Dogs: Canines, Japan, and the Making of the Modern Imperial World* (Ithaca, NY: Cornell University Press, 2011), 130.
135. "Chosŏn kwa Manju kan e kukkyŏng kyŏngbi hoeŭi," *Tonga ilbo*, January 10, 1933.
136. Matsuda, *Nihon no Chōsen shokuminchi shihai to keisatsu*, 542–544; "Kokkyō keibi renraku tagō ni kansuru ken," National Archives of Korea, CJA0002478.
137. Antō-shō Kōsho Sōmuchō Sōmuka, *Antō-shō kōsho nenpō: Kōtoku ninen* (Antō [Dandong]: Dōchō, 1936), 119.
138. "Yahon kukwŏn ŭi chŏngni ro kukkyŏng kyŏngbi e isang," *Maeil sinbo*, January 29, 1935.
139. "Manshū kara no hikiage taikensha: Takamura Eizō-san."
140. Dongbei kang Ri lianjun shiliao bianxiezu, *Dongbei kang Ri lianjun shiliao*, vol. 1 (Beijing: Zhonggong dangshi shiliao chubanshe, 1987), 159.
141. Dongbei kang Ri lianjun shiliao bianxiezu, *Dongbei kang Ri lianjun shiliao*, vol. 1, 114.
142. "Kukkyŏng ŭi pijŏk sugoe Kim Ilsŏng kyŏnggi," *Samchŏlli*, October 1, 1937.
143. For a detailed study of guerrilla groups' attempts to fight against health problems such as frostbite, see Chang Seyun, "Manju chiyŏk Hanin hangil mujang tujaeng seryŏk ŭi shiksaenghwal kwa pogŏn wisaeng," *Hanguk kŭnhyŏndaesa yŏn'gu* 28 (March 2004): 78–115.

144. This temperature is a full -2.6 degrees colder than the lowest-ever observed temperature in Japan proper, -41 Celsius, at Asahikawa, Hokkaido, in 1902.
145. An underfloor heating system used in traditional Korean homes.
146. Heian Hokudō Keisatsubu, *Kokkyō keibi*, 53–56.
147. "Kokkyō no omoide o kataru," *Ōsaka Asahi shinbun Seisen ban*, June 12, 1942; Kuromitsu Yoshiko, "Gesshū kyūjū en de kokkyō keibi junsa buchō no kakei," *Shufu no tomo*, August 1, 1934, 164.
148. For the script of a January 1936 broadcast transmitted through the Japanese Empire entitled "An evening of comfort for border patrol," see Kobayashi, *Kokkyō to sono keibi*.
149. "Hokusen kokkyō keibi," *Asahi gurafu*, July 15, 1936, 1–9.
150. Scholars have previously analyzed this film for its propagandistic theme of ethnic harmony between Japanese officials and colonized Koreans. See, for example, Naoki Mizuno, "A Propaganda Film Subverting Ethnic Hierarchy?: Suicide Squad at the Watchtower and Colonial Korea," *Cross-Currents: East Asian History and Culture Review* 2, no. 1 (2013): 63–87; Takashi Fujitani, *Race for Empire: Koreans as Japanese and Japanese as Americans during World War II* (Berkeley: University of California Press, 2011), 306–323.
151. Fujitani, *Race for Empire*, 307–308.
152. *Suicide Squad at the Watchtower* was not the first Japanese film to depict the Sino-Korean border. An earlier 1925 silent production entitled *Daichi ha hohoemu* (The continent smiles) prominently featured a scene where the main protagonist narrowly escaped death at the hands of vengeful Korean bandits along the Yalu River. Reflecting the earlier decade's emphasis on the thawing and flourishing seasons, this scene took place during the Yalu summer rather than winter. The film was evidently well-received at the time, though budget considerations prevented the directors from engaging in actual location shooting along the Yalu. Unfortunately, film scholar Yang Insil notes that no known extant copy of the film reel survives to this day. For more on the film and how it was received, see Yang Insil, "1920 nendai shikaku media no ichidanmen: 'Daichi ha hohoemu' to 'Chōsen,'" *Ritsumeikan sangyō shakai ronshū* 43, no. 1 (June 2007): 35–57.

4. ENVIRONMENTS OF YALU RIVER SMUGGLING

1. Zeikan Gaishi Hensan Iinkai, *Manshūkoku zeikan gaishi* (Shinkyō [Changchun]: Keizaibu Kanseika, 1944), 302–303; "Andong hyŏn segwalli ŭi p'okhaeng," *Tonga ilbo*, August 7, 1936.
2. Facets of the Yalu River underground economy have been covered by historians in Japan, China, and South Korea, though none examine this transnational issue using sources in all three major East Asian languages. See Yao Jingzhi, "20 shiji 30 niandaichu Dongbei de zousi wenti" (MA thesis, Xiamen University, 2006); Tanaka Ryūichi, "'Manshūkoku' keisatsu to chiiki shakai: keizai keisatsu no katsudō to sono mujun o chūshin to shite," *Chungang saron* 32 (December 2010): 259–266; and Yi Ŭnja, "Chungil chŏnjaeng ijŏn sigi Chungguk ŭi kukkyŏng tosi Andong ŭi ijumin—kyoryu wa kaltŭng ŭi ijungju," *Chungguk kŭnhyŏndaesa* 62 (June 2014): 95–127. Previous English-language historiography on smuggling and Japanese expansion in Northeast Asia has focused primarily on drug trafficking and the Kwantung Army's lucrative opium monopoly. On the links between Japanese expansionism and opium smuggling, see John M. Jennings, *The Opium Empire: Japanese Imperialism and Drug Trafficking in Asia, 1895–1945* (Westport, CT: Praeger, 1997); and Miriam Kingsberg, *Moral Nation: Modern Japan and Narcotics in Global History* (Berkeley: University of California Press, 2013).
3. While noting the difficulties that come with a concept that is inherently situational (trade deemed smuggling by officials on one side of the border is licit trade to

the other, and vice versa), I use the term "smuggling" in any context where the activity in question deliberately seeks to evade or defraud customs regulation on either side of the river. The legally marginal practices of smuggling have increasingly moved to the center of historians' attention. Eric Tagliacozzo's work on smuggling in British and Dutch colonial Southeast Asia and Philip Thai's research on smuggling in modern China both demonstrate, for example, the links between customs regulation and the emergence of modern political economies. Eric Tagliacozzo, *Secret Trades, Porous Borders: Smuggling and States along a Southeast Asian Frontier* (New Haven, CT: Yale University Press), 2005; Philip Thai, *China's War on Smuggling: Law, Economic Life, and the Making of the Modern State, 1842–1965* (New York: Columbia University Press, 2018).

4. For a representative discursive study of Manchukuo, see Prasenjit Duara, *Sovereignty and Authenticity: Manchukuo and the East Asian Modern* (Lanham, MD: Rowman & Littlefield, 2004).

5. For one eighteenth-century smuggling account, see Seonmin Kim, *Ginseng and Borderland: Territorial Boundaries and Political Relations between Qing China and Chosŏn Korea, 1636–1912* (Berkeley: University of California Press, 2017), 109.

6. On the Kwantung Leased Territory's government-general and its specific administrative responsibilities, see Emer Sinéad O'Dwyer, *Significant Soil: Settler Colonialism and Japan's Urban Empire in Manchuria* (Cambridge, MA: Harvard University Asia Center, 2015), 6–8.

7. According to "Notes on China and Chinese Subjects," *Mesny's Chinese Miscellany*, April 2, 1896, the Imperial Customs Service managed twenty-four ports in China and also helped oversee four ports in Korea as of 1896. Philip Thai notes that the Maritime Customs Service had a presence in almost fifty Chinese ports by 1930. Thai, *China's War on Smuggling*, 30.

8. Zhongguo bianjiang shi di yanjiu zhongxin, *Dongbei bianjiang dang'an xuanji* [hereafter *DBDX*] (Guilin: Guangxi shifan daxue chubanshe, 2007), 62:96.

9. See, for example, "Hanmin nai yi ru shi ye," *Shen bao*, June 6, 1910; "P'yŏnganpukto: Tonae," *Maeil sinbo*, May 21, 1914; "Yŏpchŏn ŭl milsuip," *Maeil sinbo*, November 27, 1918.

10. *DBDX*, 61:136–219.

11. "Kukkyŏng segwan pŏmch'ik chŭngga," *Tonga ilbo*, July 15, 1922.

12. See note 10.

13. Zeikan Gaishi Hensan Iinkai, *Manshūkoku zeikan gaishi*, 301.

14. Zeikan Gaishi Hensan Iinkai, *Manshūkoku zeikan gaishi*, 174.

15. The record of Yosano's travel to Andong can be found in Yosano Akiko and Yosano Tekkan, *Manmō yūki* (Osaka: Ōsaka Yagō Shoten, 1930), 92–98. For an English translation of Yosano's travelogue, see Yosano Akiko, *Travels in Manchuria and Mongolia: A Feminist Poet from Japan Encounters Prewar China*, trans. Joshua Fogel (New York: Columbia University Press, 2001).

16. A February 1931 newspaper article counted a total of 1,736 people who crossed the bridge during a one-hour interval on the previous January 31, a figure that averages to roughly twenty-nine people per minute. "Apkang ch'ŏlgyo ilil kan tonghaeng insu," *Maeil sinbo*, February 5, 1931.

17. Chōsen Bōeki Kyōkai, *Chōsen bōekishi* (Keijō [Seoul]: Tōyō Keizai Shinpo Keijō Shikyoku, 1943), 342; Nakamura Mika, "Hutatabi Shingishū no mitsuyu ni tsuite," *Keimu ihō*, August 1935, 81.

18. "Preventive Secretary's Note No. 1," March, 15, 1932, 15. Roy Maxwell Talbot Papers, Sonoma State University Library Special Collections; Zeikan Gaishi Hensan Iinkai, *Manshūkoku zeikan gaishi*, 301.

19. Second Historical Archives of China [hereafter SHAC] 679-1-27750, "Inauguration of Preventive Service, 1929–1930," Francis Hayley Bell to Frederick Maze, January 6, 1930. This and other SHAC sources cited in this chapter accessed through Robert A. Bickers and Hans J. Van de Ven., eds, *China and the West: The Maritime Customs Service Archive from the Second Historical Archives of China*, Nanjing (Reading, Berkshire, U.K.: Primary Source Microfilm, 2004), Reels 221–222.

20. SHAC 679-1-27750, "Inauguration of Preventive Service, 1929–1930," Special Dossier for F. H. Bell, May 20, 1929.

21. Kim Tae-hyŏn, "Sinŭiju kan milmuyŏk tansok chŏngae kwajŏng kwa Chosŏn Ch'ongdokpu ŭi taeŭng," *Han'guksa yŏn'gu* 183 (December 2018): 327.

22. SHAC 679-1-27750, "Inauguration of Preventive Service, 1929–1930," "Memorandum for Colonel Hayley Bell, p.s.o., Commissioner, Appendix No. 1: Report on Liutaok'ou for Commissioner."

23. Roy Maxwell Talbot Diary, November 24, 1931, Roy Maxwell Talbot Papers, Sonoma State University Library Special Collections.

24. Roy Maxwell Talbot Diary, March 7, 1932.

25. "Kukkyŏng segwan ŏmjung," *Tonga ilbo*, December 18, 1923.

26. *DBDX*, 64:428.

27. Roy Maxwell Talbot Diary, January 20, 1932.

28. Roy Maxwell Talbot Diary, February 18, 1932.

29. "Yaggan milsu chung ŏrŭm kkŏjŏ iksa," *Chungang ilbo*, December 23, 1931.

30. Compiled from charts found in *DBDX*, 60:235–281, 436–508; 61:136–219, 376–424; 62:1–76, 181–266, 372–440; 63:1–58, 189–227, 353–405; 64:1–44, 227–254, 359–391; 66:384–412; 67:261–317; 68:118–177; 69:116–174.

31. See note 30.

32. *DBDX*, 66:436; *DBDX*, 64:448.

33. For more on cattle smuggling and border controls against veterinary disease, see Joseph Seeley, "Cattle, Viral Invasions, and State-Society Relations in a Colonial Korean Borderland," *Journal of Korean Studies* 28, no. 1 (March 2023): 5–31.

34. "Preventive Secretary's Note No. 1," 17.

35. "Kukkyŏng esŏ ŏttŏn chaptongsani," *Kaebyŏk*, August 1, 1923.

36. Chang Sŏngsik, *Sinŭiju taegwan* (Sinŭiju: Munhwadang, 1931), 176.

37. Yi, "Chungil chŏnjaeng ijŏn sigi Chungguk ŭi kukkyŏng tosi Andong ŭi ijumin," 104.

38. Yi, "Chungil chŏnjaeng ijŏn sigi Chungguk," 120. In 1934 prominent Korean leaders of the Andong branch of the pro-Japanese Korean People's Association (Chosŏn inminhoe) were implicated in a gold-smuggling scheme. See "Andong Chosŏn inminhoe chŏngbu hoejang ŭl kŏmgŏ," *Chosŏn ilbo*, April 29, 1934.

39. *DBDX*, 66:444–449.

40. SHAC 679-1-27750, "Inauguration of Preventive Service, 1929–1930," "Memorandum for Colonel Hayley Bell, p.s.o., Commissioner, Appendix No. 6: Smuggling by Koreans."

41. Thai, *China's War on Smuggling*, 78–79.

42. "Antō ni okeru mitsuyunyū torishimari mondai," Japan Center for Asian Historical Records [hereafter JACAR], B13081194000, 319.

43. "Antō ni okeru mitsuyunyū torishimari mondai," JACAR, B13081194000, 319.

44. "Antō ni okeru mitsuyunyū torishimari mondai," JACAR, B13081194000, 319–320.

45. "Antō mitsuyunyū torishimari mondai (sono ato no keika)," JACAR, B1308 1215400, 261.

46. "Preventive Secretary's Note No. 1," 21–22;" Antō mitsuyunyū torishimari mondai (sono ato no keika)," 270–271.
47. "Preventive Secretary's Note No. 1," 21–22;" Antō mitsuyunyū torishimari mondai (sono ato no keika)," 270–271.
48. "Shingishū Antō kan mitsuyu torishimari ni kansuru ken," National Archives of Korea, CJA0002442.
49. "Mitsuyu torishimari ni motozuku Chōsenjin kyūsai mondai," JACAR, B09040549200, 348.
50. "Mitsuyu torishimari ni motozuku Chōsenjin kyūsai mondai," JACAR, B09040549200, 347.
51. "Shingishū Antō kan mitsuyu torishimari ni kansuru ken."
52. Compare *DBDX*, 69:116–174 and "Shingishū Antō kan mitsuyu torishimari ni kansuru ken," 287–405.
53. "Mitsuyu torishimari ni motozuku Chōsenjin kyūsai mondai," 369.
54. Antō mitsuyunyū torishimari mondai (sono ato no keika)," 245; SHAC 679-1-27750, "Inauguration of Preventive Service, 1929–1930," "Memorandum for Colonel Hayley Bell, p.s.o., Commissioner, Appendix No. 5: Smuggling across the Yalu from Korea to Liutaokow: conditions of, and preventions concerning."
55. Kim Taehyŏn, "Sinŭiju Andong kan milmuyŏk," 345–347. Japanese bureaucrats in the colonial Korean government also expressed an unwillingness to devote needed funds to reemployment projects, despite pleas from the Japanese consul in Andong. See "Torishimari kisoku kōfugo no jōkyō," JACAR, B09040549100.
56. Roy Maxwell Talbot Diary, September 17, 1931, and September 19, 1931.
57. Zeikan Gaishi Hensan Iinkai, *Manshūkoku zeikan gaishi*, 177.
58. "Preventive Secretary's Note No. 1," 25.
59. Roy Maxwell Talbot Diary, December 17, 1931.
60. Zeikan Gaishi Hensan Iinkai, *Manshūkoku zeikan gaishi*, 177.
61. "Kongyŏn han 'mil'such'ulgye tae konghwang sidae torae!" *Tonga ilbo*, April 21, 1932.
62. Roy Maxwell Talbot Diary, February 10, 1932.
63. Roy Maxwell Talbot Diary, March 30, 1932.
64. Nakamura Mika, "Shingishū no mitsuyu," *Keimu ihō*, December 1934, 78–86, and January 1935, 88–96.
65. Nakamura Mika, "Shingishū no mitsuyu," *Keimu ihō*, December 1934, 84.
66. Sinŭiju Siminhoe, *Sinŭiju shichi* (Seoul: Sinŭiju Siminhoe, 1969), 223–224.
67. "Sinŭiju koksang wit'ak chohap ch'angnip kyehoek," *Chungwae ilbo*, January 25, 1928.
68. Chang Sŏngsik, *Sinŭiju taegwan* (Sinŭiju: Munhwadang, 1931), back matter.
69. "Kŭmgoe sagŏn p'an'gyŏl," *Tonga ilbo*, November 27, 1932.
70. Kaneko Chūta, "Manshūkoku no mitsubōeki," *Shin tenchi*, July 1934, 27.
71. "Ŭiju-gun kamdŭng ŭi p'an'gyŏl," *Tonga ilbo*, June 13, 1921.
72. In 1934, for example, Han donated 600 yen to the construction of a new school in Sinŭiju and was also involved in an organization raising funds to create an athletic stadium in the same city. "Sinŭiju che-i pogyo kibonkŭm kibuja," *Chosŏn ilbo*, November 4, 1934; "P'yŏngbuk p'yŏn ki il 'undongjang' ŭl mokp'yo ro," *Tonga ilbo*, January 9, 1934.
73. Chōsen Bōeki Kyōkai, *Chōsen bōekishi*, 349.
74. Nakamura Mika, "Shingishū no mitsuyu," *Keimu ihō*, December 1934, 86.
75. "Segwansa ŭi imbu nant'a," *Sidae ilbo*, November 23, 1924.
76. "Kukkyŏng milsuip pihwa," *Samch'ŏlli*, January 1, 1933. For a full English-language translation of this short story, see Jovanne Tan Li Qi, trans., "Secret Story of

Cross-Border Smuggling," in Sayaka Chatani, ed., "Grassroots Operations of the Japanese Empire Translated Primary Sources for Teaching Purposes," https://www.japaneseempire.info/post/secret-story-of-cross-border-smuggling (accessed September 7, 2023).

77. Ch'oe Chŏnggŏn, "Milsu sangsŭpja," *Sin kajŏng*, August 1934, 14–17.

78. "Salt" was originally published in several installments from May to October 1934. An English translation of Kang Kyŏngae's short story can be found in Theodore Hughes et al., *Rat Fire: Korean Stories from the Japanese Empire* (Ithaca, NY: Cornell University Press, 2013), 212–265. For further analysis, see Miseli Jeon, "Violent Emotions: Modern Japanese and Korean Women's Writing, 1920–1980" (PhD diss., University of British Columbia, 2004), 109–116.

79. "Kokkyō zeikan no hiwa," *Mansen*, February 1, 1936.

80. "Apkang kyŏlbing ttara kyŏnggye samŏm," *Tonga ilbo*, December 23, 1933.

81. Heian Hokudō, *Heian hokudō tōkei nenpō: Shōwa jū nen* (Shingishū [Sinŭiju]: Heian Hokudō, 1937), 10.

82. "Milsu jŏnsŏn ŭi amyakcha Chosŏnin man manmyŏng tolp'a," *Tonga ilbo*, November 29, 1935.

83. Shingishū Zeikan, *Shingishū minato ippan* (Shingishū [Sinŭiju]: Shingishū Zeikan, 1932), 24; Shingishū Zeikan, *Shingishū minato ippan* (Shingishū [Sinŭiju]: Shingishū Zeikan, 1937), 33.

84. Zaiseibu, *Zeikan jimu gaiyō: Harupin, Antō Tomon no bu* (Shinkyō [Changchun]: Zaiseibu, 1934), 221.

85. Zeikan Gaishi Hensan Iinkai, *Manshūkoku zeikan gaishi*, 33.

86. Zeikan Gaishi Hensan Iinkai, *Manshūkoku zeikan gaishi*, 33.

87. Antō Shōkō Kōkai, *Antō sangyō keizai gaikan* (Antō [Dandong]: Antō Shōkō Kōkai, 1942), 54–55.

88. "I chŏn 'chamsang' hyŏpwi hanŭn chomyŏngdŭng kwa tamjŏnggyŏn," *Tonga ilbo*, November 15, 1934.

89. "Shinbunshi sakujo chūi kiji yoshi 'Tōa nippō,'" *Chōsen shuppan keisatsu geppō 75 go*, November 15, 1934.

90. "Amnokkang bingsang gui si," *Maeil sinbo*, January 20, 1936.

91. Chōsen Bōeki Kyōkai, *Chōsen bōekishi*, 355; "Ibŏn en Andong hyŏnsŏ e pulsang sagŏn," *Tonga ilbo*, April 26, 1934.

92. "Andong, Sinŭiju segwan ŭi milsudan pangŏjin," *Tonga ilbo*, March 30, 1934.

93. "Shingishū no mitsuyu," December 1934, 85.

94. "Che 46 hwa segwan yasa (9)," *Chungang ilbo*, June 14, 1975.

95. "Suguk kihaeng (chong)," *Tonga ilbo*, August 22, 1936

96. SHAC 679-1-27750, "Inauguration of Preventive Service, 1929–1930," "Memorandum no. 11."

97. Nakamura Mika, "Shingishū no mitsuyu," *Keimu ihō*, January 1935, 92.

98. "Milsusŏn ŭl koŭi ro ch'unggyŏk," *Tonga ilbo*, May 26, 1936.

99. P'okhaeng han Andong segwalli ku myŏng e ge yesim ch'ŏnggu," *Tonga ilbo*, August 11, 1936; "Ren zhao si zousi chuan bei jianshi chuan peng chen," *Shenjing shibao*, May 26, 1936.

100. "Apkang myŏngnanghwa wi hae segwansa hoengp'o ŏmgŭm rŭl," *Maeil sinbo*, June 4, 1936.

101. "Kakkoku ni okeru mitsuyunyū kankei zakken: Manshūkoku no bu," JACAR, B09040535600, 149.

102. "Ch'wich'e ŭi chŏkkŭkhwa ro milsuŏpcha tae konghwang," *Maeil sinbo*, November 8, 1936.

103. "Kukkyŏng kyŏngbijin kanghwa," *Tonga ilbo*, December 11, 1937.

5. DAM CONSTRUCTION AND "MANCHURIAN-KOREAN UNITY"

1. Antō Shōkō Kōkai, *Antō sangyō keizai gaikan* (Antō: Antō Shōkō Kōkai, 1942), 135.
2. Yamada Ryūichi, interview by author, August 9, 2015.
3. Aaron Stephen Moore, "'The Yalu River Era of Developing Asia': Japanese Expertise, Colonial Power, and the Construction of the Sup'ung Dam," *Journal of Asian Studies* 72, no. 1 (February 2013): 115–139.
4. See Hirose Teizō, "'Manshūkoku' ni okeru Suihō Damu kensetsu," *Niigata Kokusai Jōhō Daigaku Jōhō Bunka Gakubu kiyō* 6 (March 2003): 1–25; Moore, "'The Yalu River Era of Developing Asia."
5. Noritake Kazuo, *Ōryokkō* (Tokyo: Daiichi Shuppan Kyōkai, 1943), 164.
6. Minami Manshū Tetsudō Kabushiki Kaisha Sangyōbu, *Ōryokkō keizaiken chōsa hōkokusho* (Dairen [Dalian]: Mantetsu Sangyōbu, 1937), preface; Harada Kiyoshi, *Suihō hatsudenjo kōji taikan* (Amagasaki: Doken Bunkasha, 1942), 20.
7. In a recent study of the Sino-Korean border at the Tumen River, Nianshen Song claims that the "voiding of the boundary" in 1931 caused Manchuria and Korea to be easily "integrated under the domination of Japanese imperialism." Nianshen Song, *Making Borders in Modern East Asia: Tumen River Demarcation, 1881–1919* (Cambridge, UK: Cambridge University Press, 2018), 259. Nonetheless, scholarship by Aaron Stephen Moore, Chŏng Angi, and others has similarly highlighted disunity rather than cohesion along the wartime Manchurian-Korean border by looking at intraimperial rivalries. See Moore, "'The Yalu River Era of Developing Asia," 120; Chŏng Angi, "1936 nyŏn Sŏnman sunoe ŭi 'Tomun hoedam' kwa 'Mansŏn iryŏ,'" *Manju yŏn'gu* 12 (December 2011): 181–209; Tanaka Ryūichi, "Tairitsu to tōgō no 'Mansen' kankei: 'Naisen ittai,' 'Gozoku kyōwa,' 'Mansen ichinyo' no shosō," *Hisutoria* 152 (1996); Im Sŏngmo, "Chungil chŭnjaeng chŏnya Manjuguk-Chosŏn kwangyesa ŭi somyo: 'Il-Man ilch'e' wa 'Man-Sŏn iryŏ' ŭi kaltŭng" *Yŏksa hakpo* 201 (March 2009): 165–202.
8. Heian Hokudō Keisatsubu, ed., *Kokkyō keibi* (Shingishū [Sinŭiju]: Heian Keishō Henshūbu, 1936), 35; Nakamura Mika, "Shingishū no mitsuyu," *Keimu ihō*, January 1935, 92.
9. Louise Young, *Japan's Total Empire: Manchuria and the Culture of Wartime Imperialism* (Berkeley: University of California Press, 1998), 22.
10. Im, "Chungil chŭnjaeng chŏnya Manjuguk-Chosŏn kwangyesa ŭi somyo," 170–171.
11. Carter J. Eckert, *Offspring of Empire: The Koch'ang Kims and the Colonial Origins of Korean Capitalism, 1876–1945* (Seattle: University of Washington Press, 1991), 155. For further discussion of how Korean and Japanese businessmen in Korea perceived the opportunities of the Japanese invasion of Manchuria, see Eckert, 154–181.
12. Eckert, *Offspring of Empire*, 77.
13. "Chosŏn Manju kan injae kyohwan Ch'ongdok, Ch'onggam kyŏlŭi," *Tonga ilbo*, August 26, 1936.
14. Chŏng, "'Tomun hoedam' kwa 'Mansŏn iryŏ,'" 181; Im, "Chungil chŭnjaeng chŏnya Manjuguk-Chosŏn kwangyesa ŭi somyo," 183.
15. Hirose, 'Manshūkoku' ni okeru Suihō Damu kensetsu," 5.
16. "Ōryokkō oyobi Tomonkō kakyō ni kansuru oboegaki oyobi gijiroku," Japan Center for Asian Historical Records [hereafter JACAR], B13091027800.
17. "Ōryokkō kyōdō gijutsu iinkai no ken," JACAR, B09030253700.
18. Minami Manshū Tetsudō Kabushiki Kaisha Keizai Chōsakai, *Manshū suiun hōsaku* (Dairen [Dalian]: Minami Manshū Tetsudō Kabushiki Kaisha Keizai Chōsakai, 1936), 7–13.

19. A 1922 proposal by the deputy commissioner of the Andong customs T. T. Ferguson for joint management of the river and a definitive delineation of the river border can be found in Japanese translation in Minami Manshū Tetsudō Kabushiki Kaisha Shomubu Chōsaka, *Tashitō no kenkyū* (Dairen [Dalian]: Minami Manshū Tetsudō Kabushiki Kaisha, 1926), 28–36.

20. "16. Manshūkoku," JACAR, B09030266300.

21. Antō Kōseikyoku, *Keizai kasen 'Ōryokkō' no bekken* (Antō [Andong]: Manshūkoku Kokumuin Kōtsūbu Antō Kōseikyoku, 1935), 140. More about Shaw's larger extended family and their lives in semicolonial China can be found in Peter Stursberg, *No Foreign Bones in China: Memoirs of Imperialism and Its Ending* (Edmonton: University of Alberta Press, 2002).

22. Shaw vehemently denied these allegations, though British diplomats in China blamed Shaw's "cantankerous disposition" for exacerbating tensions. "Manchuria Travel Memorandum: Conditions at Antung," British Foreign Office, China File 371/18049, 178. Foreign Office Files for China, 1919–1980, Sources from The National Archives, UK, Adam Matthew Digital database (https://www.amdigital.co.uk/collection/foreign-office-files-for-china-1919-1980).

23. Minami Manshū Tetsudō Kabushiki Kaisha Keizai Chōsakai, *Manshū suiun hōsaku*, 12–13.

24. For a detailed look at the politics surrounding Shaw and his fractious encounters with local Japanese authorities along the border, see Han Ch'ŏlho, "1930 nyŏndae Ilje ŭi Joji El Sho [George L. Shaw] t'anap ch'ukch'ul kongjak kwa kŭ sŏngkyŏk," *Han'guk minjok undongsa yŏn'gu* 69 (2011): 151–190.

25. Tao Mian, *Yalu Jiang sushuo: 19 shiji-20 shiji zhongye lueduo jishi* (Shenyang: 2010), 174–179.

26. Moore, "'The Yalu River Era of Developing Asia,'" 120, 119.

27. Minami Manshū Tetsudō Kabushiki Kaisha Chōsabu, *Ōryokkō suiryoku hatsuden chōsa keikaku shiryō* (Dairen [Dalian]: Minami Manshū Tetsudō Kabushiki Kaisha, 1940), 13.

28. Satō Toshihiko, *Doboku jinsei gojūnen* (Chūō Kōron Jigyō Shūppan, 1969), 140.

29. Moore, "'The Yalu River Era of Developing Asia,'" 121; Harada, *Suihō hatsudenjo kōji taikan*, 23.

30. Nihon Chiso Hiryō Kabushiki Kaisha, *Nihon chiso hiryō jigyō gaiyō* (Osaka and Tokyo: Nihon Chiso Hiryō Kabushiki Kaisha, 1940), 131; Morisaki Minoru, *Tōhendō* (Tōkyō: Shunjūsha 1941), 240–242.

31. Christopher Sneddon, *Concrete Revolution: Large Dams, Cold War Geopolitics, and the US Bureau of Reclamation* (Chicago: University of Chicago Press, 2015), 3.

32. Richard White, *The Organic Machine: The Remaking of the Columbia River* (New York: Hill & Wang, 1995), 58.

33. Dorothy Zeisler-Vralsted, *Rivers, Memory, and Nation-Building: A History of the Volga and Mississippi Rivers* (New York: Berghahn Books, 2015), 83.

34. Aaron Stephen Moore, *Constructing East Asia: Technology, Ideology, and Empire in Japan's Wartime Era 1931–1945* (Stanford, CA: Stanford University Press, 2013), 162–164.

35. Chōsen Ōryokkō Suiryoku Hatsuden Kabushiki Kaisha, *Ōryokkō suiryoku hatsuden keikaku no gaiyō* (Keijō [Seoul]: Chōsen Ōryokkō Suiryoku Hatsuden Kabushiki Kaisha, 1940), 4.

36. Dongbei kang Ri lianjun shiliao bianxiezu, *Dongbei kang Ri lianjun shiliao*, vol. 1 (Beijing: Zhonggong dangshi shiliao chubanshe, 1987), 297. For more on the Communist-led anti-Japanese guerrilla movement in Northeast China during this period, see Chong-Sik

Lee, *Revolutionary Struggle in Manchuria: Chinese Communism and Soviet Interest, 1922–1945* (Berkeley: University of California Press, 1983).

37. Dae-sook Suh, *Kim Il Sung: The North Korean Leader* (New York: Columbia University Press, 1988), 34–35.

38. Hyesan Kunji Py'ŏnch'an Wiwonhoe, *Hyesan kunji* (Seoul: Hyesan Kunji Py'ŏnch'an Wiwonhoe, 1999), 350–355; Kim Ilsŏng, *Segi wa tŏburŏ*, vol. 6, chap. 17.2. Ebook, https://dprktoday.com/great/memoirs (accessed September 9, 2023).

39. "Hamgyŏng kukkyŏng e chei Tonghŭng sagŏn," *Maeil sinbo*, June 6, 1937; Kankyō nandō keimubuchō to Chōsen Sōtokufu keimukyokuchō, "Kokkyō keibi no jūjitsu kyōka ni kansuru ken," Kannan keihi dai 502 go, National Archives of Korea, CJA0002478.

40. "Mugi tanyak tŭng kwangch'ong hwakch'ung ŭro kukkyŏng kyŏngbi ilchŭng kanghwa," *Maeil sinbo*, November 19, 1936.

41. Dongbei kang Ri lianjun shiliao bianxiezu, *Dongbei kang Ri lianjun shiliao*, vol. 1, 203.

42. Wada Haruki, *Kin Nichisei to Manshū kōnichi sensō* (Tokyo: Heibonsha, 1992), 265.

43. Dongbei kang Ri lianjun shiliao bianxiezu, *Dongbei kang Ri lianjun shiliao*, vol. 2 (Beijing: Zhonggong dangshi shiliao chubanshe, 1987), 404.

44. Tsūka-shō Kōsho, *Kōtoku gonendo fukō kōsaku jisseki hōkokusho* (Tsūka-shō Kōsho, 1939), manuscript, Takushoku University Library.

45. Satō, *Doboku jinsei gojūnen*, 137.

46. Moore, "The Yalu River Era of Developing Asia," 130–131.

47. Tsūka-shō Kōsho, *Tsūka-shō gairan* (Tsūka-shō Kōsho, 1940), 326.

48. The Maritime Customs, *Decennial Reports on the Trade, Industries, etc. of the Ports Open to Foreign Commerce, and on Conditions and Development of the Treaty Port Provinces*, vol. 1 (Shanghai: Statistical Dept. of the Inspectorate General of Customs, 1924), 61; Tani Mitsuyo, *Ōryokkō* (Shinkyō [Changchun]: Manshūkoku Tsūshinsha, 1937), 7–8.

49. "Tashitō rinkō tetsudō to Ōryokkō ryūiki no kaihatsu," *Manshū nippō*, February 28, 1935.

50. Minami Manshū Tetsudō Kabushiki Kaisha Sangyōbu, *Ōryokkō keizaiken chōsa hōkokusho*, 556; "Tasa-do ch'ŏldo hoesa owŏl kyŏng ch'angnip ch'onghoe," *Tonga ilbo*, February 21, 1935.

51. "Ōryokkō ni okeru Senman chikkō to toshi keikaku," *Shokugin chōsa geppō*, February 1940, 40.

52. Tani, *Ōryokkō*, 8.

53. For more detailed discussions of the Dadong harbor project, see Koshizawa Akira, "Daitōkō no keikaku to kensetsu (1937–1945)—Manshū ni okeru mikan no dai kibo kaihatsu purojekuto," *Nihon dobokushi kenkyū happyō ronbunshū* 6 (1986): 223–234; Moore, *Constructing East Asia*, 139–148.

54. "Taedonghang ŭi kŏnsŏl," *Mansŏn ilbo*, January 13, 1940.

55. "Tashitō minato o ooini riyō," *Ōsaka Asahi shinbun Seisen ban*, June 11, 1940.

56. Tani Mitsuyo, *Taitōkō to hōko Tōhendō* (Shinkyō [Changchun]: Manshū Jijō Annaijo, 1940), 48–49; Manabe Gorō, *Tōhendō annai* (Dairen [Dalian]: Ajia Shuppan Kyōkai, 1940), 99.

57. Minami Manshū Tetsudō Kabushiki Kaisha, *Manshū suisan jigyō hōsaku* (Dairen [Dalian]: Minami Manshū Tetsudō Keizai Chōsakai, 1935), 209.

58. "Sementŭ ŭi yuha ro Amnokkang baekŏ kamso," *Chosŏn ilbo*, June 1, 1938.

59. "Hŏta han ŏmin ŭl hŭisaeng," *Maeil sinbo*, September 9, 1940.

60. "Shirauo no gyoken o meguri," *Ōsaka Asahi shinbun Seisen ban*, April 2, 1941.

61. "Shirauo mondai yōyaku kaiketsu," *Ōsaka Asahi shinbun Seisen ban*, April 8, 1941.
62. Harada, *Suihō hatsudenjo kōji taikan*, 75. Variations of this phrase can be found throughout this publication and in other period reporting on the Sup'ung Dam.
63. Moore, "The Yalu River Era of Developing Asia," 130.
64. Moore, "The Yalu River Era of Developing Asia," 127–130.
65. Chūō Nikkan Kyōkai, *Chōsen denki jigyōshi* (Tokyo: Chūō Nikkan Kyōkai, 1981), 439.
66. Moore, "The Yalu River Era of Developing Asia," 123.
67. Satō, *Doboku jinsei gojūnen*, 143–144.
68. Satō, *Doboku jinsei gojūnen*, 147.
69. David Fedman, "The Saw and the Seed: Japanese Forestry in Colonial Korea, 1895–1945" (PhD diss., Stanford University, 2015), 453.
70. Patrick Caffrey, "The Forests of Northeast China, 1600–1960: Environment, Politics, and Society" (PhD diss., Georgetown University, 2002), 232–233.
71. "Daikibo no Chōsen seishi," *Keijō nippō*, October 20, 1917.
72. Fedman, "The Saw and the Seed," 212; Antō Shōkō Kōkai, *Antō keizai gaiyō* (Antō [Dandong]: Antō Shōkō Kōkai, 1938), 42–44.
73. Jae Soo Bae et al., "Forest Transition in South Korea: Reality, Path and Drivers," *Land Use Policy* 29 (January 2012): 202; Caffrey, "The Forests of Northeast China," 320, 326.
74. Chōsen Sōtokufu, *Chōsen buraku chōsa hōkoku. Dai 1-satsu, Kadenmin raiju Shinajin* (Keijō [Seoul]: Chōsen Sōtokufu, 1924), 1.
75. "Paektusan ŭl nŏmŏ tongp'o tŭl ŭl ch'ajasŏ," *Tonga ilbo*, March 26, 1932.
76. Michael E. Robinson, *Korea's Twentieth-Century Odyssey: A Short History* (Honolulu: University of Hawai'i Press, 2007), 83.
77. Murayama Jōzō, *Manshū no shinrin to sono shizenteki kōsei* (Hōten [Shenyang]: Hōten Ōsaka Yagō Shoten, 1943), 73–74.
78. Yun Ch'iho, *Yun Ch'iho ilgi*, July 31, 1935. Accessed through National Institute of Korean History Korean History Database (Kuksa P'yŏnch'an Wiwŏnhoe Han'guksa Deit'ŏbeisŭ), db.history.go.kr.
79. "Taedonghang sa gae piŏpchang," *Mansŏn ilbo*, August 11, 1940.
80. "Apkang Sup'ung 'ttaem' esŏ inbu shipsam myŏng sisang," *Mansŏn ilbo*, December 29, 1939.
81. Hirose, "'Manshūkoku' ni okeru Suihō Damu kensetsu," 18–20.
82. Tao, *Yalu Jiang sushuo*, 164.
83. Tao, *Yalu Jiang sushuo*, 164.
84. Harada, *Suihō hatsudenjo kōji taikan*.
85. Harada, *Suihō hatsudenjo kōji taikan*, 92–99.
86. For full text of their addresses and others who spoke at the event, see Harada, *Suihō hatsudenjo kōji taikan*, 7–16.
87. "Amnokkang ilbu ka kyŏlbing ch'ianhyŏ," *Mansŏn ilbo*, Jan 19, 1941.
88. Antō Shōkō Kōkai, *Antō sangyō keizai gaikan*, 135.
89. Tamaoki Shōji, "Chōsen no suiryoku hatsuden ni tsuite," T50 (unpublished oral history interview, Tōyō Bunka Kenkyūsho, Gakushūin University, 1960).
90. "Kokkyō Dai issen, "Dai nisen keisatsukan haichi kankei."
91. Noritake, *Ōryokkō*, 164.
92. Antō Shōkō Kōkai, *Antō sangyō keizai gaikan*, 128–135.
93. Wada, *Kin Nichisei to Manshū kōnichi sensō*, 265.
94. "Hishu Yō Seiu no saiki," *Ōsaka Asahi shinbun Seisen ban*, September 3, 1940.
95. Wada, *Kin Nichisei to Manshū kōnichi sensō*, 289–292.

96. Mine Kenichi, "Suihō damu sobyō," *Chōsen*, January 1944, 55.
97. "Sekai ichi no yōgyojō" *Maeil sinbo*, January 30, 1944. For more on colonial development of the Sup'ung Reservoir for aquaculture and its postcolonial legacies, see Joseph Seeley, "Dammed Fish: Piscatorial Developmentalism and the Remaking of the Yalu River," in David Fedman, Eleana J. Kim, and Albert L. Park, eds., *Forces of Nature: New Perspectives on Korean Environments* (Ithaca, NY: Cornell University Press, 2023), 48–59.
98. Mantetsu sangyōbu, "Ōryokkō suiryoku hatsuden ni okeru gyodō oyobi shūbatsuro ni kansuru ni, san no chosa kekka," in Liaoning Sheng danganguan, ed., *Mantie diaocha baogao*, vol. 14 (Guilin: Guangxi shifan daxue chubanshe, 2005), 167.
99. "Suihō suiden damu riyō ōgakari no tansuigyō shiyō," *Seisen nippō*, March 5, 1938.
100. "Segye il ŭi ingong hosu," *Maeil sinbo*, July 4, 1941.
101. "Taeyang ŭi tamsŭo," *Maeil sinbo*, August 13, 1944.
102. "Sup'ung ŭi tamsŭo," *Maeil sinbo*, February 14, 1944.
103. Kate McDonald, *Placing Empire: Travel and the Social Imagination in Imperial Japan* (Berkeley: University of California Press, 2017), xv.
104. See, for example, Minami Manshū Tetsudō Kabushiki Kaisha, *Chōsen Manshū tabi no shiori* (Tokyo: Minami Manshū Tōkyō Shisha, 1938), 68–69.
105. Iino Shōtarō, "Ōryokkō suiden no kankōteki kachi," *Shingishū shōkō kōgi geppō*, September 1940, 4.
106. Moore, "The Yalu River Era of Developing Asia," 115. For more on how science figured in Japanese wartime discourse, see Hiromi Mizuno, *Science for the Empire: Scientific Nationalism in Modern Japan* (Stanford, CA: Stanford University Press, 2008).
107. "Pingjŏm ha ŭi Amnokkang molji," *Mansŏn ilbo*, February 1, 1940.
108. "Ōryokkō o shōkai seyo," *Ōryoku*, January 5, 1909, 13. For more on the timber raft controversy, see Hirose Teizō's article on the issue: "Shokuminchiki Chōsen ni okeru Suihō hatsudenjo kensetsu to ryūbatsu mondai," *Niigata Kokusai Jōhō Daigaku Jōhō Bunka Gakubu kiyō* 1 (March 1998): 39–58, as well as Moore, "The Yalu River Era of Developing Asia," 124–126.
109. Satō, *Doboku jinsei gojūnen*, 149.
110. Wang Tongsheng et al., ed., *Yalu Jiang liuyu lishi ziliao huibian*, vol. 2 (Dandong, China: Dandong shi wei, 2007), 588.
111. "Kakkoku ni okeru mitsuyunyū kankei zakken: Manshūkoku no bu," JACAR, B09040535600, 149.
112. Asano Toyomi, *Teikoku Nihon no shokuminchi hōsei: Hōiki tōgō to teikoku chitsujo* (Nagoya: Nagoya Daigaku Shuppankai, 2008), 425–431.
113. Zaiseibu zeimushi, *Zeimu tōkei nenpōsho, Dai-go kai* (Shinkyō [Changchun]: Manshukoku Keizaibu Zeimushi, 1938), 12; *Zeimu tōkei nenpōsho, Dai-roku kai* (Shinkyō: Manshukoku Keizaibu Zeimushi, 1939), 10; *Zeimu tōkei nenpōsho, Dai-shichi kai* (Shinkyō: Manshukoku Keizaibu Zeimushi, 1940), 10.
114. On economic police in Korea and Manchukuo, see Hŏ Yŏngnan, "Chŏnsi ch'ejegi (1937–1945) saenghwal p'ilsup'um tongje yŏn'gu," *Kuksagwan nonch'ong* 88 (2000): 289–330; Tanaka Ryūichi, "'Manshūkoku' keisatsu to chiiki shakai: keizai keisatsu no katsudō to sono mujun o chūshin to shite," *Chungang saron* 32 (December 2010): 237–271.
115. Zeikan Gaishi Hensan Iinkai, *Manshūkoku zeikan gaishi*, 189. There are some slight discrepancies between the smuggling data reported in this volume and the *Zeimu tōkei nenpōsho* cited in note 113, but unfortunately the *Zeimu tōkei nenpōsho* only goes up to 1941.
116. "Ap'yŏn chaebaeji pyŏnkyŏng ŭro chaeMan dongp'o taegonghwang," *Chosŏn ilbo*, October 23, 1935.

117. "Chaebae changnyŏ han ap'yŏn ŭl Chosŏn kkaji changnyŏ?" *Tonga ilbo*, October 16, 1935. Scholars have devoted considerable attention to the Manchukuo opium monopoly, though little of this looks at Manchuria-Korea relations. For recent work, see Norman Smith, *Intoxicating Manchuria: Alcohol, Opium, and Culture in China's Northeast* (Vancouver: University of British Columbia Press, 2012); and Miriam Kingsberg, *Moral Nation: Modern Japan and Narcotics in Global History* (Berkeley: University of California Press, 2013).

118. On the Government-General of Chosen opium monopoly, see John M. Jennings, "The Forgotten Plague: Opium and Narcotics in Korea under Japanese Rule, 1910–1945," *Modern Asian Studies* 29, no. 4 (1995), 795–815.

119. Pak Kang, "1930 nyŏndae Manju chiyŏk ŭli ap'yŏn chaebae wa Hanin, kŭrigo pijŏk," *Han'guk Minjok undongsa yŏn'gu* 92 (2017): 198.

120. Nakamura, "Shingishū no mitsuyu," 89.

121. Hagiwara Gunsō, "Sen-Man kokkyō chitai ni okeru ahen mitsuyu hanzai ni taisuru ichi kōsatsu," *Kenyū*, November 1941, 53–55.

122. "Apgang kyŏlbing ŭl iyong milsugun kyŏkchŭng," *Maeil sinbo*, January 30, 1942.

123. Chōsen Bōeki Kyōkai, *Chōsen bōekishi* (Keijō [Seoul]: Tōyō Keizai Shinpo Keijō Shikyoku, 1943), 354–356.

124. Manshūkoku chianbu keimushi, *Manshūkoku keisatsushi* (Matsuyama: Katō Toyotaka, 1976), 625.

125. Antō Shōkō Kōkai, *Angi keizai kondan kaigi jiroku* (Antō [Dandong]: Antō Shōkō Kōkai, 1941), 11.

126. Antō Shōkō Kōkai, *Angi keizai kondan kaigi jiroku*, 9–10.

127. Antō Shōkō Kōkai, *Angi keizai kondan kaigi jiroku*, "Angi kōri bukko taishōhyō."

128. "Amnokkang man kŏnnŭ myŏn il sŏk e ku wŏn iik," *Mansŏn ilbo*, November 23, 1940. One sŏk is equivalent to roughly 140 kilograms.

129. "Mitsuyushutsusha kan no gōtō jiken ni kansuru ken," Korean National Archives, CJA0004016.

130. One sen is one one-hundredth of one yen. One rin is one one-thousandth of one yen. From Moore, "The Yalu River Era of Developing Asia," 121.

131. Moore, "The Yalu River Era of Developing Asia," 121–122.

132. Antō Shōkō Kōkai, *Angi keizai kondan kaigi jiroku*, 27–28.

133. Kōtsūbu Daijin Kanbō Shiryōka, *Kōtsūbu yōran* (Shinkyō [Changchun]: Kōtsūbu Daijin Kanbō Shiryōka, 1944), 230.

134. For more on the Japanese wartime empire, see Peter Duus, Ramon H. Myers, and Mark R. Peattie, eds., *The Japanese Wartime Empire, 1931–1945* (Princeton, NJ: Princeton University Press, 1996).

135. "Manp'osŏn ŭi chŏnt'ong," *Tonga ilbo*, January 28, 1939; Nagatsuka Riichi, *Kubota Yutaka* (Tokyo: Denki Kōhōsha, 1966), 221.

136. Satō, *Doboku jinsei gojūnen*, 157.

137. Nagatsuka, *Kubota Yutaka*, 221; Doboku Gakkai Nihon Dobokushi Henshū Iinkai, *Nihon dobokushi: Taishō gannen - Shōwa15 nen* (Tokyo: Doboku Gakkai, 1973), 1171.

138. Satō, *Doboku jinsei gojūnen*, 158.

139. Doboku Gakkai, *Nihon dobokushi*, 1171.

140. Harada, *Suihō hatsudenjo kōji taikan*, 9.

141. Zeikan Gaishi Hensan Iinkai, *Manshūkoku zeikan gaishi*, 112.

142. "Nichi-Man kan no kanzei o menjo," *Ōsaka Asahi shinbun*, April 30, 1944; "Nichi-Man kan sanhin ni kanzei zenmen menjo," *Ōsaka Mainichi shinbun*, April 30, 1944.

143. "B-29 igi Chosŏn chinip," *Maeil sinbo*, February 15, 1945.

CONCLUSION

1. Associated Press, "Border Patrol Agents Fight Drug War on St. Lawrence River," syracuse.com, February 15, 2011, https://www.syracuse.com/news/2011/02/border_patrol_agents_fight_dru.html; "St. Lawrence River smuggling in spotlight after drownings," *CBC News*, September 5, 2015, https://www.cbc.ca/news/canada/ottawa/st-lawrence-border-smuggling-1.3217298; J. David Goodman, "They Built the Wall. Now Some in Texas Fear It May Fall," *New York Times*, January 5, 2023, https://www.nytimes.com/2023/01/05/us/texas-private-border-wall.html.

2. Transboundary Waters Assessment Programme, "Transboundary Waters Systems—Status and Trends," United Nations Environment Programme, January 2016, https://uneplive.unep.org/media/docs/assessments/transboundary_waters_systems_status_and_trends_crosscutting_analysis.pdf.

3. Laura Packer, "6 Ways the Border Wall Could Disrupt the Environment," *National Geographic*, https://www.nationalgeographic.com/environment/article/how-trump-us-mexico-border-wall-could-impact-environment-wildlife-water (accessed September 11, 2023).

4. For more on the links between climate change and border-making in the contemporary moment, see Simon Dalby, "Unsustainable Borders: Globalization in a Climate-Disrupted World," *Borders in Globalization Review* 2, no. 2 (spring/summer 2021): 26–37.

5. Nancy Langston, *Where Land and Water Meet: A Western Landscape Transformed* (Seattle: University of Washington Press, 2009).

6. Ling Zhang, *The River, the Plain, and the State: An Environmental Drama in Northern Song China, 1048–1128* (Cambridge, UK: Cambridge University Press, 2016); Roderick I. Wilson, *Turbulent Streams: An Environmental History of Japan's Rivers, 1600–1930* (Leiden: Brill, 2021); Richard White, *The Organic Machine: The Remaking of the Columbia River* (New York: Hill & Wang, 1995).

7. Kimberley Anh Thomas, "The River-Border Complex: A Border-Integrated Approach to Transboundary River Governance Illustrated by the Ganges River and Indo-Bangladeshi Border," *Water International* 42, no. 1 (January 2017): 34–53; C. J. Alvarez, *Border Land, Border Water: A History of Construction on the US-Mexico Divide* (Austin: University of Texas Press, 2019).

8. Kim Mansŏn, *Amnokkang: han wŏlbuk chakka ka oech'ŏ purŭn haebang ŭi norae!: Kim Mansŏn chakp'umjip* (Seoul: Kip'ŭn Saem, 1989), 145–156.

9. On this period of North Korean history, see Suzy Kim, *Everyday Life in the North Korean Revolution, 1945–1950* (Ithaca, NY: Cornell University Press, 2013).

10. "Antō, Shōtoku chiku jijō," November 2, 1953, *Chūkyō jijō*, riku 677 (September 14, 1955), Diplomatic Archives of the Ministry of Foreign Affairs of Japan (Tokyo), Post-WWII record, A'-0237, 19.

11. Chen Jian, *China's Road to the Korean War: The Making of the Sino-American Confrontation* (New York: Columbia University Press, 1994), 108. For more on border policing in this era, see Kim Sŏnho, "Pukhan ŭi kyŏnggye/kukkyŏng insik kwa Puk-Chung chŏpkyŏng chiyŏk kyŏngbi (1945–1947): kukkyŏng kyŏngbitae rŭl chungsim ŭro," *Tongbuga yŏksa nonch'ong* 71 (2021): 354–388.

12. Ch'oe Yŏng, "Amnokkang taean 'Chungguk kungmindang chunganggun' pipŏb haengwi chosa," Pukchosŏn inmin wiwŏnhoe waemuguk, RG 242, SA 2005, Item #36.2, National Archives Collections of Foreign Documents Seized, National Archives and Records Administration, Scan of archival document accessed through National Library of Korea website, https://www.nl.go.kr/NL/contents/N20401020000.do.

13. "Zhong-Han guojing jiufen," Records of the Ministry of Foreign Affairs, Academia Historica (Taipei), 020-010202-0003.

14. For an in-depth study of the Korean War, see Sheila Miyoshi Jager, *Brothers at War: The Unending Conflict in Korea* (New York: W. W. Norton, 2013).

15. War Memorial of Korea, "6.25 chŏnjaengsil," https://www.warmemo.or.kr/front/exhibition/exhibit.do?bbsId=1401 (accessed July 6, 2022).

16. Translation from Adam Cathcart, "Japanese Devils and American Wolves: Chinese Communist Songs from the War of Liberation and the Korean War," *Popular Music & Society* 33, no. 2 (May 2010): 213–215.

17. Charles Grutzner, "G.I.'s in Korea Battle Cold and Enemy, Too," *New York Times*, November 19, 1950.

18. One Chinese local history claims that American forces bombed the Yalu River bridges near Andong a total of 5,391 times between October 1950 and August 1951. Liaoning Sheng weiyuanhui wenshi ziliao weiyuanhui, *Yalu jiang pan de fengbei: Liaoning kangmei yuanchiao jishi* (Shenyang: Liaoning renmin chubanshe, 1990), 57.

19. Takahashi Yoshikazu, Kojima Shintarō, and Mya San Wai, "Chōsen Sōtokufu Tetsudōkyoku ni yoru fukushazaikei torasu kyōryō no kaihatsu to taidan seinō," *Doboku Gakkai ronbunshū D2 (dobokushi)*, 76, no. 1 (2020), 28.

20. Du Wenwen, "Lishi zhaopian 'Zhongguo renimin zhiyuanjun kua guo Yalujiang' dansheng jingguo," *Zhongguo jun wang*, December 27, 2016, http://www.81.cn/jwzl/2016-12/27/content_7426237.htm.

21. David Halberstam, *The Coldest Winter: America and the Korean War* (New York: Hyperion, 2007).

22. Wang Huazhong, "Yalu Flood Forces 99,000 to Evacuate," *China Daily*, August 23, 2010, http://www.chinadaily.com.cn/china/2010-08/23/content_11186198.htm.

23. Mun Dong Hui, "Two Tragedies Caused by North Korea's 'COVID-19 Phobia,'" *Daily NK*, April 27, 2021, https://www.dailynk.com/english/two-tragedies-caused-north-korea-covid-19-phobia/.

24. One best-selling memoir by a North Korean migrant that features an icy crossing over the Yalu River is Hyeonseo Lee's *Girl with Seven Names: A North Korean Defector Story* (London: William Collins, 2016).

Bibliography

PRIMARY SOURCES

Archives

    Archives of the Institute of Modern History, Academia Sinica (Taipei, Taiwan)
    Diplomatic Archives of the Ministry of Foreign Affairs of Japan (Tokyo, Japan)
    Hoover Institution Archives (Stanford, CA)
    Japan Center for Asian Historical Records (JACAR) (https://www.jacar.go.jp/)
    Kanagawa Prefectural Archives (Yokohama, Japan)
    Liaoning Provincial Archives (Shenyang, China)
    National Archives and Records Administration (College Park, MD)
    National Archives of Japan (Tokyo, Japan)
    National Archives of Korea (Taejŏn, South Korea)
    The National Archives of the Presbyterian Church, USA (Philadelphia, PA)
    National Institute of Korean History Korean History Database (Kuksa P'yŏnch'an Wiwŏnhoe Han'guksa Deit'ŏbeisŭ) (https://db.history.go.kr/)
    Records of the Ministry of Foreign Affairs, Academia Historica (Taipei, Taiwan)
    Sonoma State University Library Special Collections (Rohnert Park, CA)
    Yūhō Bunko, Tōyō Bunka Kenkyūjo, Gakushūin University (Tokyo, Japan)

Newspapers

    Asahi shinbun
    Aspen (Colorado) *Daily Times*
    Chosŏn ilbo
    Chungwae ilbo
    Dagong bao
    Hwangsŏng sinmun
    Japan Times
    Keijō nippō
    Maeil sinbo
    Manshū nippō
    Mansŏn ilbo
    New York Times
    Ōsaka Asahi shinbun Seisen ban
    Seisen nippō
    Shen bao
    Shengjing shibao
    Sidae ilbo
    Times (London)
    Tonga ilbo
    Yishi bao

Magazines, Journals, and Bulletins
  Asahi gurafu
  Chōsen (1908–1911)
  Chōsen (1920–1944)
  Chōsen shūppan keisatsu geppō
  Dongfang zhanyou
  Engineering
  Fortnightly Review
  Heihoku keishō
  Huashang lianhe bao
  Kaebyŏk
  Keimu ihō
  Kenyū
  Kingu
  Mansen
  Mesny's Chinese Miscellany
  Ōryoku
  Samch'ŏlli
  Shingishū shōkō kōgi geppō
  Shokugin chōsa geppō
  Shufu no tomo
  Sin kajŏng
  Wanguo shangye yuebao

Adachi, Kinnosuke. *Manchuria: A Survey.* New York: R. M. McBride, 1925.
Antō Kōseikyoku. *Keizai kasen 'Ōryokkō' no bekken.* Antō [Andong]: Manshūkoku Kokumuin Kōtsūbu Antō Kōseikyoku, 1935.
Antō-ken Shōgyō Kaigisho. *Antō shi.* Antō [Dandong]: Antō-ken Shōgyō Kaigisho, 1920.
Antō-shō Kōsho Sōmuchō Sōmuka. *Antō-shō kōsho nenpō: Kōtoku ninen.* Antō [Dandong]: Dōchō, 1936.
Antō Shōkō Kōkai. *Antō keizai gaiyō.* Antō [Dandong]: Antō Shōkō Kōkai, 1938.
——. *Angi keizai kondan kaigi jiroku.* Antō [Dandong]: Antō Shōkō Kōkai, 1941.
——. *Antō sangyō keizai gaikan.* Antō [Dandong]: Antō Shōkō Kōkai, 1942.
——. *Antō-shō no iseki.* Antō [Dandong]: Antō Shōkō Kōkai, 1942.
Bickers, Robert A., and Hans J. Van de Ven., eds. *China and the West: the Maritime Customs Service Archive from the Second Historical Archives of China, Nanjing [SHAC].* Reading, Berkshire, U.K.: Primary Source Microfilm, 2004.
Chang Sŏngsik. *Sinŭiju taegwan.* Sinŭiju: Munhwadang, 1931.
China: The Maritime Customs. *Decennial Reports, 1922–1931.* Shanghai, 1933.
Chinese Maritime Customs Service. *Decennial Reports on the Trade, Industries, etc. of the Ports Open to Foreign Commerce, and on Conditions and Development of the Treaty Port Provinces.* Shanghai: Statistical Dept. of the Inspectorate General of Customs, 1924.
Ch'oe Chŏnghwa. *Sakchu kunji.* Seoul: Sakchu Kunminhoe, 1991.
Ch'oe, Yŏngho, Peter H. Lee, and Wm. Theodore de Bary, eds. *Sources of Korean Tradition, Volume II: From the Sixteenth to the Twentieth Centuries.* New York: Columbia University Press, 2000.
Chŏng Mungi. *Amnokkang ŏbo,* 1940. Manuscript, Yonsei University Library.
Chōsen Bōeki Kyōkai. *Chōsen bōekishi.* Keijō [Seoul]: Tōyō Keizai Shinpo Keijō Shikyoku, 1943.

Chōsen Ōryokkō Suiryoku Hatsuden Kabushiki Kaisha. *Ōryokkō suiryoku hatsuden keikaku no gaiyō*. Keijō [Seoul]: Chōsen Ōryokkō Suiryoku Hatsuden Kabushiki Kaisha, 1940.
Chōsen Sōtokufu. *Chōsen buraku chōsa hōkoku. Dai 1-satsu: Kadenmin raiju Shinajin.* Keijō [Seoul]: Chōsen Sōtokufu, 1924.
——. *Chōsen Sōtokufu tōkei nenpō: taishō 9 nen*. Keijō [Seoul]: Chōsen Sōtokufu, 1921.
——. *Chōsen Sōtokufu tōkei nenpō: taishō 13 nen*. Keijō [Seoul]: Chōsen Sōtokufu, 1926.
Chōsen Sōtokufu Kansokujo. *Chōsen Sōtokufu Kansokujo kishō gonenhō: Shōwa gannen yori Shōwa 5-nen ni itaru*. Zinsen [Inch'ŏn]: Chōsen Sōtokufu Kansokujo, 1931.
Chōsen Sōtokufu Keimukyoku. *Chōsen keisatsu no gaiyō*. Keijō [Seoul]: Chōsen Sōtokufu Keimukyoku, 1925–1941.
——. *Kōtō keisatsu kankei nenpyō*. Keijō [Seoul]: Chōsen Sōtokufu Keimukyoku, 1930.
——. Zaiman Senjin to Shina kanken: tsuketari Manshū ni okeru hainichi undō. Keijō [Seoul]: Chōsen Sōtokufu Keimukyoku, 1930.
Chōsen Sōtokufu Suisan Shikenjō. *Ōryokkō no sakana*. Fuzan [Pusan]: Chōsen Sōtokufu Suisan Shikenjō, 1940.
Chōsen Sōtokufu Tetsudōkyoku. *Chōsen testudōshi*. Keijō [Seoul]: Chōsen Sōtokufu Tetsudōkyoku, 1929.
——. *Ōryokkō kyōryō kōji gaikyō*. Keijō [Seoul]: Chōsen Sōtokufu Tetsudōkyoku, 1911.
——. *Ōryokkō kyōryō kōji hōkoku*. Keijō [Seoul]: Chōsen Sōtokufu, 1912.
Davis, Richard Harving, et al. *The Russo-Japanese War: A Photographic and Descriptive Review of the Great Conflict in the Far East*. New York: P. F. Collier & Son, 1904.
Dongbei kang Ri lianjun shiliao bianxiezu. *Dongbei kang Ri lianjun shiliao*. Beijing: Zhonggong dangshi shiliao chubanshe, 1987.
General Staff, War Office. *The Russo-Japanese War: Reports from Officers Attached to the Japanese Forces in the Field*. Tokyo: Ganesha Publishing, 2000.
Government-General of Chosen. *The Third Annual Report on Reforms and Progress in Korea (1909–1910)*. Seoul: Chōsen Sōtokufu, 1910.
Guo Tingyi et al. *Qing ji Zhong Ri Han guanxi shiliao*. Taibei Shi: Zhongyang yanjiuyuan jindaishi yanjiusuo, 1972.
Guojia tushuguan gujiguan, ed. *Guojia tushuguan guancang Qingdai minguo diaocha baogao congkan*. Beijing: Beijing Yanshan chubanshe, 2007.
Harada Kiyoshi. *Suihō hatsudenjo kōji taikan*. Amagasaki: Doken Bunkasha, 1942.
Hattori Seiichi. *Tsūzoku seishin senki*. Tokyo: Tōkyō Tosho Shuppan, 1897.
Heian Hokudō. *Heian hokudō tōkei nenpō: Shōwa jū nen*. Shingishū [Sinŭiju]: Heian Hokudō, 1937.
Heian Hokudō Keisatsubu. *Kokkyō keibi*. Shingishū [Sinŭiju]: Heian Keishō Henshūbu, 1936.
——. *Kokkyō no mamori*. Shingishū [Sinŭiju]: Heian Hokudō Keisatsubu, 1933.
Hyesan Kunji Py'ŏnch'an Wiwonhoe. *Hyesan kunji*. Seoul: Hyesan Kunji Py'ŏnch'an Wiwonhoe, 1999.
Imperial Maritime Customs. *Treaties, Conventions, etc., between China and Foreign States*, vol. 2. Shanghai: Statistical Department of the Inspectorate General of Customs, 1908.
Ishimaru Gin'ichi. *Kokkyō shashin daikan*. Shingishū [Sinŭiju]: Ōkō Nippōsha, 1929.
Kang, Hildi. *Under the Black Umbrella: Voices from Colonial Korea, 1910–1945*. Ithaca, NY: Cornell University Press, 2001.
Kim Chŏngju, ed. *Chōsen tōchi shiryō* [*CTS*]. Tokyo: Kankoku Shiryō Kenkyūjo, 1970–1972.

Kim Ilsŏng. *Segi wa tŏburŏ*. Pyongyang: Chosŏn Nodongdang Ch'ulp'ansa, 1992–1996.
Kim Mansŏn. *Amnokkang: han wŏlbuk chakka ka oech'ŏ purŭn haebang ŭi norae!: Kim Mansŏn chakp'umjip*. Seoul: Kip'ŭn Saem, 1989.
Kobayashi Kaneshige. *Kokkyō to sono keibi*. Keijō [Seoul]: Chōsen Sōtokufu Keibi Engōkai, 1936.
Kodama Toshimitsu. *Natsukashi no Nihon uta zenshū*. Kagoshima-shi: Chiran Tokkō Irei Kenshōkai, 1972.
Kōno Yahei. *Kokkyō keibi kinenshū*. Shingishū [Sinŭiju]: Heian Keishō Henshūbu, 1937.
Kosako Shintarō. *Kokkyō no hana*. Shingishū [Sinŭiju]: Shingishū Insatsu Kabushiki Kaisha, 1936.
"Kōsōhei gaikyō." Unpublished manuscript, University of California, Berkeley, Library.
Kōtsūbu Daijin Kanbō Shiryōka. *Kōtsūbu yōran*. Shinkyō [Changchun]: Kōtsūbu Daijin Kanbō Shiryōka, 1944.
Lautensach, Hermann. *Korea: A Geography Based on the Author's Travels and Literature*. Translated by Katherine and Eckart Dege. Berlin: Springer Verlag, 1988.
Lee, Hyeonseo. *Girl with Seven Names: A North Korean Defector Story*. London: William Collins, 2016.
Liaoning Sheng danganguan, ed. *Mantie diaocha baogao*. Guilin: Guangxi shifan daxue chubanshe, 2005.
Liaoning Sheng dangshi bianweihui. *Dongbei kang Ri douzheng shilunji: di 1 ji*. Shenyang: Liaoning Sheng dangshi bianweihui, 1986.
Liaoning Sheng weiyuanhui wenshi ziliao weiyuanhui. *Yalu jiang pan de fengbei: Liaoning kangmei yuanchiao jishi*. Shenyang: Liaoning renmin chubanshe, 1990.
MacMurray, John Van Antwerp, ed.. *Treaties and Agreements with and Concerning China, 1894–1919*. New York: Oxford University Press, 1921.
Manabe Gorō. *Tōhendō annai*. Dairen [Dalian]: Ajia Shuppan Kyōkai, 1940.
"Manchuria Travel Memorandum: Conditions at Antung." British Foreign Office, China File 371/18049. Foreign Office Files for China, 1919–1980, Sources from The National Archives, UK, Adam Matthew Digital database (https://www.amdigital.co.uk/collection/foreign-office-files-for-china-1919-1980)
Manshūkoku chianbu keimushi. *Manshūkoku keisatsushi*. Matsuyama: Katō Toyotaka, 1976.
Masuda Tadao. *Manshū kokkyō mondai*. Tokyo: Chūō Kōronsha, 1941.
Minami Manshū Tetsudō Kabushiki Kaisha Chōsabu. *Ōryokkō suiryoku hatsuden chōsa keikaku shiryō*. Dairen [Dalian]: Minami Manshū Tetsudō Kabushiki Kaisha, 1940.
Minami Manshū Tetsudō Kabushiki Kaisha. *Chōsen Manshū tabi no shiori*. Tōkyō: Minami Manshū Tōkyō Shisha, 1938.
———. *Manshū suisan jigyō hōsaku*. Dairen [Dalian]: Minami Manshū Tetsudō Keizai Chōsakai, 1935.
Minami Manshū Tetsudō Kabushiki Kaisha Chōsaka. *Manshū no suisangyō*. Dairen [Dalian]: Minami Manshū Tetsudō Kabushiki Kaisha, 1931.
Minami Manshū Tetsudō Kabushiki Kaisha Keizai Chōsakai. *Manshū suiun hōsaku*. Dairen [Dalian]: Minami Manshū Tetsudō Kabushiki Kaisha Keizai Chōsakai, 1936.
Minami Manshū Tetsudō Kabushiki Kaisha Sangyōbu. *Ōryokkō keizaiken chōsa hōkokusho*. Dairen [Dalian]: Mantetsu Sangyōbu, 1937.
Minami Manshū Tetsudō Kabushiki Kaisha Shomubu Chōsaka. *Tashitō no kenkyū*. Dairen [Dalian]: Minami Manshū Tetsudō Kabushiki Kaisha, 1926.

Mishima Sōsen. *Nichi-Ro gekisen Ōryokkō*. Tokyo: Kinkōdō Shoseki, 1904.
Mizokami Sadao. *Nichi-Ro sensō jūgunki: gun'i no jinchū nikki*. Kyoto: Shibunkaku Shuppan, 2004.
Morisaki Minoru. *Tōhendō*. Tokyo: Shunjūsha 1941.
Murakami Masatsugu. *Manshūkoku oyobi shūhen ni okeru sho kasen no tōketsu*. Dairen [Dalian]: Minami Manshū Tetsudō Kabushiki Kaisha Chōsakyoku, 1944.
Murayama Jōzō. *Manshū no shinrin to sono shizenteki kōsei*. Hōten [Shenyang]: Hōten Ōsaka Yagō Shoten, 1943.
Nagatsuka Riichi. *Kubota Yutaka*. Tokyo: Denki Kōhōsha, 1966.
Nihon Chiso Hiryō Kabushiki Kaisha. *Nihon chiso hiryō jigyō gaiyō*. Osaka and Tokyo: Nihon Chiso Hiryō Kabushiki Kaisha, 1940.
Nishida Mataji and Nakamuta Gōrō. *Ōryokkō ryūiku shinrin sagyō chōsa fukumeisho*. Tokyo: Nōshōmushō Sanrinkyoku, 1905.
Noritake Kazuo. *Ōryokkō*. Tokyo: Daiichi Shuppan Kyōkai, 1943.
Ōryokkō Saiboku Kōshi, ed. *Ōryokkō ringyōshi*. Antō [Dandong]: Ōryokkō Saiboku Kōshi, 1919.
Ōsaki Mineto. *Ōryokkō: Man-Kan kokkyō jijō*. Tokyo: Maruzen, 1910.
Qing Guangxu chao Zhong Ri jiaoshe shiliao. Beijing: Gugong bowuyuan, 1932.
Railway Bureau Government-General of Chosen. *Report on the Construction of the Yalu River Bridge*. Ryūzan [Yongsan]: Chōsen Sōtokufu Tetsudōkyoku, 1914.
Satō Toshihiko. *Doboku jinsei gojūnen*. Chūō Kōron Jigyō Shuppan, 1969.
Shimizu Yoshihiro. *Shintai gunjin yōbun*. Osaka: Hamamoto Meishōdō, 1895.
Shingishū shi. Osaka: Shōbunkan Insatsujo, 1911.
Shingishū Zeikan. *Shingishū minato gaiyō*. Shingishū [Sinŭiju]: Shingishū Zeikan, 1938.
——. *Shingishū minato ippan*. Shingishū [Sinŭiju]: Shingishū Zeikan, 1932–1937.
Sinŭiju Siminhoe. *Sinŭiju shichi*. Seoul: Sinŭiju Siminhoe, 1969.
Statistical Department of the Inspectorate General of Customs. *Decennial Reports on the Trade, Industries etc. of the Ports Open to Foreign Commerce and on the Condition and Development of the Treaty Port Provinces: 1902–1911, Volume 1: Northern and Yangtze Ports*. Shanghai: Statistical Department of the Inspectorate General of Customs, 1913.
Tamon Jirō, *Tamon Jirō Nichi-Ro sensō nikki*. Tokyo: Fuyō Shobō, 1980.
Tani Mitsuyo. *Manshū kasenshi*. Shinkyō [Changchun]: Manshū Jijō Annaijo, 1940.
——. *Ōryokkō*. Shinkyō [Changchun]: Manshūkoku Tsūshinsha, 1937.
——. *Taitōkō to hōko Tōhendō*. Shinkyō [Changchun]: Manshū Jijō Annaijo, 1940.
Tsūka-shō Kōsho. *Fukō kōsaku jisshi keikaku gaiyō*. Tsūka-shō kōsho 1939. Manuscript, Takushoku University Library.
——. *Kōtoku gonendo fukō kōsaku jisseki hōkokusho*. Tsūka-shō Kōsho, 1939. Manuscript, Takushoku University Library.
——. *Tsūka-shō gairan*. Tsūka-shō Kōsho, 1940.
Ueda Gunji. *Kokkyō nihyaku ri*. Keijō [Seoul]: Kokkyō Nihyaku Ri Hakkōjo, 1929.
Wada Takashi. *Shingishū shi*. Shingishū [Sinŭiju]: Shimada Sōbunkan, 1911.
Wang Tongsheng et al., ed. *Yalu Jiang liuyu lishi ziliao huibian*. Dandong: Dandong shi wei, 2007.
Wiwŏn Kunji P'yŏnch'an Wiwŏnhoe. *Wiwŏn kunji*. Seoul: Wiwŏn Kunji P'yŏnch'an Wiwŏnhoe, 1971.
Yi Sŭngch'un, *Ōryokkō jōryū shinrin shakubatsu jigyō annai*. Hu'chang: Ōryokkō Jōryū Shinrin Shakubatsu Jigyō Annai Hakkōsho, 1931.

Yosano Akiko. *Travels in Manchuria and Mongolia: A Feminist Poet from Japan Encounters Prewar China*. Edited and translated by Joshua Fogel. New York: Columbia University Press, 2001.
Yosano Akiko and Yosano Tekkan. *Manmō yūki*. Osaka: Ōsaka Yagō Shoten, 1930.
Yu Yunfeng. *Andong Xian zhi*, 1931. Reprint in *Zhongguo fangzhi congshu. Dongbei difang: di 18 hao*. Taibei: Chengwen Chubanshe, 1974.
Yuasa Chikusanjin. *Kōta yawa*. Tokyo: Shinsakusha, 1924.
Zaiseibu. *Zeikan jimu gaiyō: Harupin, Antō Tomon no bu*. Shinkyō [Changchun]: Zaiseibu, 1934.
Zaiseibu zeimushi. *Zeimu tōkei nenpōsho, dai-go kai*. Shinkyō [Changchun]: Manshukoku Keizaibu Zeimushi, 1938.
——. *Zeimu tōkei nenpōsho, dai-roku kai*. Shinkyō [Changchun]: Manshukoku Keizaibu Zeimushi, 1939.
——. *Zeimu tōkei nenpōsho, dai-shichi kai*. Shinkyō [Changchun]: Manshukoku Keizaibu Zeimushi, 1940.
Zeikan Gaishi Hensan Iinkai. *Manshūkoku zeikan gaishi*. Shinkyō [Changchun]: Keizaibu Kanseika, 1944.
Zhengxie Hunjiang Shi Linjiang Qu Weiyuanhui Wenshi Ziliao Yanjiu Weiyuanhui. *Linjiang wenshi ziliao di er ji: Linjiang guanmin ju Ri she ling douzheng zhuanji*. Hunjiang Shi, 1986.
Zhongguo bianjiang shi di yanjiu zhongxin. *Dongbei bianjiang dang'an xuanji* [*DBDX*]. Guilin: Guangxi shifan daxue chubanshe, 2007.

SECONDARY SOURCES

Alvarez, C. J. *Border Land, Border Water: A History of Construction on the US-Mexico Divide*. Austin: University of Texas Press, 2019.
Ambaras, David. *Japan's Imperial Underworlds: Intimate Encounters at the Borders of Empire*. Cambridge, UK: Cambridge University Press, 2018.
Asano Shunkō et al. *Hazamagumi hyakunenshi*. Tokyo: Kabushiki Kaisha Hazamagumi, 1989.
Asano Toyomi. *Teikoku Nihon no shokuminchi hōsei: Hōiki tōgō to teikoku chitsujo*. Nagoya: Nagoya Daigaku Shuppankai, 2008.
Bae, Jae Soo, et al. "Forest Transition in South Korea: Reality, Path and Drivers." *Land Use Policy* 29 (January 2012): 198–207.
Baldwin Jr., Frank P. "The March First Movement: Korean Challenge and Japanese Response." PhD diss., Columbia University, 1969.
Barclay, Paul D. *Outcasts of Empire: Japan's Rule on Taiwan "Savage Border," 1874–1945*. Berkeley: University of California Press, 2017.
Batten, Bruce L. *To the Ends of Japan: Premodern Frontiers, Boundaries, and Interactions*. Honolulu: University of Hawai'i Press, 2003.
Bello, David A. *Across Forest, Steppe, and Mountain: Environment, Identity, and Empire in Qing China's Borderlands*. Cambridge, UK: Cambridge University Press, 2015.
Biggs, David. *Quagmire: Nation-Building and Nature in the Mekong Delta*. Seattle: University of Washington Press, 2010.
Billingsley, Phil. *Bandits in Republican China*. Stanford, CA: Stanford University Press, 1988.
Breuker, Remco. "Within or Without? Ambiguity of Borders and Koryŏ Koreans' Travels During the Liao, Jin, Song and Yuan." *East Asian History* 38 (February 2014): 47–62.

Brooks, Barbara J. *Japan's Imperial Diplomacy: Consuls, Treaty Ports, and War in China, 1895–1938*. Honolulu: University of Hawai'i Press, 2000.

Caffrey, Patrick. "The Forests of Northeast China, 1600–1960: Environment, Politics, and Society." PhD diss., Georgetown University, 2002.

Cai, Wenjiao. "Coping with the Cold: Nature and State on Chosŏn Korea's Northern Frontier." PhD diss., Harvard University, 2022.

Cathcart, Adam. "Japanese Devils and American Wolves: Chinese Communist Songs from the War of Liberation and the Korean War." *Popular Music and Society* 33, no. 2 (May 2010): 203–218.

Ch'ae Yŏngguk. *1920-yŏndae huban Manju chiyŏk hangil mujang t'ujaeng*. Ch'ungch'ŏng-namdo Ch'ŏnan-si: Tongnip Kinyŏmgwan Han'guk Tongnip Undongsa Yŏn'guso, 2007.

Chang, Gordon H. *Fateful Ties: A History of America's Preoccupation with China*. Cambridge, MA: Harvard University Press, 2015.

Chang Seyun. "Manju chiyŏk Hanin hangil mujang tujaeng seryŏk ŭi shiksaenghwal kwa pogŏn wisaeng." *Hanguk kŭnhyŏndaesa yŏn'gu* 28 (March 2004), 78–115.

Chang Suho. *Chosŏn sidae mal Ilbon ŭi ŏŏp ch'imt'alsa: kaehang esŏ 1910-yŏn kkaji Ilbon ŭi ŏŏp ch'imt'al e kwanhan yŏn'gu*. Seoul: Susan Kyŏngje Yŏn'guwŏn, 2011.

Chŏng Angi. "1936 nyŏn Sŏnman sunoe ŭi 'Tomun hoedam' kwa 'Mansŏn iryŏ'" *Manju yŏn'gu*, 12 (December 2011): 181–209.

———. "20 segi ch'oyŏp Hwangch'op'y ŏng ŭi yŏngt'o punjaengsa yŏn'gu." *Yŏngt'o haeyang yŏn'gu* 13 (June 2017): 64–109.

Chŏng Chaejŏng. *Ilche ch'imnyak kwa Han'guk ch'ŏlto: 1892–1945*. Seoul: Seoul Taehakkyo Ch'ulp'anbu, 1999.

Chūō Nikkan Kyōkai, *Chōsen denki jigyōshi*. Tokyo: Chūō Nikkan Kyōkai, 1981.

Christmas, Sakura. "The Cartographic Steppe: Spaces of Development in Northeast Asia, 1895–1945." PhD diss., Harvard University, 2015.

Coox, Alvin D. *Nomonhan: Japan against Russia, 1939*. Stanford, CA: Stanford University Press, 1985.

da Cunha, Dilip. *The Invention of Rivers: Alexander's Eye and Ganga's Descent*. Philadelphia: University of Pennsylvania Press, 2019.

Dalby, Simon. "Unsustainable Borders: Globalization in a Climate-Disrupted World." *Borders in Globalization Review* 2, no. 2 (Spring/Summer 2021): 26–37.

Doboku Gakkai Nihon Dobokushi Henshū Iinkai. *Nihon dobokushi: Taishō gannen— Shōwa 15 nen*. Tokyo: Doboku Gakkai, 1973.

Driscoll, Mark. *Absolute Erotic, Absolute Grotesque: The Living, Dead, and Undead in Japan's Imperialism, 1895–1945*. Durham, NC: Duke University Press, 2010.

Duara, Prasenjit. *Sovereignty and Authenticity: Manchukuo and the East Asian Modern*. Lanham, MD: Rowman & Littlefield, 2004.

Duus, Peter. *The Abacus and the Sword: The Japanese Penetration of Korea, 1895–1910*. Berkeley: University of California Press, 1998.

Duus, Peter, Ramon H. Myers, and Mark R. Peattie, eds. *The Japanese Wartime Empire, 1931–1945*. Princeton, NJ: Princeton University Press, 1996.

Eckert, Carter J. *Offspring of Empire: The Koch'ang Kims and the Colonial Origins of Korean Capitalism, 1876–1945*. Seattle: University of Washington Press, 1991.

Elliot, Mark C. "The Limits of Tartary: Manchuria in Imperial and National Geographies." *Journal of Asian Studies* 59, no. 3 (2000): 603–646.

Esselstrom, Eric. *Crossing Empire's Edge: Foreign Ministry Police and Japanese Expansionism in Northeast Asia*. Honolulu: University of Hawai'i Press, 2009.

Fedman, David. "The Saw and the Seed: Japanese Forestry in Colonial Korea, 1895–1945." PhD diss., Stanford University, 2015.

———. *Seeds of Control: Japan's Empire of Forestry in Colonial Korea*. Seattle: University of Washington Press, 2020.
Freitas, Frederico. *Nationalizing Nature: Iguazu Falls and National Parks at the Brazil-Argentina Border*. Cambridge, UK: Cambridge University Press, 2021.
Fujitani, Takashi. *Race for Empire: Koreans as Japanese and Japanese as Americans during World War II*. Berkeley: University of California Press, 2011.
Gao Jian-hua et al. "Sediment Transport in Yalu River Estuary." *Chinese Geographical Science* 13, no. 2 (2003): 157–163.
Haag, Andre. "Fear and Loathing in Imperial Japan: The Cultures of Korean Peril, 1919–1923." PhD diss., Stanford University, 2013.
Halberstam, David. *The Coldest Winter: America and the Korean War*. New York: Hyperion, 2007.
Han Ch'ŏlho. "1930 nyŏndae Ilje ŭi Joji El Sho (George L. Shaw) t'anap ch'ukch'ul kongjak kwa kŭ sŏngkyŏk." *Han'guk minjok undongsa yŏn'gu* 69 (2011): 151–190.
Hirata, Koji. "Made in Manchuria: The Transnational Origins of Socialist Industrialization in Maoist China." *American Historical Review* 126 no. 3 (September 2021): 1072–1101.
Hirose Teizō. "'Manshūkoku' ni okeru Suihō Damu kensetsu." *Niigata Kokusai Jōhō Daigaku Jōhō Bunka Gakubu kiyō* 6 (March 2003): 1–25.
———. "Shokuminchiki Chōsen ni okeru Suihō hatsudenjo kensetsu to ryūbatsu mondai." *Niigata Kokusai Jōhō Daigaku Jōhō Bunka Gakubu kiyō* 1 (March 1998): 39–58.
Hŏ Yŏngnan. "Chŏnsi ch'ejegi (1937–1945) saenghwal p'ilsup'um tongje yŏn'gu." *Kuksagwan nonch'ong* 88 (2000): 289–330.
Hughes, Theodore, et al. *Rat Fire: Korean Stories from the Japanese Empire*. Ithaca, NY: Cornell University Press, 2013.
Im Sŏngmo. "Chungil chŭnjaeng chŏnya Manjuguk-Chosŏn kwangyesa ŭi somyo: 'Il-Man ilch'e' wa 'Man-Sŏn iryŏ' ŭi kaltŭng." *Yŏksa hakpo* 201 (March 2009): 165–202.
Jager, Sheila Miyoshi. *Brothers at War: The Unending Conflict in Korea*. New York: W. W. Norton, 2013.
Jennings, John M. "The Forgotten Plague: Opium and Narcotics in Korea under Japanese Rule, 1910–1945." *Modern Asian Studies* 29, no. 4 (1995), 795–815.
———. *The Opium Empire: Japanese Imperialism and Drug Trafficking in Asia, 1895–1945*. Westport, CT: Praeger, 1997.
Jeon, Miseli. "Violent Emotions: Modern Japanese and Korean Women's Writing, 1920–1980." PhD diss., University of British Columbia, 2004.
Jian, Chen. *China's Road to the Korean War: The Making of the Sino-American Confrontation*. New York: Columbia University Press, 1994.
Kang Ch'angil. "Chōsen shinryaku no butsuriteki kiban to shite no Chōsengun." In *Nikkan rekishi kyōdō kenkyū hōkokusho: dai 3 bunka hen gekan*, edited by Nikkan Rekishi Kyōdō Kenkyūkai, 411–434. Tokyo: Nikkan Rekishi Kyōdō Kenkyūkai, 2005.
Kang Sŏkhwa. "Chosŏn hugi P'yŏngan-do chiyŏk Amnokkang byŏn ŭi pangŏ ch'egye." *Han'guk munhwa* 34 (December 2004): 167–199.
Kanno Naoki. "Chōsen-Manshū hōmen kara mita Terauchi Masatake zō no ichi danmen: Ōryokkō Saiboku Kōshi nado to no kankei o tsūjite." *Higashi Ajia kindaishi* 16 (March 2013): 97–113.
———. "Ōryokkō Saiboku Kōshi to Nihon no Manshū shinshutsu—shinrin shigen o meguru taigai kankei no hensen." *Kokushigaku* 172 (August 2000): 45–76.

Kawada Etsu, ed. *Kindai Nihon sensōshi: Nisshin, Nichi-Ro sensō*. Tokyo: Dōdai Keizai Konwakai, 1995.
Kim, Elena. *Making Peace with Nature: Ecological Encounters along the Korean DMZ*. Durham, NC: Duke University Press, 2022.
Kim, Kwangmin. "Korean Migration in Nineteenth-Century Manchuria: A Global Theme in Modern Asian History." In *Mobile Subjects: Boundaries and Identities in the Modern Korean Diaspora*, edited by Wen-Hsin Yeh, 17–37. Berkeley, CA: Institute of East Asian Studies, 2013.
Kim, Seonmin. *Ginseng and Borderland: Territorial Boundaries and Political Relations between Qing China and Chosŏn Korea, 1636–1912*. Berkeley: University of California Press, 2017.
Kim Sŏnho. "Pukhan ŭi kyŏnggye/kukkyŏng insik kwa Puk-Chung chŏpkyŏng chiyŏk kyŏngbi (1945–1947): kukkyŏng kyŏngbitae rŭl chungsim ŭro." *Tongbuga yŏksa nonch'ong* 71 (2021): 354–388.
Kim, Sun Joo, ed. *The Northern Region of Korea: History, Identity and Culture*. Seattle: University of Washington Press, 2010.
Kim, Suzy. *Everyday Life in the North Korean Revolution, 1945–1950*. Ithaca, NY: Cornell University Press, 2013.
Kim Taehyŏn. "Sinŭiju Andong kan milmuyŏk tansok chŏngae kwajŏng kwa Chosŏn Ch'ongdokpu ŭi taeŭng." *Han'guksa yŏn'gu* 183 (December 2018): 319–356.
Kingsberg, Miriam. *Moral Nation: Modern Japan and Narcotics in Global History*. Berkeley: University of California Press, 2013.
Koshizawa Akira. "Daitōkō no keikaku to kensetsu (1937–1945)—Manshū ni okeru mikan no dai kibo kaihatsu purojekuto." *Nihon dobokushi kenkyū happyō ronbunshū* 6 (1986): 223–234.
Kreitman, Paul. *Japan's Ocean Borderland: Nature and Sovereignty*. Cambridge, UK: Cambridge University Press, 2023.
Kwong, Chi Man. *War and Geopolitics in Interwar Manchuria: Zhang Zuolin and the Fengtian Clique during the Northern Expedition*. Boston: Leiden, 2017.
Langston, Nancy. *Where Land and Water Meet: A Western Landscape Transformed*. Seattle: University of Washington Press, 2009.
Larsen, Kirk. *Traditions, Treaties, and Trade: Qing Imperialism and Chosŏn Korea, 1850–1910*. Cambridge, MA: Harvard University Asia Center, 2008.
Lattimore, Owen. *Manchuria: Cradle of Conflict*. New York: Macmillan, 1932.
Lee, Chong-Sik. *The Politics of Korean Nationalism*. Berkeley: University of California Press, 1963.
——. *Revolutionary Struggle in Manchuria: Chinese Communism and Soviet Interest, 1922–1945*. Berkeley: University of California Press, 1983.
Liu, Jing, and Yan Piao. "Expansion, Contestation, and Boundary Making: Chosŏn Korea and Ming China's Border Relations over the Yalu River Region." *International Journal of Korean History* 25 (2) August 2020: 105–142.
Lone, Stewart. *Japan's First Modern War: Army and Society in the Conflict with China, 1894–1895*. New York: St. Martin's Press, 1994.
Mainichi Shinbunsha. *Nihon shokuminchishi 1: Chōsen*. Tokyo: Mainichi Shinbunsha, 1978.
Matsuda, Hiroko. *Liminality of the Japanese Empire: Border Crossings from Okinawa to Colonial Taiwan*. Honolulu: University of Hawai'i Press, 2018.
Matsuda Toshihiko. *Nihon no Chōsen shokuminchi shihai to keisatsu: 1905-1945-nen*. Tokyo: Azekura Shobō, 2009.
——. "1910 nendai ni okeru Chōsen Sōtokufu no kokkyō keibi seisaku." *Jinbun Gakuhō* 106 (April 2015): 53–79.

Matsusaka, Yoshihisa Tak. *The Making of Japanese Manchuria, 1904–1932*. Cambridge, MA: Harvard University Asia Center, 2001.
McDonald, Kate L. "The Boundaries of the Interesting: Itineraries, Guidebooks, and Travel in Imperial Japan." PhD diss., University of California, San Diego, 2011.
———. *Placing Empire: Travel and the Social Imagination in Imperial Japan*. Berkeley: University of California Press, 2017.
Merrill, John Espy. "American Official Reactions to the Domestic Policies of Japan in Korea, 1905–1910." PhD diss., Stanford University, 1954.
Mezzadra, Sandro, and Brett Nielson. *Border as Method, or the Multiplication of Labor*. Durham, NC: Duke University Press, 2013.
Miller, Ian Jared, Julia Adeney Thomas, and Brett L. Walker, eds. *Japan at Nature's Edge: The Environmental Context of a Global Power*. Honolulu: University of Hawai'i Press, 2014.
Mitter, Rana. *The Manchurian Myth: Nationalism, Resistance, and Collaboration in Modern China*. Berkeley: University of California Press, 2000.
Mizuno, Hiromi. *Science for the Empire: Scientific Nationalism in Modern Japan*. Stanford, CA: Stanford University Press, 2008.
Mizuno, Naoki. "A Propaganda Film Subverting Ethnic Hierarchy?: Suicide Squad at the Watchtower and Colonial Korea." *Cross-Currents: East Asian History and Culture Review* 2, no. 1 (2013): 62–88.
Moon, Yumi. *Populist Collaborators: The Ilchinhoe and the Japanese Colonization of Korea, 1896–1910*. Ithaca, NY: Cornell University Press, 2013.
Moore, Aaron Stephen. *Constructing East Asia: Technology, Ideology, and Empire in Japan's Wartime Era 1931–1945*. Stanford, CA: Stanford University Press, 2013.
———. "'The Yalu River Era of Developing Asia': Japanese Expertise, Colonial Power, and the Construction of Sup'ung Dam." *Journal of Asian Studies* 72, no. 1 (2013): 115–139.
Mostern, Ruth. *The Yellow River: A Natural and Unnatural History*. New Haven, CT: Yale University Press, 2021.
Muscolino, Micah. *The Ecology of War in China: Henan Province, the Yellow River, and Beyond, 1938–1950*. Cambridge, UK: Cambridge University Press, 2015.
———. "Fisheries Build Up on the Nation: Marine Environmental Encounters between Japan and China." In *Japan at Nature's Edge: The Environmental Context of a Global Power*, edited by Ian Jared Miller et al., 56–72. Honolulu: University of Hawai'i Press, 2013.
Nail, Thomas. *Theory of the Border*. Oxford, UK: Oxford University Press, 2016.
Nash, Linda. "The Agency of Nature or the Nature of Agency?" *Environmental History* 10, no. 1 (January 2005): 67–69.
Nikkan Rekishi Kyōdō Kenkyūkai, ed. *Nikkan rekishi kyōdō kenkyū hōkokusho: dai 3 bunka hen gekan*. Tokyo: Nikkan Rekishi Kyōdō Kenkyūkai, 2005.
O Pyŏnghan. "1906-nyŏn Ilbongun Andonghyŏn kunjŏngsŏ ŭi hagu chosa sŏnggyŏk kwa ŭiŭi." *Hanguk kŭnhyŏndaesa yŏngu* 80 (March 2017): 69–95.
O'Dwyer, Emer Sinéad. *Significant Soil: Settler Colonialism and Japan's Urban Empire in Manchuria*. Cambridge, MA: Harvard University Asia Center, 2015.
O'Gorman, Emily, and Andrea Gaynor. "More-Than-Human Histories." *Environmental History* 25, no. 4 (October 2020): 711–735.
Oliveras-Gonzalez, Xavier. "Beyond Natural Borders and Social Bordering: The Political Agency of the Lower Rio Brave/Grande." *Geopolitics*, https://doi.org/10.1080/14650045.2021.2016706.

Paek Ŭlsŏn. "Kankoku kokuyūrin ni okeru basshutsu, ikurin jigyō no tenkai katei ni kansuru shiteki kenkyū." *Hokkaidō Daigaku nōgakubu enshūrin kenkyū hōkoku* 47, no. 1 (1990): 1–70.
Pak Kang. "1920 nyŏndae majŏk kwa Hanin, kŭrigo ap'yŏn." *Han'guk minjok undongsa yŏn'gu* 88 (2016): 41–80.
———. "1930 nyŏndae Manju chiyŏk ŭli ap'yŏn chaebae wa Hanin, kŭrigo pijŏk," *Han'guk Minjok undongsa yŏn'gu* 92 (2017): 179–210.
Paine, S. C. M. "The Chinese Eastern Railway from the First Sino-Japanese War until the Russo-Japanese War." In *Manchurian Railways and the Opening of China: An International History*, edited by Bruce A. Elleman and Stephen Kotkin, 13–36. Armonk, NY: M. E. Sharpe, 2010.
Park, Alyssa M. *Sovereignty Experiments: Korean Migrants and the Building of Borders in Northeast Asia, 1860–1945*. Ithaca, NY: Cornell University Press, 2019.
Park, Hyun Ok. *Two Dreams in One Bed: Empire, Social Life, and the Origins of the North Korean Revolution in Manchuria*. Durham, NC: Duke University Press, 2005.
Pietz, David A. *The Yellow River: The Problem of Water in Modern China*. Cambridge, MA: Harvard University Press, 2015.
Pritchard, Sarah. *Confluence: The Nature of Technology and the Remaking of the Rhone*. Cambridge, MA: Harvard University Press, 2011.
Qi Feng. "Jindai Andong haiguan yanjiu." MA thesis, Liaoning University, 2014.
Reardon-Anderson, James. *Reluctant Pioneers: China's Northward Expansion, 1644–1937*. Stanford, CA: Stanford University Press, 2005.
Robinson, Michael E. *Korea's Twentieth-Century Odyssey: A Short History*. Honolulu: University of Hawai'i Press, 2007.
Rogaski, Ruth. *Knowing Manchuria: Environments, the Senses, and Natural Knowledge on an Asian Borderland*. Chicago: University of Chicago Press, 2022.
Sahlins, Peter. *Boundaries: The Making of France and Spain in the Pyrenees*. Berkeley: University of California Press, 1989.
Saya Makito. *The Sino-Japanese War and the Birth of Japanese Nationalism*. Translated by David Noble. Tokyo: International House of Japan, 2011.
Schlesinger, Jonathan. *A World Trimmed with Fur: Wild Things, Pristine Places, and the Natural Fringes of Qing Rule*. Redwood City, CA: Stanford University Press, 2017.
Schmid, Andre. *Korea between Empires, 1895–1919*. New York: Columbia University Press, 2002.
Scott, James. *Weapons of the Weak: Everyday Forms of Peasant Resistance*. New Haven, CT: Yale University Press, 1985.
Seeley, Joseph. "Cattle, Viral Invasions, and State-Society Relations in a Colonial Korean Borderland," *Journal of Korean Studies* 28, no. 1 (March 2023): 5–31.
———. "Dammed Fish: Piscatorial Developmentalism and the Remaking of the Yalu River." In *Forces of Nature: New Perspectives on Korean Environments*, edited by David Fedman, Eleana J. Kim, and Albert L. Park, 48–59. Ithaca, NY: Cornell University Press, 2023.
Seow, Victor. *Carbon Technocracy: Energy Regimes in Modern East Asia*. Chicago: University of Chicago Press, 2021.
Shin, Gi-Wook, and Michael Robinson, eds. *Colonial Modernity in Korea*. Cambridge, MA: Harvard University Asia Center, 1999.
Shirane, Seiji. *Imperial Gateway: Colonial Taiwan and Japan's Expansion in South China and Southeast Asia, 1895–1945*. Ithaca, NY: Cornell University Press, 2022.

Sin Chubaek. *Manju chiyŏk Hanin ŭi minjok undongsa, 1920-45: minjokchuŭi undong mit sahoejuŭi undong kyeyŏl ŭi taerip kwa yŏndae rŭl chungsim ŭro*. Seoul: Asea Munhwa, 2002.
Siniawer, Eiko Maruko. *Ruffians, Yakuza, Nationalists: The Violent Politics of Modern Japan, 1860-1960*. Ithaca, NY: Cornell University Press, 2011.
Skabelund, Aaron. *Empire of Dogs: Canines, Japan, and the Making of the Modern Imperial World*. Ithaca, NY: Cornell University Press, 2011.
Smith, Norman. *Intoxicating Manchuria: Alcohol, Opium, and Culture in China's Northeast*. Vancouver: University of British Columbia Press, 2012.
Smith, Norman, ed. *Empire and Environment in the Making of Manchuria*. Vancouver: University of British Columbia Press, 2017.
Sneddon, Christopher. *Concrete Revolution: Large Dams, Cold War Geopolitics, and the US Bureau of Reclamation*. Chicago: University of Chicago Press, 2015.
Steinberg, John W. "Operational Overview." In *The Russo-Japanese War in Global Perspective: World War Zero*, edited by John W. Steinberg et al., 105-128. Leiden: Brill, 2005.
Stephens, Holly. "Agriculture and Development in an Age of Empire: Institutions, Associations, and Market Networks in Korea, 1876-1945." PhD diss., University of Pennsylvania, 2017.
Suh, Dae-sook. *Kim Il Sung: The North Korean Leader*. New York: Columbia University Press, 1988.
Song, Nianshen. *Making Borders in Modern East Asia: The Tumen River Demarcation, 1881-1919*. Cambridge, UK: Cambridge University Press, 2018.
Stursberg, Peter. *No Foreign Bones in China: Memoirs of Imperialism and Its Ending*. Edmonton: University of Alberta Press, 2002.
Tagliacozzo, Eric. *Secret Trades, Porous Borders: Smuggling and States along a Southeast Asian Frontier*. New Haven, CT: Yale University Press, 2005.
Tanaka Ryūichi. "'Manshūkoku' keisatsu to chiiki shakai: keizai keisatsu no katsudō to sono mujun o chūshin to shite." *Chungang saron* 32 (December 2010): 237-271.
——. "Tairitsu to tōgō no 'Mansen' kankei: 'Naisen ittai,' 'Gozoku kyōwa,' 'Mansen ichinyo' no shosō," *Hisutoria* 152 (1996).
Tao Mian. *Yalu Jiang sushuo: 19 shiji-20 shiji zhongye lueduo jishi*. Shenyang: 2010.
Thai, Philip. *China's War on Smuggling: Law, Economic Life, and the Making of the Modern State, 1842-1965*. New York: Columbia University Press, 2018.
Thomas, Kimberley Anh. "The River-Border Complex: A Border-Integrated Approach to Transboundary River Governance Illustrated by the Ganges River and Indo-Bangladeshi Border." *Water International* 42, no. 1 (January 2017): 34-53.
Tian, Mo. "The Baojia System as Institutional Control in Manchukuo under Japanese Rule (1932-45)." *Journal of the Economic and Social History of the Orient* 59, 4 (2016): 531-554.
Takahashi Yoshikazu, Kojima Shintarō, and Mya San Wai. "Chōsen Sōtokufu Tetsudōkyoku ni yoru fukushazaikei torasu kyōryō no kaihatsu to taidan seinō." *Doboku Gakkai ronbunshū D2 (dobokushi)* 76, no. 1 (2020): 16-31.
Tobe Ryōichi. "Chōsen chūton Nihongun no jitsuzō: chian, bōei, teikoku." In *Nikkan rekishi kyōdō kenkyū hōkokusho: dai 3 bunka hen gekan*, edited by Nikkan Rekishi Kyōdō Kenkyūkai, 387-409. Tokyo: Nikkan Rekishi Kyōdō Kenkyūkai, 2005.
Tsing, Anna. *The Mushroom at the End of the World: On the Possibility of Life in Capitalist Ruins*. Princeton, NJ: Princeton University Press, 2015.
Tsutsui, William M. "The Pelagic Empire: Reconsidering Japanese Expansion." In *Japan at Nature's Edge: The Environmental Context of a Global Power*, edited by

Ian Jared Miller, Julia Adeney Thomas, and Brett L. Walker, 21–38. Honolulu: University of Hawai'i Press, 2014.
Uchida, Jun. *Brokers of Empire: Japanese Settler Colonialism in Korea, 1876–1945.* Cambridge, MA: Harvard University Asia Center, 2011.
Urbansky, Sören. *Beyond the Steppe Frontier: A History of the Sino-Russian Border.* Princeton, NJ: Princeton University Press, 2021.
Wada Haruki. *Kin Nichisei to Manshū kōnichi sensō.* Tokyo: Heibonsha, 1992.
Wadewitz, Lissa K. *The Nature of Borders: Salmon, Boundaries, and Bandits on the Salish Sea.* Seattle: University of Washington Press, 2012.
Wang Ju. "1927 nen no iwayuru Rinkō jiken ni kansuru shohoteki bunseki." *Chūgoku kenkyū geppō* 401 (July 1981): 39–58.
White, Richard. *The Organic Machine: The Remaking of the Columbia River.* New York: Hill & Wang, 1995.
Wickman, Thomas M. *Snowshoe Country: An Environmental and Cultural History of Winter in the Early American Northeast.* Cambridge, UK: Cambridge University Press, 2018.
Wilson, Roderick I. *Turbulent Streams: An Environmental History of Japan's Rivers, 1600–1930.* Leiden: Brill, 2021.
Winichakul, Thongchai. *Siam Mapped: A History of the Geo-Body of a Nation.* Honolulu: University of Hawai'i Press, 1994.
Xu Wanmin. *Zhong Han guangxi shi: jindai juan.* Beijing: Shehui kexue wenxian chubanshe, 2.
Yamamoto Susumu. "Shindai Ōryokkō ryūiki no kaihatsu to kokkyō kanri." *Kyūshū Daigaku tōyōshi ronshū* 39 (April 2011): 145–176.
Yamamoto, Takahiro. *Demarcating Japan: Imperialism, Islanders, and Mobility, 1855–1884.* Cambridge, MA: Harvard University Press Asia Center, 2023.
Yang, Daqing. *Technology of Empire: Telecommunications and Japanese Expansion in Asia, 1883–1945.* Cambridge, MA: Harvard University Asia Center, 2011.
Yang Insil. "1920 nendai shikaku media no ichidanmen: 'Daichi ha hohoemu' to 'Chōsen.'" *Ritsumeikan sangyō shakai ronshū* 43, no. 1 (June 2007): 35–56.
Yao Jingzhi. "20 shiji 30 niandaichu Dongbei de zousi wenti." MA thesis, Xiamen University, 2006.
Yi Chusŏn. "Ōryokkō chūshū o meguru Kan-Shin keisō to teikoku Nihon: Kōsōhei no jirei o chūshin ni." *Nihon rekishi* 763 (December 2011): 54–71.
Yi Sŭngsu. "Amnokkang myŏngch'ing ko." *Han'guk minjok munhwa* 81 (March 2022): 29–52.
Yi Ŭnja. "Chungil chŏnjaeng ijŏn sigi Chungguk ŭi kukkyŏng tosi Andong ŭi ijumin— kyoryu wa kaltŭng ŭi ijungju." *Chungguk kŭnhyŏndaesa* 62 (June 2014): 95–127.
Young, Louise. *Japan's Total Empire: Manchuria and the Culture of Wartime Imperialism.* Berkeley: University of California Press, 1998.
Yun, Peter. "Rethinking the Tribute System: Korean States and Northeast Asian Interstate Relations, 600–1600." PhD diss., University of California, Los Angeles, 1998.
Zatsepine, Victor. *Beyond the Amur: Frontier Encounters between China and Russia, 1850–1930.* Vancouver: University of British Colombia Press, 2017.
Zeisler-Vralsted, Dorothy. *Rivers, Memory, and Nation-Building: A History of the Volga and Mississippi Rivers.* New York: Berghahn Books, 2015.
Zhang, Ling. *The River, the Plain, and the State: An Environmental Drama in Northern Song China, 1048–1128.* Cambridge, UK: Cambridge University Press, 2016.
Zhang Zhongyue. *Qing dai yi lai Yalu Jiang liuyu yimin yanjiu.* Jinan: Shandong renmin chubanshe, 2017.

Index

activists: anti-Japanese, 66, 77, 79, 84, 122; Korean independence, 2, 65, 68, 78–79
agricultural settlers, 6
Ai River, 43–44, 48
Andong: battle with Russia at, 47; Fengtian Fisheries Bureau branch of, 31; illicit border trade in, 95–101, 104–5, 108–13, 134–36; railway bridge from (see Yalu River Railway Bridge); "summer defense" at, 78; timber processing near, 127, 133; violence in, 27, 37, 39, 91; winter sports at, 80
Andong Chamber of Commerce, 101, 105, 136
Andong customs, 96–98, 100, 103–4, 108–11, 113, 134
Andong-Sinŭiju corridor, 111, 133, 135
animals, 4; effects of overharvesting on, 6; as nonhuman actors, 10; movement across border, ix; use by border police, 86, 109
Asia-Pacific War, 134, 145. See also World War II

Bank of Korea, 120
"Big Sword Society," 79
border crossers, 3–4, 10–11, 13, 79, 90, 118; body-searches of, 110; female border crossers, 106; illicit, 5, 21, 140; mobility of, 141
border industrialization, 126
borderland: boomtowns in, 17, 52; border-crossing in, 12; border-making in, 2; human and nonhuman actors in, 15, 42, 64, 147; policing of bandits in, 66; seasonal changes in, 8, 11; timber industry in, 18, 34, 39; violence in, 68
border-making, 116, 142; agency in, x; global, 3; imperial, 9, 13–15, 18, 40, 90, 114; at Sino-Korean border, 13; along Yalu River, 2, 11, 119
border officials, 14; Chinese officials, 65, 69; complicity in smuggling, 102; confrontations with timbermen, 35; cross-border cooperation between, 113, 133; Japanese officials, 2, 65–66, 69, 79, 90, 121; plans for "summer defense," 78; radio broadcasts about, 89; surveillance of river traffic by, 69; use of animals, 86; use of surveillance technologies, 84; wintertime policing by, 80; wives of, 88; writings about seasonal weather, 66–67
border police: and border-making, 9; Chinese vs. Japanese, 78; and guerrillas, 71, 117, 122; and seasonal cycles, 80, 87–88, 90; and smuggling, 2, 103, 140, 147; and Sup'ung Dam, 123, 130; use of animals by, 86; use of body searches, 110; wives of, 76
border residents, 66, 110, 134
border security: and dams, 120; seasonal effects on, 7, 15, 68, 73–76, 80–84, 87–89, 122
Brooklyn Bridge, 57

Canada, 140
carrier pigeons, use by border police, 86
cattle, cross-border smuggling of, 99
Changbai, 69, 73–74, 77–78, 110, 122, 134
Chiang Kai-shek, 79, 100
China, "Open Door Policy" of, 54, 160n64
Chinese Civil War, 143–44
Chinese coolie labor, 57; work in pneumatic caissons, 58
Chinese Communist Party, 121, 143–44
Chinese Maritime Customs Service, 93, 95, 97, 100–101, 113
Chinese Nationalists, 79, 143–44. See also Republic of China
Chinese Yalu crossing, 146
Ch'oe Hyŏn, 123, 131
Ch'ŏksik Hyŏphui ("Colonization Association"), 23
Ch'ŏngch'ŏn River, 57
Cho'san County, 38
Chōsen Army, 87
Chōsen Nitrogenous Fertilizer Company, 120
Chunggangjin: temperatures in, 74, 78, 88; timber collection near, 36
Cold War, 144
Colonization Association. See Ch'ŏksik Hyŏphui
"conquest of nature," 116, 126, 129–30, 137, 139
continental adventurers. See tairiku rōnin

195

counterinsurgency, 87–88, 122, 131, 139
customs agents: collaboration with border police, 2, 9, 11,15, 141; impersonator of, 136; and seasonal cycles, 130; and smugglers, 91–96, 99–101, 103–6, 109–13, 134; rogue agents, 112
customs office: in Andong, 103, 108–9, 113; in Changbai, 110; in Manp'ojin, 136

Daan Steamship Company, 119, 133
Dadong, harbor project at, 123–24, 128–29, 137
Dalian, 93, 101, 105
Dandong. *See* Andong
deforestation vs. afforestation, 61, 73, 127, 147
Democratic People's Republic of Korea. *See* North Korea
dogs: negative depictions of, 109; as patrol animals, 86
Dongbiandao, 22, 39, 70, 124
Dongbiandao Development Company, 123

"economic police" (keizai keisatsu), 134
"economic river," 116, 133
extraterritoriality, 53, 93, 99, 114, 119, 134

Fengtian, 52, 79, 101
Fengtian-Andong line, 60
Fengtian Clique, 9, 69
Fengtian Fisheries Bureau, 31
"fire-field farmers," 127–28, 134. *See also* Hwajŏnmin
First Army, 47–50, 52
First Route Army, 131
fish: cross-border movement of, 32, 40; fisheries, 18, 30–32, 125, 131; hatchery at Sup'ung Reservoir, 131; sashimi, 88; seasonal movements of, 14; species of, 30; Yalu icefish, 18, 31, 34, 124–25
fisheries, 18, 30–32, 125, 131
fishermen, 10–11; Chinese, 18, 30–32, 124–25; Japanese, 125; Korean, 31
fishing, 21, 28, 30–32, 124, 132
fishing rights, 9, 30, 116, 124–25, 142
flooding: and border-making, 40; and climate change, 141; link to deforestation, 127; during spring and summertime (*see* seasonal flooding); large-scale in 1909, 36, 38; of Sup'ung Dam site, 129; of Ŭiju Dam caisson, 139
"flourishing season," 15, 66, 71–72, 76, 80, 90
fluid mobilities, 65, 90
Forest Management Bureau, 33–34, 36–39, 76

Four Closed Counties, 5, 7
France, 47

Germany, 47, 121
Government-General of Korea: and border security, 82, 87, 117; bridge construction by, 118; Communications Bureau of, 120; counterinsurgency measures by, 131; elimination of customs, 138; Police Affairs Bureau of, 74, 77; Railway Bureau of, 62, 132; and smuggling, 104, 112; weather observation station of, 78; and Yalu River Railway Bridge, 62–63
Grand Coulee Dam, 121
Guadalcanal, battle of, 137
guerrillas: attacks on police stations, 76; attacks on telecommunications, 84; and dam construction, 120, 123, 132; and Mitsuya Agreement, 77; relations with villagers, 72–74; seasonal patterns of, 2, 11, 65–67, 71, 81–84, 87, 90, 109; Poch'ŏnbo raid, 122 (*see also* Kim Il-sung)
gunboat imperialism, 93

Han Munhwan, 104–5, 171n72
Han settlers, 21
Hansŏng. *See* Seoul
human vs. nonhuman: as actors, 10, 15, 18, 151n30; and bridge construction, 41–42; mobilities of, 9, 17, 64, 116, 121, 141–42 (*see also* liquid geographies); nonhuman environments, 3, 13; nonhuman stories, 11
Hun River, 69, 73, 77–78, 87
Hushan, 43–44
Hwach'ang township, 73
Hwajŏnmin, 127–28. *See also* "fire-field farmers"
Hwangch'op'yŏng, 18–19, 21–29, 39, 144
Hwanggumpyong. *See* Hwangch'op'yŏng
Hyesanjin, 70, 78

"icebound season": and "bandit suppression," 67, 90; and border security, 15, 78, 80–82, 87; and bridge construction, 59; disappearance of, 130, 135; and natural resources, 80; and seasonal border-making, 11; and seasonal river changes, 9; and smuggling, 98, 102, 106, 108–9, 113
Inch'ŏn, 144
industrialization: and border security, 120, 132; link to border pacification, 123; and "Manchurian-Korean unity," 121; as military strategy, 112; Sup'ung Dam, 126, 141
Itō Hirobumi, 23–24

INDEX

Japan: Foreign Ministry of, 101–2; Imperial Navy of, 119
"Japanese-Manchukuo unity," 130
Japanese protectorate of Korea: policing of fishing rights, 30 (*see also* Korean Fisheries Law); Railroad Bureau of, 56; and river island sovereignty, 24; and timber monopoly, 32–37; and Yalu River Railway Bridge, 42, 54, 56, 62
Japanese settlers, 17, 23, 25, 69, 117
Japan-Korea Annexation Treaty, 40
Japan-Korea Protectorate Treaty, 23, 51
Ji'an, 69, 71, 109, 133, 137
Jiuliancheng: walled city of, 43–44, 47, 52; Battle of, 45
Joint Committee, 118–19
Jurchen/Manchu language, 4

Kaesŏng, 4
Kando, 19, 74
"Kando question," 19
Kanggye County, 77
Keijō, 13, 70. *See also* Seoul
Kim Il-sung, 65, 84, 88, 122–23, 131, 143
King Kwanggaet'o Stele, 4, 149n6
Kiso, 36
Koguryŏ, 4
Koike Shin'ichi, 56, 59, 62–63
Kojong, 33
Kŏmjŏngdo, island of, 48
Korea-Manchukuo border, 138, 142
Korean Fisheries Law, 30–31
Korean Ministry of Agriculture, Commerce, and Industry. *See* Nongsanggongbu
Korean People's Association, 170n38. *See also* smuggling
Korean War, 16, 144–47
Kuandian, 69
Kwantung Army, 79, 111–12, 117–18, 134
Kwantung Leased Territory, 93, 101,104

Liaodong Peninsula, 47
Liao River Railway Bridge, 57
Linjiang, 37, 69, 109, 122, 134
liquid geographies: and bridge construction, 41–42, 60, 62, and dam construction, 116; definition of, 9–10; efforts to control, 14, 16–17, 19, 29, 137, 140; and guerrillas, 121, 132; and resistance of timbermen, 40; seasonality of, 11, 54, 90, 144; and smuggling, 65, 91–93, 96, 103, 105, 114
Liudaogou, district of, 95–96

logging, 28, 34–36, 73, 127. *See also* timber industry
London, Jack, 50

MacArthur, Douglas, 144
Manchukuo: "bandit suppression" in, 80–81, 86, 87, 90, 122–23; border policing of, 67; guerrilla raids in, 131; industrialization projects in, 115–16, 118, 120–21; puppet state of, 9,14, 79, 142; and smuggling, 91–92, 104, 108–14, 134–35
Manchukuo Army, 109, 131
Manchukuo Bureau of Transportation, 137
Manchukuo customs, 91–92, 103–4, 108–13, 117, 138. *See also* border officials
Manchu people, 5
Manchuria: American bombing raids in, 139; and bridge construction, 41–42, 46; environment of, 12; guerrillas from, 81–82, 87–88, 131; Japanese occupation of, 9, 16, 65, 80, 86, 90, 103; Korean independence movement in, 68, 77; and liquid geographies, 92, 121;"mounted bandits" from (*see* "mounted bandits"); and Russo-Japanese War, 7, 23; seasonal boundaries of, 50, 91; and seasonal violence, 15; and smuggling, 94, 99, 104–7, 110, 135–36; Trans-Siberian railroad across, 33; and Yalu River Railway Bridge, 51, 63
Manchurian Incident, 15, 67, 79–82, 87, 103–4, 107, 113
"Manchurian-Korean unity": and "bandit suppression," 122; and infrastructural development, 118, 120–21, 126, 139; and liquid geographies, 116; and ongoing border tensions, 16, 123–24, 135, 142; relation to seasonal violence, 13
Manp'ojin, 133, 136–37
Mao'ershan, 37
Mao Zedong, 145
March First Independence Movement, 67–69, 79, 84, 105
May Fourth Movement, 67–68, 77
Meiji Restoration, 7
Mekong River, 11
"Memorandum Concerning Bridges on the Yalu and Tumen Rivers," 118
"Memorandum on the Formation of a Joint Manchurian-Korean Technical Committee on the Yalu River," 118
Mexico, 11, 140–41
Midway, battle of, 137
Mihara Kunitarō, drowning of, 44

Minami Jirō, 112, 117, 130
"Mitsuya Agreement," 77
Miyake Heikichi, 45
mobilities: of border-crossers, 66, 90; of borderland communities, 147; of human vs. nonhuman actors, 2, 11, 17, 30, 41–42, 64, 116; of smugglers, 92. *See also* liquid geographies
monsoonal rains: and border security, 73; and "flourishing season," 66; ginseng harvest during, 5; hardships for laborers, 129; infrastructure to channel, 52; and sedimentation, 20
more-than-human, 3, 10, 142. *See also* human vs. nonhuman
"mounted bandits" (mazei, majŏk): attacks on river boats, 69–70; "bandit suppression," 67, 76, 86–87, 122, 131–32; seasonal incursions by, 6, 66, 73, 81, 89–90; "self-defense groups" against, 85; surveillance of, 84, 92
Mt. Paektu/Changbai, 3, 5
Mukden. *See* Fengtian

Nongsanggongbu, 23
Noritake Kazuo, 86, 115, 130
Northeast China, 4, 33, 50, 67, 79, 88, 128
Northeast People's Revolutionary Army, 79, 82, 121
Northeast United Anti-Japanese Army. *See* Northeast People's Revolutionary Army
"Northern Korea Border Patrol Song," relation to weather reportage, 74
North Hamgyŏng Province, 134
North Korea: during Chinese Civil War, 143; Poch'ŏnbo raid, 122; and riparian sovereignty, 19, 29 (*see also* Hwangch'op'yŏng); and seasonal border-making, 65, 88, 144; UN march to Yalu, 145
North P'yŏngan Province, 52, 76, 87, 102; cross-border rivalries of, 124; police counterinsurgency, 73; police fatalities, 74; rape by police in, 77
North P'yŏngan Province Police Affairs Bureau, 80, 84

Okabe Saburō, 23–28, 39
opium, 8, 10, 73–74, 104, 128, 134–35
Orientalism, 57

Parhae, 4
Pearl Harbor, 137
People's Republic of China, 1, 29, 144
"People's Volunteer Army," 145

piscatorial colonialism, 30
pneumatic caissons, 51, 56–57, 59
poaching, 30–32
Poch'ŏnbo, 122
Port Arthur, 47
"power of water," 127, 139
propeller boats, 66, 69–70, 78, 123, 143
Provincial Military Railroad Department of Japanese Imperial Army, 51
Pusan, 51, 136
Pyŏngyang, 43

Qing dynasty: and Chinese Maritime Customs Service, 93, 100; collapse of, 69; and fishing rights, 30–32; Foreign Ministry of, 27; and river island sovereignty, 19–23, 29; and river sovereignty, 56, 60; and Sino-Japanese War, 33, 43, 46; and timber industry, 35–39, 127–28

Railroad Bureau of the Japanese protectorate government, 56
reeds, 14, 24, 32; harvesters of, 23, 26, 29; harvesting season, 18, 25; types of, 22. *See also* Hwangch'op'yŏng
Republic of China, 27, 63, 79, 127, 143–44
"Righteous Army," 67
Rio Grande River, 140
"riparian relations," 141
riparian sovereignty, 56, 111, 114, 133
Russia: Battle of the Yalu River, 49–50; expansion into Manchuria, 12; feared invasion by, 54; Russo-Japanese War, 7–8, 23, 26, 33, 52; and Yalu River Crisis, 46–48
Russo-Japanese War, 7, 15, 17; bandits fighting in, 25–26; bridge construction during, 41–42; cause of, 33; and Jack London, 50; military timber harvesting during, 35; and tourism, 132; and Yalu River Railway Bridge, 52–54

Saitō Makoto, alleged assassination attempt, 70
Sakchu, county of, 76, 85
Satō Toshihiko, 123, 127, 137
"Scientific Japan," 115, 132
seasonal border making, 11, 65, 92, 123, 141, 144
seasonal flooding, 2, 9, 11, 20, 32, 40, 53; and border security, 73, 90; and border surveillance, 66; effects on bridge construction, 42, 56, 59–61; effects on river course, 119; effects on river trade, 123–24; and ginseng harvest, 5. *See also* monsoonal rains
Second Army, 47

INDEX

Second Sino-Japanese War, 113, 127
"self-defense corps," 82, 84–85
"self-defense groups," 85
Seoul: railway line to, 52, 64; Russian embassy in, 33
Shandong Peninsula, 21, 35
Shanghai, 31, 38, 79, 103–4
Shaw, George, 119, 174n22
Shinkyō, 118, 136
Sindo, island of, 21–22
Sino-British Imperial Railways of North China, 57
Sino-Japanese War, 7, 15, 17, 33, 41–43, 46–47, 52
Sino-Japanese Yalu River Timber Company, 127
Sino-Korean border: "conquest of nature" at, 129; environments of, 12–13; and fishing rights, 30; liquid geographies of, 9, 17, 19, 90; and "Manchurian-Korean unity," 117; opium harvesting at, 73; policing of, 71; seasonal landscapes of, 107; Sino-Japanese War on, 43; timber industry along, 34, 39; violence at, 27, 38; and Yalu River Railway Bridge, 40
Sinŭiju: bridge construction near, 53; Chamber of Commerce of, 132, 135; dam construction near, 120, 133; smuggling in, 92–94, 97, 99, 102, 104–6, 108; role in timber industry, 34, 70; winter sports at, 80; and Yalu River Railway Bridge, 62
Sixth Army Division, 46
smuggling: decline in, 134–35; "deliberate underenforcement of, 101; among "fire-field farmers," 128; Korean role in, 99, 102,104–5; after Manchurian Incident, 104; masculine" vs. "feminine," 93, 105–6; by merchants, 93; seasonal patterns of, 16, 90, 92, 97–98, 108–9, 113; via railway bridge, 94–95; via small creeks, 96
So-Hwangch'op'yŏng, 21
South Hamgyŏng Province, 69, 74, 134–35
South Korea, 14, 110, 144
South Manchuria Railway Company, 92–93, 119–20, 124, 132, 138
sovereignty, 12–13; border officials' claims to, 32; Chinese, 15, 31–32, 63, 78, 90, 92; contested, 21, 25, 31, 60; ill-defined zones of, 92, 113; Korean, 19, 29, 51, 62; Manchukuo, 16, 92, 123; river island, 21–22, 24, 27–29; Sino-Korean, 18, 23, 30; territorial, ix
Soviet-Manchukuo border, 139
Soviet Union, 131, 143, 145
St. Lawrence River, 140
Sugujin, 43–44

Suicide Squad at the Watchtower (film), 89, 168n152
"summer defense," 6, 78
Sup'ung Dam: "bandit suppression" at, 122–23; construction of, 16, 114; effects of on river ecology, 11, 115, 124, 139, 145–46; effects of on river transit, 133; as effort to "conquer nature," 126, 130; and fish farming, 131; as hallmark of "Scientific Japan," 132; as imperial infrastructure, 120; recurring disasters at, 128–29; relation to global industrialization, 121; and seasonal changes, 116; and smuggling, 135
surveillance: of boat traffic, 66, 69; and border engineering, 14; challenges of during wintertime, 65, 82; of dam laborers, 128; of guerrillas, 82, 84, 116, 123 (*see also* "mounted bandits"); of Korean migrants, 68; of political dissidents, 66, 92; of smugglers, 95–96, 102, 108; use of railroad bridge for, 118; and violence,10,13,15
Swire Trading Company, 119

Taegil, 82–85
Tae-Hwangch'op'yŏng, 21
Taewŏn'gun, 21
Taiping Rebellion, 7
tairiku rōnin, 19, 26. *See also* "continental adventurers"
Talbot, Roy Maxwell, 97–98, 103–104
Tasa-do, harbor project at, 123–24, 137
Tasa-do Railway Company, 124
Terauchi Masatake, 52, 62, 63
territoriality, 12–13
Three Eastern Provinces. *See* Manchuria
Tianjin, 73
"timber bandits" (mokpi), 35, 39
timber imperialism, 35, 37, 39
timber industry, 18, 32, 34–35, 39, 55, 80
timber rafts: disappearance of, 115; effects of dam construction on, 133, 136; surveillance of, 66, 69; use in smuggling, 134; use in timber industry, 34–36, 39, 55
Tonghua, 7, 122, 131, 144
"Tonghŭng Incident," 82, 122
"T'osŏng Incident," 82
tourism, 132
trade, 8, 24, 54, 94, 96, 140, 147; cross-border, 7, 42, 63, 99, 118–19; of ginseng, 5; illicit, 15, 92–93, 99, 110–11, 134, 136, 139; of opium, 135; regional, 64; on river, 29, 69, 116, 123; smuggling, ix, 102; timber, 35, 38
Trans-Siberian Railroad, 33
Treaty of Aigun, 7

Trotsky, Leon, 121
Tumen Conference, 118, 122
Tumen River: bridges across, 118; guerrilla and smuggling activity along, 74, 106; as northern boundary of Protectorate of Korea, 7–8, 40; sovereignty and territoriality along, 12, 19; timber industry near, 33

Ŭiju, 52; dam project at, 137–39; violence of customs officials, 106; walled city of, 5, 43
Unbong Dam, 137
United Nations, 140, 144
United States of America, 11, 14, 60–61, 121, 137, 140, 143–44

War Memorial of Korea Museum, 144
World War II, 16, 139, 143, 145

Yalu-Hun River Waterfront Police, 69, 73, 77–78, 87, 165n82
Yalu River, Battle of the, 50
Yalu River basin: ginseng extraction in, 5; mineral extraction in, 123; tairiku rōnin in, 26; timber industry in, 32, 60–61, 127 (*see also* deforestation vs. afforestation)
"Yalu River Crisis," 33, 47
Yalu River Hydropower Company, 120, 130, 133, 136
Yalu River Melody, 69, 133, 163n28
Yalu River Railway Bridge: bombing of, 145, 180n18; construction of, 40, 42, 51, 56, 62; illicit economy across, 65, 93–95, 106, 113, 135; as Japanese military project, 63; laborers on, 56–57,160n74
Yalu River Timber Company, 33–34, 36–39, 120, 127–28
Yalu River Transport Company, 70
Yang Jingyu, 123, 131
Yangsan, 76
Yellow Sea, 3, 30, 43, 48, 67
Yi Honggwang, 82–83, 166n111. *See also* Northeast People's Revolutionary Army
Yi Ok-hyun, 2
Yi Sŏnggye, 4
Yongamp'o, 23, 67
Yongyŏn, 1
Yoshino, 36

Zhang Zuolin, 68–69, 77, 120; Fengtian Clique of, 9

www.ingramcontent.com/pod-product-compliance
Lightning Source LLC
Chambersburg PA
CBHW031436160426
43195CB00010BB/752